# Construction for Profit

# Construction for Profit

**Kenneth O. Gooch**
Chairman of the Board

**John Caroline**
President

The Builder's Institute
Pleasanton, California

Reston Publishing Company, Inc.
*A Prentice-Hall Company*
Reston, Virginia

**Library of Congress Cataloging in Publication Data**

Gooch, Kenneth O
    Construction for profit.

    Originally presented in part, in a Builder's Institue seminar.
    Includes index.
    1. Construction industry—Management.
I. Caroline, John, joint author. II. Title.
HD9715.A2G646.   624'.068   80-16245
ISBN 0-8359-0938-7

© 1980 by
Reston Publishing Company, Inc.
*A Prentice-Hall Company*
Reston, Virginia 22090

All rights reserved. No part of this book may be reproduced in any way, or by any means, without permission in writing from the publisher.

10  9  8  7  6  5  4  3  2  1

Printed in the United States of America

# Contents

**Preface  ix**

**Introduction  1**
    The Landshapers  1

**1  Preliminary Site Study  5**
    Selecting the Project and Site  5
    Decision to Proceed and Property Acquisition  17

    Forms:
        100: Preliminary Site Study  10-12
        110: Cost and Profit Study of the Tentative Program  13-16

**2  Feasibility Study  19**
    Gathering Information  19
    The Market Feasibility Study  27

    Forms:
        200: Site Feasibility Study  20-26
        220: Market Study of a Regional Area (Outline)  28-32
        240: Market Study of a Specific Site  33-52

**3  Forward Planning Stage  53**
    Planning and Mobilization  53
    Legal Organization of a Construction Company  62
    Project Design Implementation  75
    Contracts and Purchasing  83
    Letting the Bid  103
    Accounting  104

Finance 113
Money Management 118

Forms:

300: Forward Planning Schedule 54-61

305: Site Design 78-80

306: Building Design 81-82

310: Invitation to Bid 90-92

320: Bid Proposal—Subcontractors 93-96

325: Bid Proposal—Suppliers 97-98

330: Bid Summary Sheet 99-102

360: Financial Feasibility Study 114-116

370: Finance Package Checklist 117

## 4 Cost and Profit 121

Cost and Profit Analysis 121

Forms:

400: Cost and Profit Analysis (Face Sheet) 122-127

410: Work in Process Budget—Indirect 129-130

420: Work in Process Budget—Direct 131-134

430: Product Line Detail Support (Work Sheet) 135-136

440: Financing/Tax Budget 137-138

450: Model Excess Budget 139-140

## 5 Construction 141

Mobilization 141
Contracts 142

Forms:

500: Construction Contract Checklist 146-148

510: Subcontract Agreement 149-154

520: Subdivision Schedule 156-158

530: Weekly Construction Schedule 159-162

540: Quality Control—Outline Form 163-168

550: Quality Control—Itemized Form 169-189

Contents / vii

560: Field-Color Schedule Card  190–192
570: Employee Record Card  193–195
580: Timecard  197
590: Job Summary  199

## 6  Marketing and Sales  201
Marketing  201
Marketing Evaluation: One Project  218

Forms:
600: Sales and Marketing Planning Checklist (New Homes Pre-Opening)  223–233
650: Agreement for Sale of Real Estate  234–243
660: Exterior Color Selections  244–248
670: Interior Color Schedule  249–250
680: Field-Color Schedule Card  251–252
690: Change Order  253–256

## 7  Warranty and Follow-Through  257
Warranty  257
Warranty Agreement  262

Forms:
700: Warranty Checklist  258–261
705: One-Year Warranty  263–270
710: Compliance Inspection Report  271–274
720: One-Month Inspection Form  275–278

**Epilogue**  279

**Index**  281

# Preface

This book was written in response to a need for an easy-to-read, comprehensive guide to making a profit in the construction and development process.

Our primary purpose is to present the fundamentals of the construction business as it is practiced in the United States today by entrepreneurial merchant builders, general contractors, and subcontractors who represent the major sector of the construction industry. They are the businessmen and craftsmen who create the homes, offices, and light industrial facilities that contribute to our environment, economy, and way of life.

The emphasis in this book is on practical examples for building for profit. It is real-life, day-to-day information with usable forms based on proven and successful techniques and business management methods which are discussed in simple down-to-earth language. It is directed both to those who have mastered the mechanics of the construction industry and want to know more about the methods of running the business end of it and to those who are new or relatively inexperienced in building. The subject matter will also be of considerable interest to architects, engineers, real estate land and project specialists, and professors and students in universities or technical institutions which offer courses in construction.

The information in this book was originally presented, in part, in our highly successful Builder's Institute seminar. It was conceived as a seminar with a book as a compendium of information by builders for builders. The scope of the project has been greatly increased with this book as the outcome of that endeavor.

In this book we are making available the business methods that work for us as a prime example of construction for profit.

For over a quarter of a century, since 1954, I have been a builder and building consultant. The business methods I developed during that time have resulted, thus far, in a total value of involvement of almost half a billion dollars. Now, as President, Ken Gooch Construction Inc.; Chairman of the Board, The Builder's Institute, Inc.; and member of the National Association of Home Builders, Building Industry Association, and American Institute of Building Designers, I can share those methods and the exciting experience of that involvement.

John Caroline, the co-author of *Construction for Profit* and chief guiding force of our seminar subsidiary, is the creator of many of the control systems used in this book. He is a builder and has been in the building business since 1959, involved with over a half-billion-dollars' construction. He is President of Caroline-Knudson, Inc., and President, The Builder's Institute, Inc.

In order to cover the subjects of this handbook and our original seminar adequately we called upon the expert consultants who work with us on our building ventures to cover their specialties. Our experts are:

*Legal*: John Paul Hanna, attorney, author of *The California Condominium Handbook* and *The Complete Layman's Guide to the Law*, and member of the Real Property Section of the American Bar Association.

*Marketing*: Gary Ryness, President of The Ryness Company, noted lecturer, and authority on home marketing, sales, and financing for home builders.

*Contract Administration:* John Van de Roovaart, Vice President, Caroline-Knudson, Inc.; Vice President, The Builder's Institute, Inc.; and President. Rovart, Inc.

*Accounting*: Jerry Blackmore, CPA, Principal of the firm of Allen & Blackmore, Inc., and member of the California Society of Certified Public Accountants and the American Institute of CPAs.

The fields that these men cover are an integral part of any profitable building enterprise. Along with the other practical information included herein, it is hoped that this book will serve adequately in your future building and development endeavors, whether it be one small adventure or a career of multi-million-dollar ventures.

                                                                 Kenneth O. Gooch
                                                                Pleasanton, California

# Construction for Profit

# Introduction

## THE LANDSHAPERS

In the beginning there was the land. And upon that land strode men and women of vision and daring to shape living, working, and playing environments for the people of the great civilizations of our earth. Their efforts are timeless; their endeavors and accomplishments legend. These people were and are the landshapers.

The landshapers are the builders; developers; land owners, big and small; monarchs; leaders of industry; individuals and multifaceted conglomerates—all with one thing in common—the shaping of the land and the construction within and upon that land.

## THE CONSTRUCTION INDUSTRY

The construction industry, which includes both building and development, is the largest private enterprise in the United States today. It is the bulwark of the American economy. It is the most evident and sensational of materialistic achievements. Great fortunes have been made, and the potential and opportunity are always there. Tradesmen have risen through the ranks to head their own companies. Students of business, engineering, architecture, construction, law, and anthropology have acquired or hired the skills to gain a spot in the building industry. The ranks of builders include former mailmen, milkmen, train engineers, bankers, clerks, clergy, factory workers, and soldiers. They come from all walks of life and from all backgrounds. There is no typical builder prototype as there is no typical prototype building.

**Unlimited Opportunities.** The building and development industry is the greatest industry in the world today. The opportunities are unlimited. An individual can take any part in it—from listing the land, supplying the nails, or digging the foundations to doing it all or overseeing it all. The individual can be a project designer, a carpenter, a contractor, or the head of the largest building company in the country; and that individual can have a sense of accomplishment as the project rises from nothing to final fruition. There is no feeling better than the inner satisfaction of a job well done, and each participant in whatever phase can have that feeling.

**High Failure Rate.** The building industry, despite the tremendous opportunities for success, has one of the highest bankruptcy or failure rates of any business today. Construction contractors have a business failure rate of almost 15 percent per year and, of these failures, 50 percent have been in business five years or more. The reason is the relative ease that contractor status is achieved. Many contractors have little formal training in business administration; their construction management expertise has been acquired the hard way through time-consuming and costly on-the-job training. And, some contractors never do recognize the importance of good management; they never know where they stand until the project is finished and the final tabulations are made.

**Network of Control Systems Needed.** There is a need in the building industry for a network of control systems which will enable the developer or contractor to formulate, record, and monitor the construction process from the first day until the end; to know where he stands, down to the last penny; to know what effect yesterday's rain and tomorrow's labor strike will have on his cash flow, his scheduling, and his start of future jobs.

In an industry where bids are still given on the backs of envelopes and agreed upon by a handshake, and large amounts of money are discussed over the hood of a pickup truck, there is room for improvement and that improvement will mean increased profit.

For those who are more experienced, a network of control systems will act as an easy reference or guide that will add to their pool of knowledge and increase their effectiveness.

**Repetitive Process.** The construction process and construction projects, in general, need not be complex. By formalizing the procedures, each phase is shown as a series of events and this series is repetitive. Each project follows the same course from start to finish as the project that preceded it and the ones that will follow. Most people follow this procedure intuitively, some by being bumped along the line of progress. Each step must be completed and each decision made before the next step is taken. A network of control systems is set up like a road map, to be used as a guide along the easiest and most prosperous route to the final destination.

The authors, individually and through their separate companies and associated projects, have been using a network of control systems for almost 20 years, continually improving and updating it. They have the expertise and the contracting, project packaging, and consulting experience gained from over one billion dollars worth of construction involvement, and they are totally qualified to discuss the "nuts and bolts" of the building industry and discuss it at the grass-roots level. It is this knowledge that they are sharing.

# 1
# Preliminary Site Study

## SELECTING THE PROJECT AND SITE

To most of us who have been in the building business for a long time, site and project selection is usually a good, but relatively quick, look at a piece of property and the surrounding environment. We are usually looking at sites in areas we are familiar with and that are within a certain acceptable time/distance radius from our home base.

The feelings that we get for a site or project are usually based on just that—feelings. The process is automatic and intuitive. A decision on one site might take a few minutes; another, a few hours; or another, perhaps several days. But, no matter how long the study takes, the final decision is always based on cost and profit.

The following example will help illustrate the process. We are looking at a site in a nearby city. The city has been virtually closed to major building for the past five years because of the lack of sewer capacity and the environmental policy of the powers that govern. Now a few sewer permits will be allocated on a first-come basis. The rush is on. This is the only site that is available to us that is ready to go. Do we want it?

We look at the site. It looks good—relatively flat, drains well, good access, good location ("near everything", to use an old real estate term), but it is in an area where existing homes are reselling in the $70,000–$75,000 range.

We know the municipality and their requirements. We know, without thinking about it, that apartments are out because of financing and negative cash flow due to relatively low rental rates. We know single-family residential is out because of restrictive zoning and low yield; therefore, we are looking at a townhouse project. Townhouses in this city are allowed at a maximum density of ten to the acre, and we can compute the density that can be expected.

We recently completed a townhouse project in a nearby city. Using the same distribution of two-, three-, and four-bedroom units, we can compute the average floor area, and from this point, it will take a relatively short time to figure the important part of the study, the *cost and profit*.

The cost and profit exercise, which is covered in detail later in this book, shows that the average sales price would have to be $80,000. This gives us a price spread of $77,500 to $82,500.

The first question is, figuring that building construction will start in five months and move-ins in nine months, will the market in an area which now tops out at $75,000 be ready for a $77,500–$82,500 townhouse project of this magnitude? The general housing market for that half of the year based on national statistics indicates *no*. The specific housing market, based on local real estate activity and historical data, even considering pent-up demand and lack of new housing competition, indicates that the sales price is at or above the range for fast turnover.

Did we need an elaborate site and market study to get to this point? No, because we knew the area, we knew the government requirements, we knew the market, and we had our plans and costs.

But, what if we are not familiar with the market? What if we do not have a package set of plans and costs available? And what if we, our lender, or, as in the case of large out-of-state corporations, our home office prefer not to rely on our intuitive feeling about a site? We then need a systemized site and project selection method and, if further study is needed, a feasibility study which could include an in-depth site study and a market study.

The following procedures and forms are presented as a guide for an analytical approach to site and project evaluation.

## SELECTING THE PROJECT

What are the key factors crucial to profitable project selection? The project should:

1. Be the type of project that has significant market demand.
2. Have a reasonable profit with a minimum of risk and exposure.
3. Be within the limits of your company's experience and potential.
4. Be compatible with your financial structure and borrowing power.

5. Be of duration and timing to minimize the effect of rising costs and future market uncertainties.
6. Have tax advantages.
7. Be the type of project you would like to do, thus sustaining your enthusiasm and motivation.

The project should relate to your goals, both short-range and long-range, and your present interests. Are you a contractor, a builder-developer, or a land specialist? Are you interested in developing your own land or do you want only developed and ready-to-build project sites?

**Contractor.** To a contractor, selecting the project generally means selecting the work you want to bid on. For the purpose of this discussion, a contractor is defined as someone who contracts to do work for others. Even if you function only in this capacity, would you like to be in a position to advise your clients about project and site acquisition? If so, you need to be familiar with the process of land development and, hopefully, you will be drawn into a process before bid time to add your knowledge and experience to the overall program.

**Small-Volume Builder.** If you are a builder, are you a small-volume builder with gross project volume of under $750,000? If you are, you are in the same category as some 90 percent of the builders in the United States. You may prefer to stay small. Your volume permits you to exercise personal control over every part of your organization. Overhead is minimum and you may even do much of the construction labor yourself.

There are many advantages to staying small, but there are also disadvantages. You have probably experienced difficulty in obtaining land or lots at a reasonable cost. You may not be able to afford the time or money to develop land because you need to conserve your capital and time for construction. Yet you are competing with large builder-developers who enjoy the economic advantage of building on sites they have developed themselves.

**Medium-Volume Builder.** Have you stepped up activity to the point that classifies you as a medium-volume builder with a gross project value between $750,000 to $10,000,000? You have experienced the need for management and organization where responsibilities are delineated and assigned so that others perform parts of your function with and, sometimes, without your direct supervision. You enjoy better prices because of purchasing volume. You are capable of obtaining larger blocks of developed or packaged land or projects and you also have the option of developing your own raw land. You have some of the advantages of the small-volume builder with fewer of the disadvantages.

**Large-Volume Builder.** If your volume has grown over the years and your organization has developed and prospered, you may be one of the less than two percent of the builders who can be classed as a large-volume builder with a gross project value of over $10,000,000 per year. You and others in your classification will be doing the majority of the building that is going up. You have a full-scale operation, staffed to carry on large-scale business. You are capable of initiating land use and development on a grand scale. You may be multi-locational and even countrywide, and you are organized, departmentalized, and corporationalized to the fullest. To you, efficiency, economy, and communication are essential, and you realize these by employing the most advanced business procedures.

**The Procedure.** No matter where you are on the economic production ladder, small-, medium-, or large-volume, the procedure of selecting the project and developing a program is similar. If you have been in business for any length of time, the procedure is automatic. You may not consciously ask yourself what type of project you want and are geared up for, or what criteria make up a successful project. But this is where it begins and, these questions, as basic as they may seem, are the first steps in the process. Once again, determine if the project has:

1. Market demand.
2. Reasonable profit with minimum risk and exposure.
3. Requirements within your experience and potential.
4. Requirements within your financial structure.
5. Optimum duration and timing.
6. Tax advantage.
7. Qualities that will sustain your enthusiasm and motivation.

The next step is to find a site that will meet your project requirements.

## SELECTING THE SITE

The investigation of any site should take into consideration the project requirements and the following key factors crucial to profitable *site* selection:

1. Government requirements.
2. Ease of development and construction.
3. Location.
4. Marketability.
5. Terms of purchase.

Government Requirements. Are there delays anticipated for zoning? Are there building permits readily available? Are utilities and sewers in or close by with permits for hookup allocated? Are there ecological questions that need to be resolved, such as those regarding historical buildings, endangered species, archaeological findings, and air, water and noise pollution? Is annexation going to be a requirement? Is architectural review either by a local committee or the governing municipality necessary?

Ease of Development and Construction. Is the terrain such that a minimum of grading will be necessary, and will the lots be flat enough for non-stepped or split development? Does the site drain naturally tie into existing storm water inlets? Are utilities in or nearby? Are roads in or nearby?

Location. It has often been said that the three most important factors in site selection are: (1) location, (2) location, and (3) location. There are, of course, other important considerations, but this example is given to show how important location is. The location requirements vary with use. The one constant requirement is that the location be within your effective working radius.

*For residential, townhouse, or apartment sites*, the location criteria are: Is the site near shopping, schools, and transportation? Is there adequate police and fire protection, and are there hospitals and health support facilities nearby? Is the site away from airports, garbage dumps, noisy or smelly industry, and truck or train routes?

*For commercial sites*, the location criteria are: Is there major residential development nearby sufficient to support the project? Are the area's highways or streets sufficient to handle the traffic generated? Will there be enough parking and is there room for expansion?

*For individual commercial sites* not in large commercial centers, additional location requirements are: Are other commercial ventures in the area compatible to your use? What is the competition and how are they doing? Is the site easy to find?

*For industrial sites*, the industrial criteria are: Does the site have truck or train access? Is it within a reasonable distance to the residences of the work force? Are the tax requirements of the local municipality favorable or workable?

Marketability. Is the surrounding neighborhood well kept? Will it enhance the value of your site? Is there new building in the neighborhood? Is the landscaping and the general appearance in good condition? Do the people or businesses in the area look prosperous? Is your project competitive with similar enterprises in the area with regard to cost and value? How many projects like yours are for sale or lease now?

Terms of Purchase. What is the asking price? What do you or your consultants think it is really worth? How much can you pay for it and still have a profitable project? What are the terms? What terms do you want or need? Can you obtain an option on the site? How much time is allotted for a feasibility study?

## PRELIMINARY SITE STUDY—FORM 100

Form 100, Preliminary Site Study, is presented as a guide for the early stage of site investigation. It is extremely basic. The purpose at this period is to determine if the site meets certain preliminary requirements that qualify it for further study before expending the time and effort necessary for the in-depth feasibility studies that follow.

Form 100 can be used as a checklist of valuable information. It can be applied to a single developed lot or to large expanses of undeveloped land.

Form 100 can also be used as a guide in the presentation of the property to determine what kind of information you require to make a preliminary decision or to express an interest in the site. The mechanics of the form are well within the capabilities of real estate professionals, and it is not unreasonable to expect that the person showing you the parcel fill out most or all of the form.

# 100

## PRELIMINARY SITE STUDY

Site Location _____
_____

Size:   acres _____   sq. ft. _____   width _____   depth _____
_____

Anticipated land use: _____
_____

Number units or square feet _____

1. **GOVERNMENTAL REQUIREMENTS:**
   a. Present zoning _____ Required zoning _____
   b. Prospects for rezoning:   ☐ good   ☐ fair   ☐ unfavorable
      Comments: _____
      Time estimate _____
   c. Building permits:   ☐ available   ☐ allotment list   ☐ unknown
      Comments: _____
   d. Sewer permits:   ☐ available   ☐ allotment list   ☐ unknown
      Comments: _____
      Time estimate _____
   e. Ecological requirements: _____
   f. Annexation:   ☐ required   ☐ not required   ☐ unknown
      Who: _____
      Comments: _____

2. **EASE OF DEVELOPMENT:**
   a. Terrain:   ☐ flat   ☐ rolling   ☐ upslope   ☐ downslope
   b. Site drainage: _____
   c. Utility tie-ins:   ☐ in   ☐ available   ☐ unknown
   d. Roads:   ☐ adequate   ☐ need widening   ☐ need lengthening
      Comments: _____

3. **LOCATION:**
   Distance between site & builder/developers home base: miles ____ minutes ____
   Comments: _____
   a. Residential:
      Is the site near:
         shopping   ☐ schools   ☐ transportation   ☐ health facilities
         Comments: _____

b. Commercial:
   Is the site near:
   ☐ population centers   ☐ major streets   ☐ parking
   Competition: _____
   Is the site easy to find: _____
   Comments: _____
c. Industrial:
   Is the site near:
   ☐ truck route   ☐ railroad spurs   ☐ working force
   Comments: _____
   Are there city/county tax advantages: _____

4. **MARKETABILITY:**
   a. Neighborhood appearance:   ☐ well kept   ☐ average   ☐ blighted
      Comments: _____
   b. Neighborhood forecast - on its way:   ☐ up   ☐ down   ☐ no change
      Comments: _____
   c. Comparable project price range: _____
      Comments: _____

5. **AESTHETICS:**
   a. Trees:    ☐ large      ☐ medium    ☐ none
   b. View:     ☐ pastoral   ☐ marine    ☐ large vista   ☐ none
   c. Streams:  ☐ year long  ☐ seasonal  ☐ none
   d. Does the site and surroundings have natural beauty:   ☐ yes   ☐ no
      Comments: _____

6. **TERMS OF SALES:**
   a. Price: _____
   b. Terms: _____
   c. Option: _____
   d. Time for feasibility study: _____

7. **COMMENTS:** _____
   _____
   _____
   _____
   _____
   _____
   _____
   _____
   _____

Study Made By _____   Date _____

# COST AND PROFIT STUDY OF THE TENTATIVE PROGRAM—FORM 110

As part of the investigative stage, a tentative study is made to determine what type of improvement can be put on the site. In the case of residential or townhouse, the number of units will be the question. In the case of commercial or industrial, the number of buildings and amount of square footage will be the question. In many cases, it is too early to know exactly what the governing forces will allow or require. You will be looking at the site to determine capabilities and potential and to decide if the preliminary findings show that you should proceed.

It is also too early to know costs. What you need at this point is a *cost framework* to work within; a cost based on market values and similar project costs. You are trying to determine if the cost of the raw land (or developed lot, if that is what you have), when put together with everything else, will allow a decent profit.

How is the study made and by whom? The study is no more than a comparative exercise. If you have built similar projects in the same or corresponding areas, you already have most of the information. Otherwise, for the *land development cost*, you can ask your engineer to supply you with a development cost estimate for your site. At this stage, it does not have to be and will not be anything elaborate. His cost figure will only be an indication, in his professional opinion, as to what the costs might be, based on his experience. The real cost figures will not be available until after the site plan and land development plans are drawn, accepted, and bid out.

If you do not have your own figures for the *building construction cost*, use industry averages for buildings similiar in construction type, quality, and size. These averages are published by the trade magazines, by several estimating firms in book form, and by some of the larger banks and lending institutions.

*Contingencies* are the allowance for early stage estimates. In this case, because we are still in the conceptual stage, use 8 to 15 percent of the improvement costs, depending upon the source and reputed accuracy of your cost figures. A contingency is a cost added on to cover errors or unknowns.

Form 110 is a worksheet. It is the Cost and Profit Study of the Tentative Program. Use it as a guide. Simplify it or add to it. Projects do differ and the degree of complexity certainly varies. If you are buying completed lots, start with *Developed Lot Cost*. If your project is more complex, use the extra lines provided.

The two work columns are arranged for tabulation of the *estimated cost* as you actually derived it and for the *feasible cost* for the cost that you must have to make the project profitable. The estimate column is usually worked from top to bottom, while the feasible column is worked from bottom to top. Start with the profit needed and sales price anticipated. From this point work with the other fixed costs and then budget the other items.

Certain items, such as Developed Land Cost and Financing Charges, will probably be a fixed cost. The Construction Cost is a variable to the extent that detail, amenities, and size can be changed within the parameters dictated by the *Target Sales Price*. The Target Sales Price may or may not be a variable, according to the dependability and the extent of the study from which it was derived. The Sales and Marketing Budget varies with the needs for advertising, model home furnishing, landscaping, and the relative quality these items demand, depending on competition, size of project, and the duration of the sales program.

A very extensive and comprehensive cost and profit analysis is discussed in Chapter 4. It breaks down the many costs in detail. Form 110 is intended to be basic and geared for a fast preliminary evaluation where time and expense are a prime consideration.

The ability to make fast and good decisions is one of the most important requisites of business. There is an old saying: *"Opportunities are never lost, they just go to someone else."*

Good projects and sites usually go to the first qualified person or company that sees them. There is usually very little time to study or ponder a decision. That is why at this point in process there is a need for a fast, relatively easy method of formulating the required information before proceeding with or declining the project and the site.

# COST AND PROFIT STUDY OF THE TENTATIVE PROGRAM

Site Location _____

Tentative Program and Type of Improvement _____

☐ Custom Res.   ☐ Multi Res.   ☐ Townhouse   ☐ Commercial   ☐ Industrial

**Project Capabilities**

Number of units or sq. ft. Maximum _____ Minimum _____ Optimum _____

## COST STUDY

|   |   | Estimated Cost | Feasible Cost |
|---|---|---|---|
| 1. | Land Cost | | |
| 2. | Land Improvement Cost | | |
| 3. | Contingencies | | |
| 4. | Finance Charge | | |
|   | **Total Developed Lot Cost** | | |
| 5. | Construction Cost of Structure | | |
| 6. | Contingencies | | |
| 7. | Finance Charge | | |
|   | **Total Construction Cost** | | |
| 8. | Amenities (pools, tennis court) Cost | | |
| 9. | Contingencies | | |
| 10. | Finance Charge | | |
|   | **Total Cost of Amenities** | | |
|   | **Sales & Marketing Budget** | | |
|   | TOTAL COST | | |
|   | TARGET SALES PRICE | | |
|   | OVERHEAD & PROFIT | | |

Comments _____

Study made by _____ Date _____

## NOTES

# DECISION TO PROCEED AND PROPERTY ACQUISITION

You now have the preliminary information available from the investigation stage. You have Form 100, the Preliminary Site Study, and Form 110, the Cost and Profit Study of the Tentative Program.

You have enough information to determine your desire for further research. The next stage involves a feasibility study which will entail a considerable amount of time and cost, and before these studies are undertaken, you should make a commitment towards site acquisition.

Before proceeding to the next stage, the property should be tied up either by:

1. **Purchase**, contingent upon a favorable feasibility study and other contingencies you or your counsel may deem necessary.

2. **Option** to purchase.

3. **Letter of intent** with certain irrevocable clauses protecting your investment and specifying price, time, terms, etc.

4. **Other agreements**, such as participating or limited partnerships, contract of sale, first right of refusal.

No matter what form the agreement takes, it must be clear to all parties concerned that, for any reason you wish to stipulate in the written agreement, you can decide not to continue with the project if it proves unfeasible.

The sales price, terms of purchase, time schedule, and all other factors pertinent to the purchase of the property need to be clearly defined, agreed upon, and understood by all parties concerned at the earliest possible time.

Uppermost among these factors are the release or forfeit of any deposits that have been advanced and who will pay for or be liable for marketing, engineering, geological, architectural, surveying, or other expenses that might be incurred in the investigation process.

There is no standard land purchase agreement form. Although real estate companies do have their own forms and at first glance they seem to look the same, they are not always the same and certainly not standard, just as there is no standard lot and no standard real estate deal.

A purchase agreement for any large site, and even most smaller ones, should be drawn up by *your* counsel and reviewed by the sellers' counsel. Legal contracts are binding—that is what they are for—but there is some credence to the old saying that contracts are only as good as those who sign them. And there is much to be said about intent—original intent.

Legal counsel is not cheap, but it is certainly inexpensive when compared to the possible pitfalls and the cost of undoing some inadvertent and seemingly minor error.

# Feasibility Study 2

## GATHERING INFORMATION

Now that the site and project have been investigated and accepted for further study, the work on the feasibility report begins. This work consists of leg work, phone calls, and in-depth site and program study.

### SOURCES

It is at this stage that you must obtain the maximum amount of information that is available pertaining to the site.

**Catalogue Sources.** All information gathered is catalogued for future reference—specifically, from whom the information was obtained and what was said—so that there are no future misunderstandings.

**Question Sources.** The information gathered is only as good as the person who gives it to you. Question his sources and get a commitment or a feeling for the durability of the information.

**See Person In Charge.** Talk to the person in charge—you will probably need to know him or her later anyway. And, value his time and information.

**Consult Government Officials Early.** Work with your government officials (director of public works, planning director, chief building inspector, etc.) and bring them into your project early.

**Other Considerations.** A project, however, cannot be totally formalized. There is still the need for enthusiasm, motivation, and knowing when something is right for you. Will the project aid your company image? Is it something you will be proud to participate in? These are all very important factors and they are a part of the final evaluation. Sometimes you have to pay too high a price for image, pride, or ego; and the business world, in general, looks upon these luxuries as secondary to profit. Bottom-line profit is the all important factor for staying in business. It determines borrowing power and it pays your salary.

## APPROACH

The forms of the Feasibility Study give you a systematic approach to the information-gathering process. These forms are the basis for collecting the type of information you need at this stage. Many people do this type of research intuitively. The purpose of this section is to show you how to do it intentionally and systematically.

The feasibility study is broken down into four major sections:

1. Site Feasibility Study—Form 200
2. Market Study of a Regional Area—Form 220
3. Market Study of a Specific Site—Form 240
4. Market Study (Conclusions)—Form 250

# SITE FEASIBILITY STUDY—FORM 200

The Site Feasibility Study is an in-depth, cover-every-base research project. The intent of this study, as it is presented in Form 200, is to give you an outline for information collection. There is no way that this form, or any other form, could cover any and all situations without becoming too complex for use.

The guidelines for this stage of information gathering are:

1. **Research.** It will be up to you to delve, pry, and dig to your own satisfaction to obtain the information you need. Suggested sources are listed under "Market Feasibility Study" later in this chapter.

2. **Organize.** The organization, processing, and cataloguing of the material gathered must be systematized and clearly done so that it is easily understandable and accessible.

3. **Disseminate.** Most important of all, it is up to you to disseminate and distribute the necessary information to your various departments and consultants. Information locked in your files, no matter how good, is useless.

200

## THE SITE FEASIBILITY STUDY

Project Locations _____
Type of Project _____

1. **TITLE STUDY**   (From preliminary TITLE REPORT)

    A.  Legal Description   (lot, block, subdivision, street address)
        _____
        _____

    B.  Size: acres _____  Sq. ft. _____
    C.  Dimensions:   width _____  depth _____
    D.  Easements and Right of Ways _____

    E.  Encumbrances _____

    F.  Covenants and Restrictions _____

    G.  Other _____

        Comments: _____

        Source: _____ Date _____

2. **FIELD INVESTIGATION** (From visual site study and engineering data available)

    A.  Off Site
        1.  Roads: adequate site access from existing roads
            ☐ yes   ☐ no   ☐ unknown   ☐ general condition _____
        2.  Storm water: do adjacent sites drain onto site
            ☐ yes   ☐ no   ☐ unknown _____
        3.  Other: _____

            Comments: _____
            Source: _____ Date _____
    B.  On Site
        1.  Storm water: does site drain naturally to existing inlet
            ☐ yes   ☐ no   ☐ unknown _____
        2.  Existing buildings:  ☐ yes   ☐ no   Describe _____
        3.  Large trees:   ☐ yes   ☐ no   Describe _____
        4.  Other: _____

            Comments: _____

            Source: _____ Date _____

3. **COUNTY/CITY AGENCIES:** jurisdiction _____

    A. Planning
        1. Zoning
            a. Present zoning _____ required zoning _____
            b. Prospects for zoning ☐ good ☐ bad ☐ unknown
                not needed
            c. Time estimate - target dates
                Design review _____
                Planning commission _____
                Board Supervisor/City Council _____
            d. Other requirements _____
                Comments: _____
                Source: _____ Date _____

    B. Public Works and/or Engineering: jurisdiction _____
        1. Streets to the site
            a. Lengthenings req. _____
            b. Widening req. _____
            c. Other improvements _____
                Comments: _____
                Source: _____ Date _____

        2. Storm sewer to the site
            a. Lengthening req. _____
            b. Resizing req. _____
            c. Other improvements _____
                Comments: _____
                Source: _____ Date _____

        3. Geological studies ☐ available ☐ not available
                ☐ required ☐ not required _____
              Comments: _____
              Source: _____ Date _____

        4. Grading permits ☐ required ☐ not required
              Comments: _____
              Source: _____ Date _____

        5. Other requirements _____

        6. Fees _____
            Comments: _____
            Source: _____ Date _____

_____
_____
_____
_____

C. Architectural Controls  (from City/County ordinance)
   1. Density
      a. Units allowed_____ Sq. ft._____
      b. Set backs: front_____ rear_____ side_____

   2. Coverage and Open Space Requirements
      a. Building coverage_____% site area
      b. Open space_____% site area

   3. Parking ratio_____

   4. Height restrictions
      Maximum height_____ Ft._____

   5. Other requirements_____
      Is there architectural review  ☐ yes  ☐ no  who?_____
      Comments:_____
      Source:_____ Date_____

4. **BUILDING DEPARTMENT:** jurisdiction_____

  A. Building Permits  ☐ available  ☐ allotted  ☐ unknown

  B. Codes Applicable  UBS 19____  special ordinance_____

  C. Other requirements_____

  D. Fees_____
    Comments:_____
    Source:_____ Date_____

5. **UTILITIES**

  A. Sanitary Sewer:  jurisdiction_____
    1. Permits        available  ☐ allotted  ☐ not needed_____
    2. Off site lengthening req'd_____
    3. Off site resizing req'd_____
    4. Other requirements_____
    5. Fees_____
      Comments:_____
      Sources:_____ Date_____

  B. Gas:  jurisdiction_____
    1. Available  ☐ yes  ☐ no
    2. Requirements_____
    3. Fees and charges_____
      Comments:_____
      Sources:_____ Date_____

C. Electric: jurisdiction _____
   1. Available ☐ yes ☐ no _____
   2. Requirements _____
   3. Fees and charges _____
   Comments: _____
   Source: _____ Date _____

D. Water: jurisdiction _____
   1. Available ☐ yes ☐ no _____
   2. Requirements _____
   3. Fees and charges _____
   Comments: _____
   Source: _____ Date _____

E. Telephone: jurisdiction _____
   1. Available ☐ yes ☐ no _____
   2. Requirements _____
   3. Fees and charges _____
   Comments: _____
   Source: _____ Date _____

F. T.V.: jurisdiction _____
   1. Available ☐ yes ☐ no _____
   2. Requirements _____
   3. Fees and charges _____
   Comments: _____
   Source: _____ Date _____

G. Other: _____
   Comments: _____
   Source: _____ Date _____

6. **PUBLIC HEALTH:** jurisdiction _____

   A. Project Impact on existing facilities _____

   B. Recommendations and requirements: _____
   Comments: _____
   Source: _____ Date _____

7. **FLOOD CONTROL:** jurisdiction _____

   A. Is the site in a flood plain ☐ yes ☐ no

   B. Recommendations and requirements: _____

    C.   Fees_____
          Comments:_____
          Source:_____ Date_____

8. **SCHOOLS:** jurisdiction_____

    A.   Are there adequate schools   ☐ yes   ☐ no

    B.   Recommendations and requirements_____
          _____
          Fees_____
          Comments:_____
          Source:_____ Date_____

9. **PARKS:** jurisdiction_____

    A.   Recommendations and requirements_____
          _____

    B.   Fees_____
          Comments:_____
          Source:_____ Date_____

10. **LEGAL:** jurisdiction_____

    A.   Annexation   ☐ req'd   ☐ not req'd   ☐ unknown

    B.   Environmental Impact Report   ☐ req'd   ☐ not req'd
          _____

    C.   Recommendations and requirements_____
          _____
          Fees_____
          Comments:_____
          Source:_____ Date_____

11. **SPECIAL AGENCIES**_____

    A.   Recommendations and requirements_____
          _____
          Fees_____
          Comments:_____
          Source:_____ Date_____

12. **OTHERS**_____

    A.   Recommendations and requirements_____
          _____
          Comments:_____
          Source:_____ Date_____

## NOTES

# THE MARKET FEASIBILITY STUDY

The market study is tremendously important. This book could be filled with fun but not funny stories of the perils and foibles of builders who ventured down the wrong road at the wrong time, giving products away for a song on the one hand, and sitting on others for long periods of time until the market caught up to the price or, even worse, the cost.

A good market study in the beginning is worth the time or money it costs, regardless of the size of the project.

## DEFINING THE MARKET

To a giant building company, a market study will determine what part of the country, or perhaps what part of the world, is the best area to place a product. Once an area is determined, considerations are, in sequence, what city, what area of that city, what specific site, and what to put on that site.

To a medium-size builder, the market study might be two separate studies—an area or city study, followed by a study of the specific site and what to put on it.

To a smaller builder, the market study could very well start with the site and what to put on that site and the price range of the finished product.

**Start Early.** You cannot start too early on your market study. Form 100 has a section devoted to a very preliminary market study. Form 100, Item 4, addresses itself to a neighborhood appearance, comparable project price range, and market forecast. For some builders, that is all the information they require or get. But in this day of keener competition, steeply accelerating costs, and market uncertainties, it is necessary to know everything about your market as well as your product.

## TESTING AND NEED

We are living in an age of overkill. Tests are run and tests are tested and margins of error are built in as a matter of course. Government agencies run studies at seemingly huge costs for everything they do and sometimes do not do. Large pharmaceutical and manufacturing companies test some of their products for years.

The building industry also continuously tests and improves their product and the most consistent changes have been in procedures. The one procedure most needed is a good market study.

**Who Does the Market Study?** There are companies that specialize in market studies and, depending upon complexity and scope of the project, you can use one of these companies, have your marketing or real estate people do it, or do it yourself.

**Question Information.** One last caution on this subject. A market report can be slanted to favor a site or area. It can be slanted to favor one type of development over another. A market study is only as good as the person conducting it, his motivation and the information fed into the process. You must ask yourself, when you are requesting or are required to supply a market study, if you want it as a sales tool to support your intuitive desire, or if you want to know the whole story.

If you inherit the market study along with the project, question the motives of the person who initiated the study.

### SOURCES OF INFORMATION

The following can help you obtain information for a market report:

1. Nearby homeowners
2. Census Bureau
3. Builders' associations
4. Manufacturers' research reports
5. Research companies
6. Subdivision sales personnel
7. U.S. Post Office
8. Trade publications
9. Lenders
10. Elected officials
11. Chamber of Commerce
12. Realty boards
13. FHA of HUD
14. Title companies
15. Utility companies
16. City/County Building, Engineering, and Planning departments

## MARKET STUDY OF A REGIONAL AREA—FORM 220

Giant companies with their base corporate offices out of the area, and sometimes out of the state, need market studies that cover large geographical areas. They need to study market trends in smaller cities surrounding several metropolitan centers at the same time. This will aid them in determining in which areas project sites can be found. They will be looking at the overall picture of growth potential, of employment availability and progress, for any indications of market soft spots for underactivity or overactivity, and for need and demand.

This type of work is almost always done by large professional marketing companies. Some building companies are large enough to have their own people and departments to handle the market study. These studies need not be difficult or complex, and just like anything else you do in business, or life for that matter, you simply determine what you want—in this case the information needed—and then go out and get it.

The general information is available through the Chamber of Commerce and sometimes the local city/county planning department. Specific information on marketing and sales can be obtained from the local real estate multiple listing board, if there is one, or its counterpart. And the data that refers directly to the housing market may be available at the nearest office of the National Association of Home Builders or at other builders' associations. It will, of course, help immensely if you are a member of the organization from which you are requesting the information.

The Market Study of a Regional Area, Form 220, is presented in outline form as a guide to the type of information that is gathered. Your determination at this time is, first, do you need a study of a large regional area? And secondly, if you do, what information do you need? Do you need only the facts that you can get or do you need the professional opinion of an outside marketing firm?

## MARKET STUDY OF A REGIONAL AREA
## OUTLINE

I. **Location**

    A. The geographical area being studied.
    B. Square miles.
    C. General description - plains, hills, coastline, creeks, rivers, rainfall, manufacturing, agricultural business.

II. **Transportation and Access**

    A. Freeway network.
    B. Public transportation.
    C. Future road construction.
    D. Railroads.
    E. Airports.

III. **Population Growth**

    A. Tabulate population growth per city and county over past 40 years. Compute percentage or rate of growth each 10 year period.
    B. Provide forecast of new growth, where they will come from and where they will settle.
    Source: Chamber of Commerce.

IV. **Industry and Employment**

    A. List major employers and how many they employ.
    B. Compute and tabulate rate of employment growth over past 10 years, listing catagories on type of employment.
    C. Average income per household.
    Source: State Employment Department.

V. **Housing Market**

    A. The general market for the area showing number of permits over the last 5 years and the price range. And try to detect hot spots.
    B. A general study of houses presently for sale in the overall area showing any areas of concentrated activity.
    C. The general attitude of municipal jurisdiction and special interest groups towards growth and development in the area.

VI. **Conclusion**

    A statement covering the findings including any recommendations or observations.

# NOTES

# MARKET STUDY OF A SPECIFIC SITE—FORM 240

Form 240, Market Study of a Specific Site, is presented in outline form—condensed and simplified.

A market study is just like any other study. It is an investigation of each part of a whole, step by step. In the case of most sites, the steps are all the same, just the names and places change and, of course, the information.

With this form, you may try to do your own market study. The small builder normally does not spend the money for such a service and, therefore, does without it. He could, however, undertake the study himself because his projects are usually small and less complicated. For anyone else contemplating the self-study of a larger, more complex program, proceed with caution. A reasonably accurate and comprehensive market study does take time and it is a very serious and important undertaking. The outline Form 240 will tell you what data to direct qualified people to compile. It will give you a method of cataloguing the information and it will direct you in how to use it.

The outline is for a residential tract. You will note that with certain minor variations it could be adapted to commercial or industrial. The outline is a suggestion of what you might expect to receive for a market study. It is not meant to tell market researchers how to conduct their business, but if you have no other source or procedure, it is the outline we use on consultation jobs and our own projects.

Remember, this is only a guide. Each site and each project has its own unique set of circumstances and it will be up to you and your researchers to recognize and include any added requirements.

It should be remembered that much of the data gathered is derived from estimates and averages. When making predictions or conclusions from this type of information, the researcher should keep in mind that the findings are based equally on factual information and professional opinion. When you hire a market research firm, you are, therefore, paying for their data-gathering expertise and their professional opinion, and their professional opinion must be based on experience and knowledge of your specific area and product.

Form 250, Market Study—Conclusions, can be used for a listing of recommendations and additional findings.

240

# MARKET STUDY OF A SPECIFIC SITE

Prepared by_____ Date_____

Site Location_____

The general area under study_____

## The Site

Site Description (acreage, proximity, heritage, beauty, activity)

_____
_____
_____

Location and Access

| City or Destination | From Site | |
|---|---|---|
| | Miles | Driving Time |
| | | |
| | | |
| | | |
| | | |
| | | |
| | | |
| | | |

Major access routes_____

Nearby freeways_____

The freeway system_____

Public transportation_____

## The Program

Type of development anticipated (number of units, use)

_____
_____
_____
_____

35

I. SITE ANALYSIS

   A. LOCATION AND EASE OF TRANSPORTATION from the area to:

   1. **Shopping:**
      Shopping center _____
      Neighborhood shopping _____

   2. **Employment:**
      Major employment center _____
      Nearby employment locations _____

   3. **Recreation:**
      Regional parks _____
      Neighborhood parks _____

   4. **Schools** - school district:
      Grade school _____
      Intermediate _____
      High school _____
      Jr. College _____

   5. **Churches** and place of worship:
      Denomination _____
      Denomination _____

   6. **Family and friends:**
      Nearby neighborhoods _____
      Nearby neighborhoods _____

   7. **Cultural areas:**
      Major _____
      Other _____

   B. GENERAL ENVIRONMENTAL QUALITY of the area:

   1. **Amount of open space** - parks and private yard area
      _____

   2. **Aesthetic** attractiveness and cleanliness of the neighborhood
      _____

   3. **Traffic** including auto and pedestrian
      _____

   4. **Class** status of the area
      _____

   5. **Ethnic** makeup
      _____

   6. **Age** and physical conditions of nearby structures
      _____

C. **QUALITY OF SCHOOLS** in the area - capacity, crowding, busing, scholastic standing, general school program.

1. Grade school _____
_____

2. Parochial school _____
_____

3. Intermediate _____
_____

4. High school _____
_____

5. Jr. college _____
_____

6. College _____
_____

D. **THE DEGREE OF PERSONAL SAFETY** in the area - crime rate, police and fire protection, street crossing safeguards, street lighting.

_____
_____
_____
_____

E. **THE PRICE OR AVERAGE VALUE** of other homes in the neighborhood or vicinity.

$ _____ to $ _____

F. **THE TYPE OF ADJACENT STRUCTURES** - single family, townhouse, apartments, commercial, industrial.

_____
_____
_____
_____
_____
_____
_____

## II. MARKET ANALYSIS

The following information is obtained to guide the marketing program in the determination of product, price, design and merchandising. This is accomplished by studying: A. Demand and absorption; B. Competition; and C. Public attitudes.

**A. DEMAND AND ABSORPTION**

The three most important contributing factors to demand and absorption are: population growth, employment growth, and supply.

**Population Growth by Municipality** in the past 3 years

Table 1A

| City/County | Population increase by amount and percent | | | | | |
|---|---|---|---|---|---|---|
| | 1976-1977 | % | 1977-1978 | % | 1978-1979 | % |
| | | | | | | |
| | | | | | | |
| | | | | | | |
| | | | | | | |
| | | | | | | |
| | | | | | | |
| | | | | | | |

Comments: _____

**Number of Housing Units Authorized** over the past 5 years as gauged by building permits issued on all new residential single family and multiple units.

Table 1B

| City/County | 1975 | 1976 | 1977 | 1978 | 1979 |
|---|---|---|---|---|---|
| | | | | | |
| | | | | | |
| | | | | | |
| | | | | | |
| | | | | | |
| | | | | | |
| | | | | | |
| | | | | | |

Comments: _____

**Employment Growth**

Table 1C

| Name & Location | Type of Business | Number of Employees | Comments Anticipated Growth |
|---|---|---|---|
|  |  |  |  |
|  |  |  |  |
|  |  |  |  |
|  |  |  |  |
|  |  |  |  |
|  |  |  |  |
|  |  |  |  |

Comments: _____
_____
_____
_____

**Supply**

The number of units by price range now on the market in the study area.

Table 1D

| Price Range | New construction | | | Re-sales unsold | Total |
|---|---|---|---|---|---|
|  | Unsold | U/C | P/I |  |  |
| Under $ 60,000 |  |  |  |  |  |
| $ 60,000—$ 75,000 |  |  |  |  |  |
| $ 75,000—$ 85,000 |  |  |  |  |  |
| $ 85,000—$100,000 |  |  |  |  |  |
| $100,000—$125,000 |  |  |  |  |  |
| Over $125,000 |  |  |  |  |  |

U/C - under construction.   P/I - permits issued not started.

Comments: _____
_____
_____

B. **COMPETITION**

Comparative research into what the competition is marketing is obtained in a direct canvas of each comparable tract in the general market area. The purpose is to determine the market standard relative to the study site in terms of product and merchandising and to compare your program, its strengths and weaknesses against the competition. The intent is not to copy the competition; in fact, quite the opposite. It is to come up with something that will be more successful and more marketable. You will be looking at your competition for things you can improve upon and by so doing, capitalize on their experience.

The data needed is covered in the Sales and Marketing Competition Questionnaire. This form also has a section on the physical and locational characteristics of the competition for direct comparison of location, proximity, and class.

The information from the Competition Questionnaire is catalogued for easy comparison in Table 2A, Market Standards; and 2B, Physical and Locational Characteristics.

From Table 2A the following patterns or market standards are derived: Table 2C, 1. Distribution of units relative to bedrooms, sq. ft. and price; and Table 2D, 2. Absorbtion rate relative to price range.

Notes:

## SALES AND MARKETING
## COMPETITION QUESTIONNAIRE

Project Name: _____
Location: _____
Developer: _____
Person Interviewed: _____
By: _____ Date: _____

1. Date sales began _____
2. Total units planned _____
3. Units completed _____ under construction _____
4. Units sold _____
5. Type of unit, distribution and sales data

| Model | BRM | Bath | Sq. ft. | Total Amount | *Absorbtion Rate | | | Price |
|-------|-----|------|---------|--------------|------------------|---|---|-------|
|       |     |      |         |              | Total Sold | Time to sell | Rate per mo. |       |
|       | 2   |      |         |              |            |              |              |       |
|       | 3   |      |         |              |            |              |              |       |
|       | 4   |      |         |              |            |              |              |       |
|       | 5   |      |         |              |            |              |              |       |

*The absorbtion rate is calculated by dividing the number of units sold by the number of months it took to sell them:

6. Amenities
   included: _____
   _____
   _____
   Offered as extra _____
   _____

7. Unique features: _____
   _____
   Comments: _____
   _____
   _____

# PHYSICAL AND LOCATIONAL CHARACTERISTICS
## OF THE COMPETITION

1. Architectural style_____
   _____

   Type of structure_____
   _____

   Size_____
   Color_____

2. Special features_____
   _____
   _____
   _____
   _____

3. Location_____
   Distance to shopping_____
   Town center_____
   Transportation_____
   Schools_____
   _____

   Employment_____
   _____
   _____

4. General neighborhood appearance_____
   _____

   Comments:_____
   _____
   _____

## MARKET STANDARDS
### Data Catalogue from Survey of Nearby Subdivision

Table 2A

| DATA | 1 Tract Name / Location | | 2 Tract Name / Location | | 3 Tract Name / Location | | 4 Tract Name / Location | |
|---|---|---|---|---|---|---|---|---|
| Start of sales | | | | | | | | |
| No. units planned | | | | | | | | |
| Completed | | | | | | | | |
| Under construction | | | | | | | | |
| Sold | | | | | | | | |
| Unsold | | | | | | | | |
| Absorption Rate: | Month | Year | Month | Year | Month | Year | Month | Year |
| PLAN # | | | | | | | | |
| Bedrooms | | | | | | | | |
| Baths | | | | | | | | |
| Floor area | | | | | | | | |
| Number garage/CP | | | | | | | | |
| Number stories | | | | | | | | |
| Number units | | | | | | | | |
| Price per plan | | | | | | | | |
| Amenities included | | | | | | | | |
| Amenities extra | | | | | | | | |
| Comments | | | | | | | | |

## PHYSICAL AND LOCATIONAL CHARACTERISTICS

Data catalogue from Survey of Physical and Locational Characteristics of the Competition

Table 2B

|    |                                          | Project 1 | Project 2 | Project 3 | Project 4 |
|----|------------------------------------------|-----------|-----------|-----------|-----------|
| 1. | Architecture<br>Style<br>Size<br>Color   |           |           |           |           |
| 2. | Special Features                         |           |           |           |           |
| 3. | Location Distance to:<br>Shopping<br>Town<br>Transport<br>Schools<br>Employment |           |           |           |           |
| 4. | General nearby neighborhood appearance   |           |           |           |           |

Comments:

**DISTRIBUTION OF UNITS** compiled from Table 2A

Table 2C

| Type Unit | | Square foot range | | Distribution | | Price Range | |
|---|---|---|---|---|---|---|---|
| BRM | BATH | From | To | Units | % | From | To |
| 2 | | | | | | | |
| 3 | | | | | | | |
| 4 | | | | | | | |
| 5 | | | | | | | |

Comments: _____
_____
_____

**ABSORPTION RATE RELATIVE TO PRICE RANGE** from Table 2A

Table 2D

| Type Unit | Rate of Absorption | | Price Range Alternative | | |
|---|---|---|---|---|---|
| BRM | Month | Year | 1 | 2 | 3 |
| 2 | | | | | |
| 3 | | | | | |
| 4 | | | | | |
| 5 | | | | | |

Comments: _____
_____
_____

## C. PUBLIC ATTITUDE

The study of public attitude is concerned first with understanding <u>who</u> the segment of the market that relates to the study site is. This is measured by <u>neighborhood profile</u> which usually necessitates a door-to-door or telephone canvas of the households close by. Neighborhood Profile Questionnaire is the suggested questionnaire and <u>Table 3A</u> is the catalogue for this information. This data will aide in determining the neighborhood stability, migration, family make-up, age group, status, and income. This type of information is usually an indication of the market that the study site will be drawing from, and the people that will be attracted.

Public attitude is next concerned with what the people want or <u>consumers preference</u>. Data on consumer preference by region is available from several building journals: Housing, Professional Builder and Building. This information can be transferred to Table 3B. Consumer preference can also be measured in the study area as a part of the neighborhood profile - in this case it is captioned <u>neighborhood preference</u> and is catalogued in Table 3C.

NOTES:

# NEIGHBORHOOD PROFILE
## QUESTIONNAIRE

ADDRESS _____

BY _____ DATE _____

1. How long have you lived at this address?

    ☐ 0-1 year     ☐ 1-2 years     ☐ 2-5 years     ☐ 5 years or more

2. Where did you last live?

    _____

3. Number of persons in household?

    1   2   3   4   5   6   or more

4. Age group of head of household?

    ☐ under 30     ☐ 30 - 45     ☐ 45 - 65     ☐ over 65

5. Where does head of household work?

    _____

6. Head of household's occupation.

    _____

7. Combined family income range:

    ☐ under $15,000     ☐ $15-25,000     ☐ $25-35,000

    ☐ $35-50,000        ☐ $50-70,000     ☐ over $70,000

    Comments _____
    _____
    _____
    _____
    _____
    _____

## NEIGHBORHOOD PREFERENCE

What would you like to have in your next home?

1. Style: ranch_____ split_____ 1½_____ 2 story_____
2. Sq. ft._____
3. Garage: 1_____ 2_____ 3_____    Carport: 1_____ 2_____ _____
4. Bedrooms: 2_____ 3_____ 4_____ 5_____ _____
5. Baths: 1_____ 1½_____ 2_____ 2½_____ 3_____ _____
6. Living Rm: formal_____ larger_____ smaller_____ _____
7. Dining: formal_____ combined with kit. family rm._____ _____
8. Family Rm. larger_____ smaller_____ none_____ _____
9. Unfinished bonus type area:_____

Other_____

Amenities:   ■ Expected   ☒ Would pay extra for   ☐ Unwanted

- ☐ range and oven
- ☐ dishwasher
- ☐ disposal
- ☐ compactor
- ☐ microwave oven
- ☐ pantry
- ☐ ceramic counters
- ☐ air-conditioning
- ☐ central vac
- ☐ security system
- ☐ intercom

- ☐ fireplace   ☐ LR   ☐ FR
- ☐ gas log starter
- ☐ garage door opener
- ☐ walk-in closets
- ☐ spa
- ☐ sauna
- ☐ vaulted ceilings
- ☐ concrete patio
- ☐ fences   ☐ rear   ☐ side
- ☐ landscaping   ☐ front   ☐ rear
- ☐ pool

Other:_____

# NEIGHBORHOOD PROFILE
Survey of Nearby Residences

Table 3A

| Questions | Responses | | Questions | Responses | |
|---|---|---|---|---|---|
| | Number | % | | Number | % |
| 1. How long have you lived at this address?<br>0 - 1 year<br>1 - 2 years<br>2 - 5 years<br>5 years or more<br>TOTAL | | 100% | 5. Where does head of household work?<br><br>vicinity of site<br><br>next closest city<br><br>city 2<br><br>in county<br><br>travels<br>TOTAL | | 100% |
| 2. Where did you last live?<br><br>vicinity of site<br><br>next closest city<br><br>city 2<br><br>other county<br><br>out of state<br>TOTAL | | 100% | 6. Head of household's occupation?<br><br>retail, wholesale, insurance, banking, real estate, professional, scientific, government, personal service, retired semi-retired.<br><br>TOTAL | | 100% |
| 3. Number of persons in household?<br><br>1.<br>2.<br>3.<br>4.<br>5.<br>6 or more<br>TOTAL | | 100% | 7. Combined family income?<br><br>under $15,000<br>15,000-25,000<br>25,000-35,000<br>35,000-50,000<br>50,000-70,000<br>over $70,000<br>TOTAL | | 100% |
| 4. Age group of Head of Household?<br><br>Under 30<br>30 - 45<br>45 - 65<br>over 65<br>TOTAL | | 100% | | | |

Comments: _____
_____
_____

## CONSUMER PREFERENCE

Table 3B
Regional Data From _____

In the price range and region under study buyers prefer:

1. Style: by %   ranch _____   split _____   1½ _____   2 story _____   _____
2. Sq. ft. _____
3. Garages  one _____   2 _____   3 _____   carport _____   _____
4. Bedrooms: by %   2 _____   3 _____   4 _____   5 _____   _____
5. Baths: by %   1 _____   1½ _____   2 _____   2½ _____   3 _____   _____
6. Living Rm: by %   formal _____   larger _____   smaller _____   _____
7. Dining: by %   formal _____   combined with kit. _____   family rm. _____
8. Family Rm: by %   larger _____   smaller _____   _____
9. Unfinished bonus type area: _____
Other: _____

Amenities:          ■ Expected          ☑ Would pay extra for          ☐ unwanted
  ☐ Range and oven      ☐ dishwasher            ☐ garage door opener
  ☐ compactor           ☐ microwave oven        ☐ pantry
  ☐ ceramic counters    ☐ air-conditioning      ☐ central vac
  ☐ security system     ☐ intercom              ☐ fireplace ☐ LR ☐ FR
  ☐ gas log starter     ☐ walk-in closets       ☐ spa
  ☐ sauna               ☐ vaulted ceilings      ☐ concrete patio
  ☐ fences ☐ rear ☐ side  ☐ pool                ☐ landscaping ☐ front ☐ rear

## NEIGHBORHOOD PREFERENCE

Table 3C
Neighborhood Data _____

In their next home nearby residents would like to have:

1. Style: by %   ranch _____   split _____   1½ _____   2 story _____   _____
2. Sq. ft. _____
3. Garages  one _____   2 _____   3 _____   carport _____   _____
4. Bedrooms: by %   2 _____   3 _____   4 _____   5 _____   _____
5. Baths: by %   1 _____   1½ _____   2 _____   2½ _____   3 _____   _____
6. Living Rm: by %   formal _____   larger _____   smaller _____   _____
7. Dining Rm: by %   formal _____   combined with kit. family rm. _____
8. Family Rm: by %   larger _____   smaller _____   _____
9. Unfinished bonus type area: _____
Other: _____

Amenities:          ■ Expected          ☑ Would pay extra for          ☐ unwanted
  ☐ Range and oven      ☐ dishwasher            ☐ garage door opener
  ☐ compactor           ☐ microwave oven        ☐ pantry
  ☐ ceramic counters    ☐ air-conditioning      ☐ central vac
  ☐ security system     ☐ intercom              ☐ fireplace ☐ LR ☐ FR
  ☐ gas log starter     ☐ walk-in closets       ☐ spa
  ☐ sauna               ☐ vaulted ceilings      ☐ concrete patio
  ☐ fences ☐ rear ☐ side  ☐ pool                ☐ landscaping ☐ front ☐ rear

# MARKET STUDY

## CONCLUSIONS

Prepared by:_____ Date_____

Site Location:_____

_____

**A. RECOMMENDATIONS:**

1. **Type of project**_____
2. **Number of units**_____
3. **Type of units** (from Table 2A, 2C, 2B and 3C)

| Type Unit | | Square Feet | Distribution | |
|---|---|---|---|---|
| BRM | Bath | | Units | Percent |
| 2 | | | | |
| 3 | | | | |
| 4 | | | | |
| 5 | | | | |

4. **Amenities** (from Table 2A, 3B and 3C)
   Included as standard_____
   _____

   offered as extra_____
   _____

5. **Price range** relative to absorption rate and length of project (from Table 2D)

| Type Unit | Distribution | | Price Range Alternatives | | |
|---|---|---|---|---|---|
| Bedrooms | Units | Percent | 1 | 2 | 3 |
| 2 | | | | | |
| 3 | | | | | |
| 4 | | | | | |
| 5 | | | | | |
| Estimated absorption rate and time to complete project | | | | | |
| | per month | | | | |
| | per year | | | | |
| Total length of sales per price range | | | | | |

250

51

B. **ADDITIONAL FINDING:**

1. **Strength of Market** - The present and historical demand of the study area in the selected price range. (From Table 1A, 1B, 1C)
   _____
   _____

2. **Location Parameters** - The advantage and disadvantages of the location and any remedial steps. (From Site Analysis)
   _____
   _____

3. **Site Parameters** - Restrictions or restraints imposed by site contour or configuration, municipalities. (From Site Study)
   _____
   _____

4. **Price Parameters** - What are the upper limits of the competition sales prices? What unique features or offering does your site have that would justify a higher price level? (From Table 2A, 2D)
   _____
   _____

5. **Market Study** - What is being offered in your area and price range? (From Table 2A, 2B)
   _____
   _____

6. **Markets to be Sought** - The type of people to appeal to including income, household size, employment, age. (From Site Analysis, Paragraph 2D, 2E, Market Analysis Table 3A)
   _____
   _____

7. **Competitive Edge** - What to include in your program or package that will give you an advantage over your competition. This advantage can be in the form of any or all of the following: (a) Neighborhood and location; (b) Price and financing; (c) Curb appeal; (d) The plan; (e) Amenities; (f) Your reputation; (g) Salesmanship; and (h) Marketing and publicity.
   _____
   _____
   _____

   Comments:_____
   _____
   _____
   _____

# Forward Planning Stage 3

## PLANNING AND MOBILIZATION

The Forward Planning Stage of the construction process is the planning and mobilization phase which precedes the actual physical construction. In other words, it is the business administration function that is so important and so many times put off or ignored by new or relatively small businessmen. Large or medium-size established companies have their guidelines and procedures or they most surely would not still be in business. This section is dedicated to the newer company and the "little guy" who wants a bigger slice of the "construction pie" and has to compete with established and well-organized companies. For the existing companies, this section will serve as a reminder or comparison and also as a training tool for new members of the firm.

## FRONT OFFICE MANAGERIAL FUNCTIONS

The Forward Planning Stage covers what is generally the front office managerial functions. The man in the field is usually only vaguely familiar with this stage. It covers the many things that must happen before a project starts: the forming of the company; the selection of the team members; obtaining and dealing with government subdivision or zoning approvals so necessary in today's building business; commissioning and directing the design teams; setting up contracts and purchasing, which includes bidding and the office manipulations that are entailed; organizing bookkeeping and accounting; and funding or financing the project.

## 54 / Forward Planning Stage

The Forward Planning Stage covers that part of the business that keeps you in business. There is no way that a company or an individual in today's sophisticated and computerized business society can compete on any scale without doing his book work—without knowing where he stands now and at the projected end of any given job.

The Forward Planning Stage is the bookkeeping and record-keeping procedure that keeps all of the many pieces of the construction process together and on schedule. When done correctly, it will give you a record of when jobs were done or submitted for approval, when they can be expected to be completed, and what the next orderly procedure is. It takes the mystery and exclusivity out of the managerial function, allows for delegation of responsibilities, and alleviates rushed deadlines by providing for necessary lead time.

# FORWARD PLANNING SCHEDULE—FORM 300

The key form that regulates and directs the planning and mobilization phase is a central control document we call the Forward Planning Schedule. This form, filled out as events are scheduled and again when they take place, provides a checklist and logical order to follow. The Forward Planning Schedule starts with land or project acquisition or the letter of intent and continues on through to the final construction. This form, or one like it, should be your key scheduling and time documentation source and your most important business administration tool.

The Forward Planning Schedule is meant to make the builder or developer aware of many of the pitfalls encountered in building. This form is not all-encompassing and can be changed to suit each builder's specific and particular needs. The basic logical concept behind the form will hold true for most areas and most projects.

### A CHECKLIST OF FUNCTIONS

Form 300 is a checklist of important functions that may have to be performed. To the experienced builder, it will only serve as a reminder. To the people just joining the industry, it will be a valuable aid. For instance, if the individual or entity does not know that a soils report is a normal requirement in the proper planning of a development, then, of a certainty, there will be mistakes made in this area. The worst thing that can happen is remedial action, such as hurry up, catch up, do it a second time, do it late, do it again. The purpose of Form 300 is to make the builder aware of the many facets of our industry.

Some people might think this form is too detailed. Others who are used to PERT systems may think it too simplified. Most who use this form find it to be extremely versatile. This form can be used for single or multiple residential, including tracts and townhouses. It is also used for office complexes and industrial, both individual parcels and industrial parks.

## KEEPING THE BUILDING TEAM INFORMED

For large national development companies who have many employees—each one delegated a different task, such as purchasing, land acquisition, marketing—it is extremely important that the president or general manager be kept informed at all times of the progress of each project, regardless of what stage it is in. And everyone in the group can be fully apprised by the timely filling out of Form 300 on a twice-monthly basis.

The form can introduce the new builder to the many pieces that constitute a project. It can be used by the experienced developer to further communication and coordination which is necessary in bringing all of his projects to a timely and profitable conclusion.

The important thing to realize about Form 300 is that it neither starts nor ends right here. It is a basic project-scheduling document that covers the entire scope of the project, starting at the beginning and going through the entire construction process. In a file of project documents, this form would act as or be part of the cover letter. All other forms, including the all important cost and profit form, would be duly noted as to date completed and would be appropriately filled.

Form 300 is presented here in the beginning of the planning stage. It is an ongoing document that needs to be referred to and updated throughout the project. You will be going back to it in the bidding stage and the construction stage.

# FORWARD PLANNING SCHEDULE

300

Project _____  Type of Development _____
No. Acres _____  Purchase Price Per Acre _____
No. Units _____  Total Purchase Price _____
                                  Raw Land Cost Per Unit _____

| Operation | Original Date | Revision 1 | Revision 2 | Actual |
|---|---|---|---|---|
| **I. FEASIBILITY** | | | | |
| 1. Letter of Intent | | | | |
| 2. Economic & Engineering Feasibility Study Days _____ | | | | |
| 3. Enter Escrow - Close Date Extension Time _____ | | | | |
| 4. Contingencies _____ | | | | |
| 5. Feasibility Cost & Profit | | | | |
| 6. Governmental Approval Zoning Use Permits | | | | |
| 7. Board Approval | | | | |
| 8. Seller Notified of Approval | | | | |
| 9. Final Cost & Profit | | | | |
| 10. Purchase Property | | | | |
| **II. FUNDING** | | | | |
| 1. Lender | | | | |
| 2. Preliminary Package Submitted | | | | |
| 3. Final Package Submitted | | | | |
| 4. Loan Approval | | | | |

**III. ADDITIONAL COST & PROFIT SUBMITTALS**

Tract

| | |
|---|---|
| 1. | |
| 2. | |
| 3. | |
| 4. | |
| 5. | |

| Operation | Original Date | Revision 1 | Revision 2 | Actual |
|---|---|---|---|---|
| III. ADDITIONAL COST & PROFIT SUBMITTALS Tract | | | | |
| 6. | | | | |
| 7. | | | | |
| 8. | | | | |
| 9. | | | | |
| 10. | | | | |
| IV. LAND PLANNING UNITS | | | | |
| 1. Receive Land Planning Assignment Sheet | | | | |
| 2. Engineer: _____ | | | | |
| a. Authorize Preliminary Investigation | | | | |
| b. Request Map Schedule | | | | |
| c. Receive Map Schedule and Letter of Proposal | | | | |
| d. Receive Preliminary Engineering Cost Estimate | | | | |
| e. Authorize to Proceed | | | | |
| f. Receive Engineer's Final Cost Estimate | | | | |
| V. LAND PLANNER | | | | |
| 1. Authorize Preliminary | | | | |
| 2. Request Preliminary Plan | | | | |
| 3. Request Land Planner's Sched | | | | |
| 4. Receive Land Planner's Sched | | | | |
| 5. Receive Preliminary Plan | | | | |
| 6. Receive Final Layout | | | | |

| Operation | Original Date | Revision 1 | Revision 2 | Actual |
|---|---|---|---|---|
| **VI. SOILS ENGINEER** | | | | |
| 1. Authorize Soils | | | | |
| 2. Receive Preliminary Report | | | | |
| 3. Receive Final Report | | | | |
| **VII. ENVIRONMENTAL IMPACT REPORTS** | | | | |
| 1. Ordered From _____ | | | | |
| 2. Date Due in House | | | | |
| 3. Date to City for Review | | | | |
| **VII. LANDSCAPE ARCHITECT** | | | | |
| 1. Authorize Preliminary | | | | |
| 2. Receive Preliminary | | | | |
| 3. Authorize Final | | | | |
| 4. Receive Final | | | | |
| **IX. ARCHITECTURAL** | | | | |
| 1. Receive Architectural Assignment | | | | |
| 2. Architect _____ | | | | |
|    a. Authorize Prelim. Plans | | | | |
|    b. Request Arch. Schedule | | | | |
|    c. Receive Arch. Schedule | | | | |
|    d. Receive Preliminary Plans | | | | |
|    e. Authorize Final Plans | | | | |
|    f. Receive Final Concrete Layout for Land | | | | |
|    g. Receive Final Plans | | | | |
| **X. PRODUCTION COSTS** | | | | |
| 1. Bid Construction — Start: | | | | |
|    Complete: | | | | |
| 2. Prepare Cost Estimate Based on Bids — Start: | | | | |
|    Complete: | | | | |

| Operation | | Original Date | Revision 1 | Revision 2 | Actual |
|---|---|---|---|---|---|
| X. PRODUCTION COSTS (Cont.) | | | | | |
| 3. Prepare Contracts | Start: | | | | |
| | Complete: | | | | |
| 4. Prepare Final Costs | Start: | | | | |
| | Complete: | | | | |
| XI. IMPROVEMENTS | | | | | |
| 1. Street Improvement | Order: | | | | |
| | Receive: | | | | |
| 2. Receive Preliminary Engineer's Cost Estimate | | | | | |
| 3. Final Improvement Drawings | Start: | | | | |
| | Receive: | | | | |
| 4. Bid Street Improvements | Start: | | | | |
| | Complete: | | | | |
| 5. Prepare Contracts | Start: | | | | |
| | Complete: | | | | |
| 6. Receive Engineer's Final Costs | | | | | |
| 7. Prepare Final Costs | Start: | | | | |
| | Complete: | | | | |
| 8. Receive Final Map for Recording | | | | | |
| 9. Lot Grading | Start: | | | | |
| | Complete: | | | | |
| 10. Improvements | Start: | | | | |
| | Complete: | | | | |
| XII. CONSTRUCTION MODELS | | | | | |
| 1. Schedule Received for Completion of Models | | | | | |
| 2. Building Permits | Submitted: | | | | |
| | Received: | | | | |
| 3. Start Models | | | | | |

| Operation | | Original Date | Revision 1 | Revision 2 | Actual |
|---|---|---|---|---|---|
| **XII. CONSTRUCTION** | | | | | |
| **MODELS (Continued)** | | | | | |
| 4. Complete Models | | | | | |
| 5. Start Model Landscaping | | | | | |
| 6. Complete Model Landscaping | | | | | |
| **XIII. PRODUCTION UNITS** | | | | | |
| 1. Schedule | Order: | | | | |
| | Received: | | | | |
| 2. Building Permits | Submitted: | | | | |
| | Received: | | | | |
| 3. Production Units | Start: | | | | |
| | Complete: | | | | |
| 4. Common Area & Landscape | Start: | | | | |
| | Complete: | | | | |
| 5. Complete First Unit | | | | | |
| 6. Complete Final Unit | | | | | |
| **XIV. ADDITIONAL COMMENTS OR SCHEDULES** | | | | | |
| | | | | | |
| | | | | | |
| | | | | | |
| | | | | | |
| | | | | | |
| | | | | | |
| | | | | | |
| | | | | | |
| | | | | | |
| | | | | | |
| | | | | | |
| | | | | | |
| | | | | | |
| | | | | | |
| | | | | | |
| | | | | | |
| | | | | | |
| | | | | | |

# LEGAL ORGANIZATION OF A CONSTRUCTION COMPANY

In the building industry, legal questions arise in almost every facet of the construction process, from forming a company to paying workmen for their services. Anyone venturing into a new business should have a knowledge of the laws that govern, protect, and define that business.

## FORMS OF BUSINESS

The legal organization of a contracting business can take several forms. The builder has his choice between sole proprietorship, joint venture, general partnership, limited partnership, and a corporation.

The simplest form of business a builder can choose is proprietorship. In the name John Smith DBA Ace Builders, DBA means *doing business as*. All the sole proprietor has to do to get in business is hang out a sign and file a fictitious business name certificate with the county in which he is doing business.

**Joint Venture and General Partnership.** Another form of business would be a joint venture. A joint venture involves two or more parties. It is the same as a partnership, except that a joint venture is for one particular transaction. Joint ventures have the same relationship to each other as partners do in a partnership. They are as fully liable for all the debts and obligations in a joint venture as partners are. The only difference between a general partnership and a joint venture is that the joint venture is formed for one particular project—you buy a piece of land, develop it, sell it, and terminate. A partnership is one step beyond that. It is made up of two people or more who go into a general partnership together, agree to do business together, and do many projects. In either case, if the joint venture or the partnership is going to acquire title to the property, they have to file a statement. In the case of partnerships, it is called a statement of partnership; in the case of joint ventures, it is called a statement of joint venture. In the past, most joint ventures did not take title to the property. Instead, the property was placed in the names of the individuals in undivided interest because title companies were reluctant to insure title for joint ventures. But most title companies now accept a recorded statement of joint venture, which is the same as a recorded statement of the partnership. You can use a joint venture to the same extent that you can use a general partnership.

**Limited Partnership.** Limited partnership involves one or more general partners and one or more limited partners. A general partner can be you as an individual; it can be your corporation; or can be another partnership, either general or limited. It can be a general partner in a limited partnership. Limited partners are the individuals who can do nothing but contribute their money. They only have a right or certain very limited rights. Mainly, they have a right to get profits on the money they put in. They cannot lose anymore than they have put into it.

The general partner who runs the business takes all the risks and, supposedly, is rewarded with an appropriate share of the profits, though usually he has to pay the limited partners whatever they have put in, plus whatever their agreed rate of return is, before he gets his money out. Limited partnership is a convenient vehicle for financing some of your developments when you need some cash and you cannot get it from conventional sources. You could have a tax shelter involved because you have some expenses that could be written off. You can get a group of doctors, dentists, lawyers, or others to put in some money as limited partners so they can get tax shelter and some profit.

Corporation. The corporation method is probably most often used by builders who have been in the business for a long time. They do it because it limits their liability, which is very important if you're in a high-risk business—and building is a high-risk business. If you have a lot of exposure and not all of it can be insured, the only way you can protect the fortune that you have built up over the years is to limit your liability by incorporating.

In incorporating, your lawyer will tell you that there are certain procedures you have to follow to make the corporation work well. You have to adequately capitalize it. That means you have to put in enough of your own money—equity money for stock, not loans—to give the corporation a reasonable chance of being able to succeed in the building business. No one can tell you what that amount is.

An action which a creditor can use against a corporate shareholder is called *piercing the corporate veil action.* That means that if for some reason you run into financial difficulty—you cannot pay your bills, a creditor sues you, and the assets of the corporation are not sufficient to pay the debt—he can file an action to pierce the corporate veil and he can claim that you did not put enough of your own money into the corporation initially to give it a reasonable chance of succeeding in the business world. If he can prove that, and the court will use 20/20 hindsight and look back in making the determination as to whether you put in enough money, your corporate veil is pierced and he can go against you directly, personally, for whatever amount of money is left over after he takes your corporate assets.

You do not have to form a corporation and put in $50,000 to get started in business. If you put in $2,000 and then make some money, soon you can put in $10,000 or $15,000 and buy stock. If you get past this initial period, you are probably going to be all right. The main thing is that at some point, prior to the time when your creditors become involved, you had enough of your own money at risk in that corporation so that a court will say the company was adequately capitalized, saying, in effect, "Leave the guy alone; you've taken his corporation, that's all you're entitled to."

There are other grounds for piercing a corporate veil. If you fail to act like a corporation, i.e., if you do not hold regular meetings, if you do not keep regular minutes or fail to keep them up to date, if you operate as if you were really a sole proprietorship, or a partnership, and you ignore the formalities, the corporate veil may be pierced.

There is also the so-called "alter ego doctrine"—the other "self." The corporation is really you. It is not an independent entity because you have not treated it as such. It can be a wild fantasy or fiction because of a new corporation law that provides for one-man corporations. It used to be that you had to have at least three directors and some directors' meetings. It was more or less a bonafide deal. Although everybody would tend to slough off the meetings, they would dummy up the minutes once a year and they would say that the directors met at 7:30 P.M. at such and such a place, held a meeting, and passed resolutions. Well, the meeting never occurred. The minutes were signed and you are covered. A new corporation law was passed that says you can have a one-man corporation and the sole stockholder is also the chief executive officer and president, he is vice president, secretary, treasurer, chief financial officer. So what happens to the "alter ego doctrine?" Well, there has not been a case yet that has been tried on the grounds that such a corporation was really meaningless. You will find that most careful people that have one-man corporations act as if they were three-man corporations. They have meetings, and the minutes are funny if you read them. They say the directors met, and after discussion the following resolutions were passed. It is a charade that you have to go through to protect yourself. It sounds ridiculous, but your attorney will tell you, you have to do it.

## LICENSES

If you do incorporate, of course, your corporation has to be licensed. Whatever your license is, contractor's license, real estate broker's license, you have to license your corporation as well as yourself. In the state of California, in any building or construction company, no matter what form the organization takes, at least one member or employee of that firm has to be licensed. State laws vary and it is important to check this point with the state agency regulating licensing in your state.

## ATTORNEYS

At some point in your business, you are going to need the services of an attorney. It is important to know how to find an attorney, how to work with him, how he can save you money, and how to avoid paying more money than you have to for legal services.

**Get a Specialist.** The first thing you want to do is get a specialist. You would not go to a pediatrician to have your appendix out, so do not go to a tax lawyer or a trial lawyer to get answers on a real estate problem. There are attorneys within the real estate field who specialize in different areas. There are times you may need the services of different attorneys. There are very few who cover the entire spectrum of real estate law because it is a very broad field. There are some who specialize in construction problems and lien problems and those who work out the kinds of problems touched on briefly here. If you have a real estate problem, do not give it to your regular attorney. He may be fully experienced in his field, but you may lose time while he is grapling with your problem for a number of weeks.

**Environmental Specialist.** Environmental law is another special area. There are attorneys who specialize in this area. They deal with planning commissions, state boards, Federal boards, and getting big projects approved. If you have a problem, you better get someone who is familiar with the law in this area and who has the expertise. If you have a problem with processing through the local Department of Real Estate or problems with a Map Act, developing projects, or working with a city or county government, you better get someone who is experienced in those fields.

**Trial Lawyer.** If you run into litigation and get sued, your real estate attorney may or may not be a trial lawyer. If he tells you that he wants you to get someone else to handle it, get someone else. In fact, you might ask him if he feels fully comfortable handling this piece of litigation. Assure him that he is not going to lose your account, that you still want him to handle your real estate business, but you want to be sure that the litigation is handled properly. And most attorneys can understand your point of view.

**Tax Specialist.** Tax, obviously, is a specialty. When you have a tax problem, get an accountant and get a tax lawyer. There is a tendency to put off seeing a lawyer until you have a serious problem, and that is a mistake. It will cost you a lot more to solve it after it is under way than it would if you hired him in the beginning.

**Attorney's Fees.** In dealing with your attorney, you want to have a clear understanding with him in the beginning as to his areas of responsibility. You also want to have a clear understanding with him on fees. On what basis is he going to charge you? Is he going to charge you a standard hourly rate? Is he going to charge you for whatever he does for you if he thinks you have a good result or a bad one? Is he going to charge you on a flat fee basis for so much a unit for helping you with subdivision work? Work that out in advance to determine what he thinks the fees will be on a particular job. Do not make the mistake of trying to box him into a corner. You do not want your attorney locked into working on a particular job for a set fee while he is losing money on it and not even making his overhead. It is reasonable for you to ask him for an estimate.

You have to understand that most legal problems are not capable of exact definition. You can tell someone what it is going to cost to build a house, within certain limits. An attorney, with few exceptions, cannot tell you what it is going to cost exactly to handle a particular case. He can give you a range; he can say, "Well, the last two or three I did cost between $1,500 and $2,000." You can say, "Okay, that sounds all right, are you going to bill me on an hourly rate? What is it going to be?" He'll tell you and you can say, "All right, I want to be billed monthly. I want to know exactly where I stand. I don't want you to hold things back for six months and then send me a huge bill. And, if we run into any problems on this project, or if it looks like the fees are going to be higher than you estimated, let's talk about it. Tell me, I don't want any surprises."

## LEGAL PROBLEMS IN BUILDING

A builder is always exposed. In a slide situation, for example, everyone involved in the project—the builder, the architect, the civil engineer, the soils engineer, the subcontractors—will get sued and they will accuse each other. Terrible, terrible lawsuits ensue. They go on for months and years, and the depositions just mount and mount, because everyone has to have his deposition taken, and everyone is represented by an attorney. Hopefully, if you ever get into a situation like that, you will be covered by insurance. When you are served with a complaint, send it to your insurance company with a tender letter saying you tender defense to them.

There may or may not be coverage for the liability, depending upon how the complaint is worded. They will usually owe you a defense at their expense. The only thing you have to watch out for, if they accept the tender, is that you are not sandbagged somewhere along the line. If they just go through the motions of defending you, reserving their rights not to pay any judgment, and if you do not pay any attention to the lawsuit (i.e., let them handle it, and they lose it) there will be a big judgment. They have given you the free defense, but you end up having to pay some money. So, you have to watch out for that. Sometimes, even though they take the defense, you may have to have your own lawyer look over their shoulder to make sure they are doing their job properly.

One of the problems that insurance companies get into in the above situation is a conflict of interest. They may be defending several different parties for the lawsuit who really should be represented by independent counsel because one of them is more at fault than the other. But if they are representing both of them, they are in a very difficult situation. Do not allow them to defend you and someone else at the same time. If you think that someone else is the guy responsible, you have to insist on an independent counsel.

In slide situations, there are cases in which no one will ever be able to prove exactly why something happened. All we know is that it did happen, there was damage, and someone has to pay. It may be you. That is a risk, however, that you can insure against.

## LEGAL PROBLEMS IN DEVELOPMENT

**Subdivision Processing.** Any subdivision or project that you want to develop—planned unit development project, condominium, etc.—generally requires a map, Department of Real Estate processing, and processing through the city or the county. It can entail subdivision maps, building permits, changes in zoning, moritoriums, and delays.

**Time Limits.** If you are processing a subdivision map or a condominium plan, there are certain time limits that are built into the subdivision Map Act. The Map Act says, generally, that if you file a tentative map, the planning commission, if there is one, or the council if there isn't a planning commission, has a certain amount of time within which to consider that map and either approve or disapprove it, or approve it with conditions. If they have not acted on your map within a certain period of time, the code says it is deemed approved. They have to act on it unless you, the property owner or the developer, have somehow waived those time limits. What happens? You are standing at the planning commission meeting. Forty-five days have gone by since the time you filed your tentative map. The planning commission has just heard it, and the chairman says to you, "Mr. Developer, we would like more time to study this map. Would you have any objection if we postponed the hearing on this for two weeks?" If you agree, you waive your right to get automatic approval five days later, and once it's gone, it's gone forever. What should you do in that case? Well, you have some options. You could say, "Mr. Chairman, I'll be glad to agree to a continuance for ten days or two weeks, but not beyond that." And make sure that it is in the record. Or you could insist upon your right. You could say, "No, I don't want any continuances." If you do that, it's kind of a "Brinksmanship Game"; you are inviting them to deny you. However, if they deny you, you can turn to another section of the Map Act which says that if they deny you, they can only do it on certain grounds. And if they deny you and they fail to state the ground upon which they are denying you, or they state what the ground is and it is not one of those which is listed, then you can go into court. You can tell the judge that you were denied on the wrong ground, and the judge will say the map is approved.

**Vested Rights Document.** What happens if you get your map approved for 8,000-square-foot lots and you put in your off-site improvements and six months later, when you request some building permits, you find out that two weeks earlier the city council passed a new ordinance rezoning the property to 10,000-square-foot lots? Your request is denied. What should you have done? You should have kept informed of what was going on in City Hall and you should have picked up your building permits and started some work before they changed the zoning. This is what's known as the *Vested Rights Document*. You have to get a building permit, you have to start work, you have to get some concrete poured, in order to have the right to continue if they down zone your property. It does not matter how much money you have spent on other things.

**The Youngblood Case.** Here is another example of what can happen to you. Suppose you receive approval on your tentative map for one-acre lots—50 lots in an area that is zoned one-acre on a hillside. You quickly get your final map prepared and meet all the conditions. You return with a final map two months later to record it and to get it approved. Your appearance before the city council should be routine. You have your tenant map, and they say: "Oh, Mr. Developer, we cannot approve your final map because we've changed our general plan, and what was previously zoned one-acre lots is now zoned hillside/residential. We have a new slope density formula. You had 50 lots there before; you now have 25 lots. Your map is no good." What do you do then? You do not lose this time. You did, up until the California Supreme Court ruled in the *Youngblood* case that if you present a final map which is in accordance with the tentative map, and the tentative map is in accordance with the zoning and the general plan at the time it was approved, you get your final approval. In other words, it doesn't make any difference if, in the meantime, they have changed the zoning and the general plan. If they are going to approve your tentative map and you are going to spend a lot of money on the reliance of that, you should be able to get a final approval.

**The Avco Case.** But, the Youngblood case did not decide on changed zoning. Suppose you are going to pick up your building permits and they say: "Ah, Mr. Developer, we're sorry. You have a very nice map which is all approved and recorded but you don't get any building permits because we've changed the zoning before you picked up your building permit and poured your concrete." The *Avco* case is cited to you. What do you do then? The answer is unclear at this point in time. Logic would tell you that if the California Supreme Court said that they cannot change the ground rules on you and if your final map is in accordance with the tentative map, the final map should be approved. You should be able to get building permits and build on it. What good is a map if you cannot build? That issue was not before the Supreme Court in the Youngblood case. But we still have the *Avco* case. Avco spent millions of dollars on off-site improvement. Along came the Coastal Zone Initiative. They were told they did not have building permits, they did not pour concrete, so they cannot build on all those lots. There is still an area of some concern here. All you can do is be sure that if you are able to pick up a building permit, you do so as soon as possible and do some work. If you think that change is imminent, keep your ear to the ground, know what is going on in the community in which you are trying to build. If somebody is trying to force through an ordinance that will affect you, you won't be surprised and you will have time to act before they do.

Constitutional Guarantees. The Constitution says you cannot be deprived of your property without just compensation. The courts have said that as long as some reasonable economic use remains for your property, you have not been deprived of it, despite the number of restrictions and the intensity of the restrictions they have placed upon it.

The city of Palo Alto, in California, was involved in a couple of landmark decisions. One case involved 680 acres of land in the foothills which Palo Alto decided they wanted for a park, but they did not want to pay for it. Over a period of years they made it impossible for anybody to develop it. They down zoned it from one-acre lots to ten-acre lots. Then they went beyond that and said you cannot build on any portion of the property which you see from the Foothill's Park, which was up above it. This meant you had to build down in the gulleys. Then they did all kinds of things which made it literally impossible to build on that project. They did a very bad job of it. They left tracks all over the place. Memorandums went back and forth. Unprivileged memorandums which came out in discovery indicated this was all part of a conceived plan to restrict this property so that it would be retained in open space for the citizens to look at and admire. Palo Alto ended up buying it for $7,000,000 on a compromise settlement just as they were about to go to court. What the judge said before they went in for the question of damages was that the city had so restricted the use of this property as to deprive it of any economic use. They pointed out, for example, you could not farm on it. If it had been good farmland, it might have been a different case.

## ENVIRONMENTAL IMPACT REPORT

In order to do almost anything today, you have to have an environmental impact report (EIR). Sometimes you can get by with a negative declaration, which means the planning body, or council, declares that a project has so little effect on the environment that it is not worth a big study of effects. No further study is required.

Incidentally, if you are involved in a project like that and you get a negative declaration, make sure that the negative declaration is filed with the county clerk because sometimes the city will neglect to do this. After the filing, there is a set period of time—30 days—in which anyone who wants to attack that decision could bring an action. If no one brings an action within 30 days, your negative declaration is secure. If an action is brought within that time, then you may have to go back through the environmental impact hearing process, which could take a long, long time.

Suppose you secure a negative EIR and your project does not go forward. If another developer comes in sometime later, perhaps a year later, does that negative EIR still stand? Yes, if the project has not changed—if there are no increases in the number of units, changes in the density, changes in the street pattern, or other changes of a material substantial nature which could have some kind of effect on the environment that was not considered before.

When does your environmental approval time clock start running? The time clock in the negative declaration starts from the time it is filed. If you have an environmental impact report, the time clock starts from the time your project is approved. For example, as a result of an environmental impact report on a subdivision, your tentative map is approved by the planning commission. That starts the time clock running. At that point there is a notice of determination that should be filed with the county clerk which again starts the 30-day time period running. If that notice is not filed, then it becomes a 180-day period. And you do not want to get caught in a lawsuit when you are 5½ months into a project if someone decides to attack the environmental impact report. You could have cut that off in 30 days after your tentative map was approved if you had been alert to it. It is the job of the city clerk, but often they do not do it.

**Assembly Bill 884, Processing Time Limit.** In California, Assembly Bill 884 is a real weapon which you have at your disposal. Before it was passed, there was no time limit on environmental impact processing. It could take five years to process your environmental impact report. Assembly Bill 884 provides for a one-year limit from the time your application is *complete*. The word "complete" is very important because there is much dispute over what constitutes a complete application. The only way you can protect yourself in this area is to write a letter to the city planner, or whichever government official you are dealing with, and ask if your project is complete as of such and such a date and, if not, what else is needed.

You have several options. You can ask for a letter confirming that the application is complete, or you can tell the official that if you do not hear from his office within a certain number of days, you will assume the application is complete. In doing this, you are going one step beyond what the code says. The code says you are to be informed when your application is complete, but you usually are not.

After you receive confirmation of completeness, you know that you have a maximum of one year from that time. This may sound like a long period of time, but, for any major subdivision now, if you get it approved in a year, you are doing well.

## TEAM APPROACH TO DRE PROCESSING

On the processing of documents, when you have to go through a local or state department of real estate (DRE) to get your report, it is important to establish a team of people to do this for you. That team should consist of yourself, the leader of the team; the architect; the engineer; the title company; and your attorney. And there are a number of ways to handle this process. The best way is to get everyone together for a meeting, about one hour in length, at the very beginning of the project. At a typical meeting, you might say: "We're going to build a 65-unit townhouse development on this location. It's going to have a swimming pool, etc., etc., and we want to be in a position to start construction in so many months and start sales in so many months. We want to have a public report by such and such a date. And we are here to coordinate what we will do."

The architect, the engineer, and the attorney can exchange information on how the development is going to be laid out so that there will be compatibility between the architectural plans, the condominium diagram, or the subdivision map, which the engineer will do, and the legal documents (the CC and R's, and the articles and by-laws), which the attorney will do.

Even if you are beyond that stage—you already have architectural plans done and you have an engineer halfway through the map—it is still the best procedure to get the team together at this time to set up the schedule for processing through the DRE. You can ask the title company to handle all of your DRE processing for you without charge. They will do this willingly because they want your title business. Do not ask your attorney to do it because that is something you will have to pay for. Attorneys will do it and sometimes, if you get in a real bind, you may have to use them if the title company cannot perform fast enough for you. But most of the time you can ask the title company to handle your application through DRE with all the various forms and leg work that must be done.

The attorney should concentrate on doing the declaration, restrictions, by-laws of the association and, perhaps, the deposit receipt form which you have to file with the DRE. If it concerns a condominium or a complicated planned unit development, he would do the sample form deed for the title company.

If you get these people together in the beginning and have them work as a team, it will save you a lot of grief later on. It will save you having to redraft and reprocess. One of these meetings could take perhaps an hour or two, but it is the best investment you can make.

## ORGANIZING YOUR APPROACH FOR GOVERNMENT APPROVAL

Knowing what you want and what you need to accomplish it will greatly reduce the time it takes to process anything through a government agency. The terms "government red tape," "pigeon holing," "being shuffled from one department to another," are often associated with dealing with the government. In the case of building and development, there are certain procedures to follow. Once you know these procedures, the "snafus" and delays can be predicted and, in many cases, eliminated. Dealing with the government takes experience, and, in the absence of experience, it takes patience, both on your part and on theirs. Tell them what you want and ask them what they need. This way you will be prepared, and the documentation will be ready and available when needed.

Government approval is a recognized necessity in the building and development business. Very seldom do you find a large piece of land with the appropriate zoning and guaranteed permits. Government approval is something that all of us go through at one level or another from tentative map approval to building permits.

Each municipality and government jurisdiction has its own unique requirements. The fee structures vary, as does the time from submittal to approval. There are several things that affect any submittal and they are:

1. **The environmental attitude towards the project regarding:**
    a. Location.
    b. Zoning and general plan change.
    c. Proposed improvement.

2. **The complexity of the program regarding:**
    a. Type of approval needed.
    b. Available services and adequate tie-ins.

3. **The government department relative to:**
    a. Work load.
    b. Staff available.

To aid in getting government approval and speeding the process, there are several things you can do, and they are:

1. **Submit a complete package** the first time. Include cover letters and all documents needed or requested.

2. **Know exactly what you want** and how you arrived at that particular answer to your needs.

3. **Have your consultants and backup people available** for questions or additional information.

4. **Talk to the people who will be making the final decisions,** make sure there are no misunderstandings, and that you have presented your case in the best way possible.

5. **Have alternates and compromises available** in case of stalemate.

**Profit and Liquidity Must Be Retained.** In your efforts to get your project approved, the most important factor is that it still remain economically viable. The main goal of any entrepreneurial project is to make a profit, and do it in a reasonable time span.

Profitability and liquidity are directly related to sales price. If you have to pay too much for permits, rebuild an extensive utility tie-in or tributary street, or go through litigation and delay, you may no longer have a project.

**Development Time Frame.** The time frame or phase that the project area is in, especially when dealing with raw land and larger projects, has a direct bearing on its feasibility and the amount of government work involved. The key questions to this are:

1. Is the project in a study area?
2. Have other developers attempted packages on this or nearby sites?
3. Does the master plan call for the same use you require?
4. Is there neighborhood or regional environmental group action anticipated?
5. Is the general area dormant and with no foreseeable active development?
6. Is there growth in the area evidenced by activity and/or interest?

## GOVERNMENT APPROVAL CHECKLIST

The checklist on the following page is included to aid you in your government presentation. It is procedural and basic and not meant to be all inclusive or specific.

## GOVERNMENT APPROVAL CHECKLIST
## FOR ZONING OR USE PERMIT

A. Packages submitted for zoning or use permit approval to the Design Review Board, Planning Commission, and County Supervisors or City Council may include:

1. Letter of submittal and introduction _____ ☐
2. Application forms _____ ☐
3. Site plan _____ ☐
4. Site and neighborhood photographs _____ ☐
5. Preliminary plans and elevations _____ ☐
6. Architectural renderings _____ ☐
7. Site study _____ ☐
8. Environmental impact report or negative declaration _____ ☐
9. Soils and geological study _____ ☐
10. Other _____ ☐
11. Fees _____ ☐

B. The following government agencies may be part of the approval process:

1. City or County Planning Department staff preliminary meetings _____ ☐
2. Environmental studies EIR or negative declaration _____ ☐
3. Design review board zoning or use _____ ☐
4. Planning Commission zoning or use _____ ☐
5. County Supervisor or city council zoning or use _____ ☐
6. Other _____ ☐
7. Comments _____
_____
_____

# PROJECT DESIGN IMPLEMENTATION

The following work by members of the design team should be implemented or underway at this time:

1. **Site Engineer:** preparation of the tentative site plan, survey, topographical map, street layout, site drainage, sewer, grading, and improvement plans.
2. **Geologist:** soils report, geological studies, and recommendations of foundation design.
3. **Architect or Designer:** site plan coordination with site engineer, floor plans, elevations, construction details, and amenities.
4. **Landscape Designer:** preliminary landscape design, location of mounds, and amount of topsoil and soil additives in coordination with site engineer.
5. **Structural Engineer:** structural details, seismic and wind lateral load studies, and foundation design.

The work being done by the design team should be supplemented by you, your staff, and any subcontractors, material suppliers, or factory representatives that are necessary to help obtain the best, most economical, and marketable product possible.

## PROJECT DESIGN

The successful project design effort must be monitored at all times to insure that costs stay within acceptable limits. The team will add expertise to the people who are actually going to supply and build the project. The design is evaluated, revised, and improved as needed. Materials and fixtures that are readily available and competitive are specified. Standard construction techniques known to the bulk of the work force are detailed.

All of this is done, hopefully, in a way not to hinder the creativity of the design team. The burden is on them to use standard materials and methods, stay within the construction cost budget, and yet come up with a design that is unique and marketable.

**Integrated Plans.** When plans are finalized—integrating mechanical plans, landscaping plans, amenity plans, architectural specifications, engineering specifications, structural plans and all else that constitutes the finished working drawings—cost parameters are set up for color selections, floor covering, appliances, and extras, and the total package is let out for final bid.

The bidding process is covered later in this chapter. It should be pointed out here, that for a company that has been in business for any length of time and which has construction subcontractors and suppliers working on ongoing or recently completed jobs, the bidding process does not start at the completion of the working drawings and finalized program—it starts long before. It could start in the feasibility stage. It could start at the preliminary plan stage. People are drawn into the project, as needed, to consult with and to add their experience to the program. It is this interaction of design teams and consulting experts that gives real meaning to the often used and wrongfully abused phrase *"value engineered."*

## SITE AND BUILDING DESIGN

The project plans should consist of site plan, floor plans, elevations, and, in the case of townhouses, commercial or industrial sites, landscaping indication.

**Commission Design Team.** At this stage, an engineer and an architect, building designer, or your in-house design department should be commissioned to start the preliminary work.

Up to now, you have been dealing with comparables, old projects you have done, and generalities as far as the actual building is concerned. To tighten the project and to move to specifics, you should start the design process and gather all the program and decision-making information that has been generated up to this point.

**Direct Design Team.** What you know by now is what the governing forces will allow or, at least, within what limits you should operate in order to obtain the needed permits and services. You know your competition and what is available. You know your parcel of land and, from your market study, you probably have a good idea of what you want to do with it.

It is this information that you will give to your design team. Direct them as you would anyone else that works for you. Give them the approximate square footage, ultimate sales price, and theme or atmosphere you wish to have them help you to create. Then let them do it.

**Market Motivators.** Unless there is a vastly significant difference in the house design and amenities offered, the location or neighborhood will be the prime consideration of the buying public when choosing one residence over another. And the reasons that make one location or neighborhood superior to another are the adequacy, convenience, and attractiveness of shopping, parks, recreation, schools, churches, transportation, and the general socio-economic make-up of the people in the area. A great deal of time and study should be spent on fulfilling these desirable features or to compensate for the relative lack of any that cannot be provided.

**The Site Plan.** The design program must coordinate with the site plan. The lot yield is usually maximized and certainly always optimized. Lot size is the first consideration if you have a stock set of plans that you would like to use. The lot should be designed to fit the house with corresponding side, front, and rear setbacks, but it also must meet the lot coverage rules. Residential subdivisions are generally designed to fit existing house plans. Ideally, from a strictly aesthetic and architectural point of view, the opposite should be true, and in the case of some irregular or particularly exciting sites, the plans are designed to fit the land and the lot size should meet the criteria of terrain, sun orientation, trees, and view. Open space, integrated parks, cul-de-sacs, curvelinear street patterns, median strips, camper and boat storage yards—depending on your budget—are all things to think about.

**Home Design Criteria.** It is important to concentrate on quality of design and product, for that is all that distinguishes one home from another when all else, especially location and neighborhood, are equal. And the way to achieve that, is:

1. **Appearance.** The attractiveness of the home as it is first seen from the front is called curb appeal. This includes the first impression of quality of design, materials, workmanship, color, and landscaping. This first impression also must carry through to the entryway, interior decoration, cleanliness, and an overall feeling of spaciousness.

2. **The Plan.** There is no perfect plan for a merchant-type mass-produced home when you are trying to appeal to the largest segment of the market, but there are certain important considerations that are found in all good and successful plans. They are:
   a. Adaptability to living patterns.
   b. Adequate and efficient room arrangement.
   c. Circulation.
   d. Spaciousness.
   e. Openness of the plan to the outdoors and to private yards, taking full advantage of the site (view, trees, terrain).

3. **Amenities.** Some basic features have become expected standard items and unless you are appealing to the lowest end of the market range with a stripped-down shelter-type home, you should include oven and range, disposal, dishwasher, carpets, and forced-air heat. All else should be looked at very carefully.
   Try to avoid putting in features that the homeowner does not appreciate. Too often one home is compared to another strictly on square footage with little or no regard for automatic garage door operators, vacuum sys-

tems, or security systems. These things are not readily apparent; you cannot see them unless they are pointed out, therefore, they are not prestige items.

Prestige items are three-car garages, vaulted ceilings, spas, landscaping with large or specimen plants, trees and lawns, elegant powder rooms, large, sumptuous master suites, wide front elevations with a definite and acceptable style, and expensive-looking and tasteful materials.

Amenities of borderline desirability are air conditioning, microwave ovens, compactors, mirrored closet doors, backyard landscaping, fences, drapes, and design decorating service.

Amenities you get nothing or less than value for are: gold plumbing fixtures, food preparation built-ins, colored bath fixtures, wallpaper, paneling, and pools; in other words, things that not everyone wants. If they are included, buyers will take it, but these are not items they would pay extra for or really appreciate.

4. **Reputation.** The reputation of the builder, developer, and the design team for competence, value, workmanship, integrity, and fair dealing, precedes you wherever you go. It is apparent in referrals, in customers who buy a second and third house from you over the years. It follows you to the lender, the Planning Department, and the Building Inspection Department. Reputation is one of your most treasured assets.

5. **Price.** Price goes hand in hand with value. If your home is better than the competition, then people should be willing to pay more for it. If your home is inferior to the competition, then people will expect to pay less for it. If your home is better and is lower or equal in price to the competition, then people will realize the value and demand can be expected to increase accordingly. Therefore, it is important to cost engineer value into your product. Weigh one building method against another. Consider alternate materials and put your money into things that can be seen and appreciated.

## SITE DESIGN AND BUILDING DESIGN—
## FORMS 305 AND 306

Form 305 and Form 306 are site and building design procedures. These forms will provide some of the necessary information for your design team.

## SITE DESIGN

Land Planner _____

1. **Site Plan**
   A. Number of lots desired _____
   B. Lot width   min.____   max____   plan width _____
   C. Lot depth   min.____   max____   width to depth ratio _____
   D. Lot area   min.____   Max____   coverage _____
   E. Street layout ☐ gridiron ☐ curvelinear ☐ cul de sac ☐ median strip
   F. Parks and common areas integrated into design ☐ yes ☐ no
   G. Trees   ☐ leave in   ☐ optimize   ☐ take out _____
   H. Camper-boat storage yards   ☐ yes   ☐ no   where _____
   I. Grading   ☐ flat   ☐ benched   ☐ optimize   ☐ use natural grade
   J. Security gate entrance and fences   ☐ yes   ☐ no
   K. Other: _____
      Comments: _____

2. **Site Engineering**
   A. Amount of float or tolerance desired _____
   B. Height of pads above swales _____ above curb _____
   c. Backfill dirt desired ____ yds per site ____ yds total ____
   D. Large commons or parks   ☐ mounds   ☐ flat   ☐ slope ____%

3. **Target Date**
   A. Preliminary investigation _____
   B. Preliminary site plans _____
   C. Preliminary site development cost estimate _____
   D. Construction plans complete _____ approval _____
   E. Map approval _____ map recordation _____

NOTES

# 306

## BUILDING DESIGN

Architect or Designer _____

1. **Home Design**
   A. Number of separate plans desired

   |    | Plan | Bedrooms | Baths | Stories | Sq. Ft. | Price Range |
   |----|------|----------|-------|---------|---------|-------------|
   | 1. |      |          |       |         |         |             |
   | 2. |      |          |       |         |         |             |
   | 3. |      |          |       |         |         |             |
   | 4. |      |          |       |         |         |             |

   B. Design Criteria - The Floor Plan

      1. Adaptability of living patterns.
      2. Adequate and efficient room arrangement.
      3. Circulation.
      4. Spaciousness.
      5. Openness of plan to outdoors and to private yards taking full advantage of the site.

2. **Elevations**
   A. Number of Elevations per Plan _____

   B. Design Criteria - Elevations

      1. Curb appeal (attractiveness, feeling of spaciousness, quality)
      2. Materials: _____

3. **Amenities**
   A. Included: _____
   _____
   _____

   B. Extra: _____
   _____

   C. Comments: _____
   _____

4. **Target Dates**
   A. Preliminary Building Plans _____
   B. Construction plans and specifications _____
   C. Renderings or special work _____
   D. Other: _____

## NOTES

# CONTRACTS AND PURCHASING

## EARLY INVOLVEMENT

Whoever is going to be involved in the contracting and purchasing, be he part of a large corporation or one of a two- or three-man operation, must get involved in the plans early. He must get involved before the working drawings are finished. This applies both to the off-site plans and the architectural drawings. It is fundamental that he have a working knowledge of the landscaping plans, site improvement plans, and the architectural plans to eliminate expensive details before these details get out in the final plans, before the plans get approved by the building department, and before the field starts building them. The following examples show the importance of early involvement.

In a large tract of homes in Valencia, California, they were using ½" reinforcing bars 12" on center, both ways, in the concrete floor slabs. One day someone asked why they were doing that and no one had an answer. Someone else looked at the soils report. The report said the soil was non-expansive and that 6"-x-6" #10 wire mesh could be used. No one had bothered to read the soils report and make certain that the information was either relayed to the architect or that the architect carried through and put it on his drawings. It was expensive—hundreds of dollars per house—and there were many, many houses.

Another company was building conventional foundations in Walnut Creek, California. They were using 2"-x-6" mudsills on top of the foundation all the way around, and the floor joists sat on top of it—all they needed was 2" x 4". Just a small item—$20 to $30 a house—but again, no one bothered to look at the plans in the early stages.

## DESIGN ALTERNATIVES vs. COST

In your early development you have to be thinking about presenting design alternatives and estimating their cost. Usually when you are in the early stages there is still room to play with the floor plan, the exterior design, the roof layout, etc. You must be aware of design alternatives; roughly, how much more does it cost to put on a hip roof rather than gable ends? What happens if I back up my bathrooms—concentrate all of my plumbing? These are the type of ideas that have to be going through your head. Many times, the person doing the contracting or purchasing tends to be single-minded. He has tunnel vision, thinking only of cutting costs. You do not want to cut out your marketing program either, so keep these thoughts in mind and present them to someone who has the marketing authority. Remember that you cannot cut cost and cut the guts out of the house either, in terms of being able to market it.

You also have to have a working knowledge of the basic unit prices. Many times it is just quick rules of thumb—what is the cost of a plumbing fixture, a yard of carpet with pad, sheet vinyl? These are simple little things, but you have to come up with quick answers.

Working with good subcontractors and having a long-time working relationship with them pays off. You have to be able to call a subcontractor and get a quick response from him. When you are working with good people, you *will get* a quick answer.

One of the most important things any builder/developer can do in the early stages of planning is to get his subcontractors involved. When you have a preliminary set of working drawings, the floor plan, some exterior details, and maybe the roof plan, give a set of these plans to your framer, your plumber, your heating and sheet-metal man. These are the men that can tell you, for example, that if you line up your upstairs and downstairs bathrooms, costs can be lowered by $50 a house. They are critical to you. Get them involved early, long before you even think of submitting your plans to a building department, because once they are into a building department it is difficult to change details without stopping and going back again. If you have done your job correctly, by the time the plans are ready for city or county approval, all the major changes, especially the structural items, will have been completed.

## PREPARATION FOR BIDDING

When the working drawings have been submitted to the county and you are waiting for the plan check, take a complete set of plans, put your name on them and the notation, "Do Not Remove from Office." These are the plans you are going to be bidding and contracting from. When you come across anything that is unusual in the way of details or special notes, mark the plans with highlighter felt-tipped pens. If you notice anything wrong or ambiguous or incomplete, make notes. Do this so that when you go out to bid, you can relay accurate and precise information to each subcontractor. Tell them what you do or do not want done, that they will or will not supply this item or that item.

For example, you may run across quarter-inch steel framing straps on the framing details. Many people go blissfully along thinking the framer is going to supply it. What happens when your framer is ready to set your beams and discovers he has no connectors? He argues that he does not supply anything he cannot buy out of the Simpson book. What do you do?

If you had gone through and noted framing straps as an unusual item you can tell your framer you want him to supply it or you can tell him you will get it from the ornamental shop, that you will have them fabricate it and that you will supply it. To eliminate the coordination problem, have whoever installs it, supply it. This may cost an extra $5 per house because he has to make arrangements to get the framing strap, but you know that when the framer is ready to install it, he has it.

Another example is air-conditioning preparation. This usually is not on your plans; it is often a marketing-type specification. When someone says they want certain units prepared for air conditioning, what do they mean? There are about 12 items to consider to prepare a house for air conditioning. If you do two of them, is it prepared for air conditioning? If you do ten? Do you run the refrigerant lines but do not connect them? Do you supply an air-conditioning furnace? Do you supply a five-wire to the thermostat? Do you supply an air-conditioning thermostat? Again, these are thoughts that have to go through your mind before you go out to bid, because your bids can vary widely. You have to draw the lines—you have to think of all these little things.

**Be Organized.** You have the plans down and you are basically organized. You are ready to go. Whether you are big or small, you have to remember that if you are building a house from the foundation on up, you will be dealing with 20 to 25 subcontractors. If you are going to do competitive bidding, you will be dealing with about 90 to 120 subcontractors. You will have to organize them and make certain that everybody is bidding "apples to apples." It is a monumental job. You must be organized from the very beginning.

There are two big tools in the bidding process that are important. They are the *plan log* and the *bid file*. They are very simple and one has to be very diligent in terms of filling them out and keeping them current; but, if you do, when it comes time to put your budget together, when it comes time to write the contract, you are going to be certain that it is all there.

**The Plan Log.** The plan log is a very simple item. It is simply a sheet of legal paper with four columns drawn on it. The first column is for the *subcontractor's name*, the second is for the *plan number*, the third is for the *date that the subcontractor picked it up*, and the last is for the *date he returned it*.

Depending on how many types of houses you have, your plans may cost $10 to $50 a set. You have to recycle them. You cannot just distribute 120 sets of plans; you have to work off of 30 to 40 sets and get the subcontractors to turn them over.

**Plan Numbering.** There should be a date on the cover sheet of your plans. That first date is your ground-zero set of plans. Start numbering all plans 101, 102, 103, etc. Sometimes, especially in large companies, someone in the marketing department makes a major revision to the plans which may throw many of your bids out the window. How do you handle this? A new set of plans incorporating the changes is made up. How do you keep track of that? First, you must insist—and architects understand the importance of it but they seldom do it—that all revision dates be posted on the cover sheet of the architectural plans. If the plans are changed on a certain date for a certain reason, that should be noted in the revision block. The date should be posted, along with a general statement, in two or three words, of what was changed. That way you know which set of plans is current.

When you get new plans, start a new series of numbers. Start at 201, 202, 203, etc., because you are going to have to look down this plan log to find out who has been affected by the plan change. This is the only way you can keep track of it, because one week after you have the new set of plans you are going to forget which set was used for bidding. You can easily write a contract based on the old set of plans and then have arguments in the field when it comes time to build. One company actually managed to put in five complete foundations using the wrong set of plans. Who is at fault? In this case it was the subcontractor's fault. It is up to you to make certain that your subcontractor and field have the proper set of plans.

Let the subcontractors with simple takeoffs such as shower doors, windows, etc., do their takeoffs in the office. Remember, your plans are costing you from $10 to $50. Just let them come in, schedule the time, and make certain they are there. Mark the plan logs, showing what plan they took off and the date.

**Bid File.** The second item is the bid file. It is just a plain legal-sized folder with fasteners on each side. You start out with one file for each trade or major supply item that you are going to contract. You will have about 20 to 25 files. If you are going to do off-sites as well, you could have 30 of them.

For each subcontractor and major supply item, make a spread sheet using accounting paper which has approximately 14 columns. Start off on the far left with your plan numbers—Plan 100, Elevation A, B, C; Plan 200, Elevation A, B, C, etc. Then list the number of units of each plan. As the subcontractors send in their bids, write the subcontractor's name, telephone number, and the price for each plan he is quoting right down the column. Based upon the quantity which you have already listed, multiply it out and come up with a grand total at the bottom. It is all right there—you can compare them very easily.

Use the rest of the spaces at the bottom of the sheet for specifications and the items to be included or excluded. For example, who runs the flue and the venting for the water heater and the furnace? Who hooks up the gas for the furnace? Does the plumber do it or does the heating and sheet-metal subcontractor do it? If subcontractor A has it included, note it next to his bid. If subcontractor B has excluded it, note that. By the time you are finished bidding, the specifications for each contract in that phase should be identical so that you are comparing apples to apples.

You must cross-check between different, but related, contract or supply items to be sure you are covered. Have your subcontractors itemize what is included and excluded. You do not want overlaps and double coverage either.

**Invoice File.** This file serves another purpose. After you are finished with the bidding, have awarded the contract, and have written the contract (which has been signed and returned), move your bids, your signed contract, and your spread sheet over to one side of the folder. The other side of the folder becomes your invoice file. All of the incoming correspondence, the insurance form, the preliminary liens, the invoices, and copies of paid checks, are all in the folder. Now you have made one folder for that trade, for that entire job. You will have to add a few folders—perhaps five at the most—for such things as temporary toilets, miscellaneous bills, etc. This file is extremely important.

**Field Approval of Invoices.** When an invoice comes into your office, it goes to the superintendent. If the subcontractor is smart, he will get on the phone and call the superintendent and say, "I want to bill you for stocking Lots 1 through 21, is that okay?" The superintendent will say, "No, you really have not finished stocking on the last couple of houses. If you send an invoice for 1 through 19, I will okay it." If the subcontractor is smart, he will do that. All invoices are field-approved.

**Filing.** Learn to file alphabetically by trade. If you file alphabetically by subcontractor, *all* of your projects will be in the same file. But when you file by project, by trade, alphabetically, you will always find what you are looking for—even five years from now.

**Subcontractor's Checklist.** You could have a checklist for every trade. Framing, however, because it can be so complicated and involved, is the key one. This is your largest trade and the one that provides most of the functions for you. The checklist has basically two columns—labor and material. It shows whether the framer supplies the labor for a particular item or excludes it. Does he supply the material or does he exclude it? Does he supply the debris box or do you supply it? Does he put the material in the debris box or do you do it? Does he unload the cabinets and put them in the kitchens or do you? Does he unload the appliances, the windows, the millwork? These are all things that can cause misunderstanding if they are not spelled out in advance. If not specified, they can lead to one headache after another.

There is one more seemingly small item that could cost you a lot of money, especially if you have not counted on it. You need to specify that all the debris and material from this work as outlined in the contract are to be disposed of and/or removed from the job site at the expense of the subcontractor. It should be made very clear to the subcontractor from the very outset that he is responsible for cleaning up and removing his debris from the job site.

**Subcontractor Phone Bid List.** A lot of bids are received over the phones. Use a very simple form for subcontractors who phone in bids. The form forces you to record the name of the subcontractor, the project, and the date when you received it. Other pertinent information can be written at the bottom of the form. Have about 50 of these forms in your desk before starting to bid a job.

**Work with the Bidders.** While you are bidding, you have to have quick answers for the subcontractors. The subcontractors will have questions about details, about what you do or do not want, and you should have quick answers to most of these questions. Get back to them before they put your takeoff aside and start doing someone else's.

Work with the subcontractors, respect his time. If you relate to these people on a good business level, you will be working *together*. You, the contractor, are out to make a profit. You want to let the subcontractor make a profit. By working together you are both going to maximize your profits. Together, you won't have any big surprises.

**Cost Budget.** Use two forms for the cost budget—one for land development and the other for building development. The first being, of course, for the development of the on-site improvements and land; the second is related to the physical construction of the house, the apartment, the warehouse, or whatever it is that you are going to be building.

If you have done your preparatory work—spread sheets, work with the subcontractors, contract specifications, and checklists—filling out these forms is just a simple process of filling in bid amounts. These sheets are bid summary sheets and from them you derive your budget. It is just as simple as that. It can be a very brief operation. These forms serve a dual purpose. These are the numbers you can show to your bank when you are asked about your backup. They also serve as a checklist.

**Contract Payment Schedule.** At the beginning of each job, make up a contract payment schedule, in conjunction with the subcontractor, to decide how he is going to be paid on each building unit as he completes each progress phase. Drywall, for example, has three phases: stocking, hanging, and tape/texture. Progress payments are usually in a percentage form, such as 35 percent for stocking, 35 percent for hanging, and 30 percent when the tape/texture is completed and accepted. This particular contract payment schedule will show three columns, one for each phase, with the amount to be paid noted and with space to note when it was paid. This gives your bookkeeper a quick means of checking invoices and it greatly simplifies your accounting process.

## BIDDING AND SHORTCUTS

A good philosophy and some shortcuts will simplify and eliminate a lot of headaches. First of all, *negotiate, don't bid*. Have one, maybe two, subcontractors in each trade that get all of your business. In a bad year, that is business that they can count on even though it may not be a monumental tract. It keeps the bread on the table. It keeps their key people employed—they can count on you. But in a good year, when things are flying fast and furious, and there are not enough carpenters or plumbers or electricians to keep up production schedules, you will always get an electrician and a plumber to keep on schedule, no matter how many men it takes. Other people will be without electricians and plumbers because you got the manpower first.

There are bad subcontractors, and you have to weed them out from the start. There are good ones and they are the ones that you want to work with and to build lasting relationships. Meet the president, meet the owner, see what his shop is like. Grow to understand his problems. From the start you have to approach it with the attitude that everyone makes a profit and that there are no surprises. The small things that always happen on one job are picked up on the next—that is their attitude and that is how they work. A retention is just an extension of that philosophy. Anytime a subcontractor knows a contractor is going to hold a retention, he builds it into his bid. There's no point in it. Again, if you are working with good people, remember that you are working *with* them.

## BIDDING FORMS

The contract and purchasing procedures just discussed are usually learned the hard way—by years of experience. This experience is difficult to relate in just a few pages and within the general terms dictated by the scope of this book, which is an overview of the entire construction process.

This is especially true in the use of forms in this phase of the operation—forms used to tabulate and regulate the large amount of important information that is generated at this time.

Bidding is broken down into four operations:

1. Subcontractors' and Suppliers' Bid List.
2. Invitation to Bid.
3. Bid Proposal.
4. Bid Summary.

The phases overlap. You might, for example, be summarizing the bids on concrete while you are still sending out the invitations to bid the roof. You might also be bidding out several jobs at the same time with even more activity. The point is that it is important to keep things straight, and this is done by good and diligent record keeping.

## SUBCONTRACTORS' AND SUPPLIERS' BID LIST

It is the custom of the authors and our associated companies to request bids only from those subcontractors or suppliers that we want to work with. We choose our list of bidders very carefully. The bidder must meet the criteria listed below:

1. We request bids from people with whom we have first-hand experience and a positive working relationship.
2. We choose only people who are in business—not just doing business. They have a daytime support staff, they are available for discussion and follow-through, and they do their bookwork and pay their bills.
3. We accept bids from people who have good trade references and have evidence of being able to handle the volume and do the quality of work we require. We want to see something they have done and talk to the supervisors of prime contractors that they have worked for. We want to make sure that their definition of "workmanlike manner" is the same as ours.
4. We accept bids only from those able and willing to stand behind their work. Service is a prime requisite of the construction process. Prompt, efficient and cordial follow-through on warrantee work is a must.

## INVITATION TO BID—FORM 310

The Invitation To Bid is a form that we send to subcontractors and suppliers that we wish to invite to become a part of our project construction team. It is sometimes called a bid request.

The purpose of this form is to notify prospective bidders as to:

1. Project location, address, lot block, and tract number.
2. Scope of project, number of units, and size of building.
3. Time of commencement.
4. Tentative schedule of completion.
5. Where the plans and specifications can be taken off or picked up.
6. Deadline for bids.

The Invitation to Bid form can be formal or informal and it can be in letter form if preferred.

The following is our bid request Form 310. We use it as a formalized start to a very important business function, a first step that will set an attitude of professionalism and good communication.

**310**

_____
Company

_____
Address

**INVITATION TO BID**

Date_____

To_____
_____

Dear_____

You are invited to submit a bid on our next project.

**Project Location**_____
_____

**Scope of Project**_____
_____

The tentative starting date of the project is_____ and it will take approximately _____ months to complete, with a tentative completion date of_____.

Plans and specifications can be ☐ taken off ☐ picked up at _____

**Bid Deadline**_____ Date_____ 19____.

We will be using our bid proposal forms and contract forms. Please submit your bid on our form - you may use your own as addenda if so desired. Please read our contract form carefully - it will be the one you will be asked to sign if your bid proposal is accepted.

Very truly yours,

_____
Title

NOTES

# BID PROPOSALS—FORMS 320 AND 325

The bid proposal should describe or refer to everything that you want the subcontractor or supplier to do or supply. A well-detailed proposal will cover all items with no overlap into other phases or trades, and it will also cover all the work done without any gaps. In bids revised after the fact, you lose the competitive edge, deducts are more difficult to negotiate, and add-ons are usually higher than they would have been if included in the original bid.

The bid proposal form should give a detailed description of the work. The time-worn phrase *"per plans and specifications"* usually won't get it done anymore. It is still a good phrase with which to start, but in most contracts it is backed up with statements such as *"must comply with all codes and laws"* and *"includes work customarily done"* and, before long, the bidder is adding in all sorts of contingencies for work implied but not specified.

To keep this from happening to you:

1. Check all plans and specifications for correctness and relative completeness.
2. Make quantity takeoffs of all material and/or labor prior to discussion with the bidder.
3. Know exactly what you want. Listen to new ideas or cost-cutting suggestions, but defer decisions until you have evaluated the alternatives.
4. Prepare your bid packages in advance and have everything ready.
5. Develop your bid proposal, clearly defining and specifying exactly what is to be done and what is expected, what type of materials, and what brand of fixtures.

When this is done correctly and in sufficient detail, the bid proposal then becomes Exhibit "A" in the contract documents.

# 320

_____
Company

_____
Address

## BID PROPOSAL - SUBCONTRACTORS

**By** _____

_____

**Project Location** _____

_____

**Proposal**

    We propose to do the following:

_____
_____
_____
_____
_____
_____
_____
_____
_____
_____
_____
_____
_____
_____
_____
_____
_____
_____
_____
_____

**Price**

    All the above to be completed in a workmanlike manner for the sum of _____ ($_____)

This price to hold until_____ 19____ .

**Payments**

     Payments are on progress and are made in the following manner:
_____
_____

**Billing**

     Payments will be authorized on completed and verified work billed on or before the _____ day of the month, payment to be made on or before the _____ day of the following month.

**Retentions**

     Retentions of ___% totaling $_____ will be made. Total payment to be _____.

**Warrantee**

     The subcontractor will guarantee his work and material for one year from the date of _____ under the standard warrantee required by law. He will also guarantee his work for any extended time the courts or officials may require for hidden defects, errors and ommissions, negligence or any other legality.

**Lien Releases**

     The subcontractor will provide the prime contractor or owner with lien release for material and labor if so required.

**Contract Documents**

     The subcontractor will further be bound by the stipulation and requirements set forth in the contract documents - a copy of which is attached to this bid proposal form.

**Submitted By:**

| _____ | _____ | _____ |
|---|---|---|
| Name | Title | Date |

**Accepted By: and Made a Part of Contract Documents as Exhibit A**

| _____ | _____ | _____ |
|---|---|---|
| Name | Title | Date |

325

_____
Company

_____
Address

**BID PROPOSAL - SUPPLIERS**

**By** _____

**Project Location** _____

**Proposal**

We propose to do the following:

_____
_____
_____
_____
_____
_____
_____
_____
_____
_____
_____
_____
_____
_____
_____
_____
_____
_____

**Price**

All the above to be furnished for the sum of _____
($ _____ )
This price to hold until _____ 19____ .

**Payments**

Payments are on progress and are made in the following manner:
_____
_____

**Billing**

Payments will be authorized for delivered and verified material billed on or before the _____ day of the month, payment to be made on or before the _____ day of the following month.

**Retentions**

Retentions of ___% totaling $_____ will be made. Total payment to be _____.

**Warrantee**

The supplier will guarantee his product and material for one year from the date of _____ under the standard warrantee required by law. He will also guarantee his product for any extended time the courts or officials may require for hidden defects, errors and ommissions, negligence or any other legality.

**Lien Releases**

The supplier will provide the prime contractor or owner with lien release for material and manufactured items if so required.

**Contract Documents**

The supplier will further be bound by the stipulation and requirements set forth in the contract documents - a copy of which is attached to this bid proposal form.

**Submitted By:**

| _____ | _____ | _____ |
|---|---|---|
| Name | Title | Date |

**Accepted By: and Made a Part of Contract Documents as Exhibit A**

| _____ | _____ | _____ |
|---|---|---|
| Name | Title | Date |

# BID SUMMARY SHEET—FORM 330

The construction and supply bids are catalogued in a summary sheet for easy reference and transmittal. The sheet is extremely basic. There are many ways of cataloguing the bids. Some do it chronologically in construction sequence. Some do it numerically, following the CSI 16 item system. The important thing is to settle on one, whether it is one of these or your own, and strive for consistency.

It would be to your advantage to list each trade and material item needed to complete the job on your bid summary sheet. This way there will be no gaps and overlaps. If you list these categories in the beginning, you can set up your order of cataloguing and provide a space to enter each bid as it comes in.

There should be a central collection person and document, such as Form 330, for bid receiving. Bids coming in over the phone should be noted with time received and the name of the person who phoned in the bid. This note must be on an individual 8½"-x-11" sheet that is consistent with your standard bid proposal form size and it should be filed with the other written proposals. By all means, the telephone bid must be confirmed in writing on your standard form and signed and submitted as soon as possible.

# BID SUMMARY SHEET

330

Project _____

| Code. | Trade-Phase or Supply Item | Bidder Amount | Bidder Amount | Bidder Amount | Accepted Bid |
|-------|----------------------------|---------------|---------------|---------------|--------------|
|       |                            |               |               |               |              |

# BID SUMMARY SHEET

Project _____

| Code. | Trade-Phase or Supply Item | Bidder Amount | Bidder Amount | Bidder Amount | Accepted Bid |
|---|---|---|---|---|---|
| | | | | | |

# LETTING THE BID

It is not necessary to always select the low bidder. There are other reasons besides price in choosing one bidder over another, especially if the bids are close. It may be worth it to pay a little more for experience, proven craftsmanship, or a "heavy" (someone who is geared up for high-volume production). Therefore, to allow for flexibility to choose, there is no need for a formal bid opening or a hard and fast bidding deadline. Bids should not be peddled or bidders manipulated one against the other. And fair play and good human relations should be followed at all times. Bidders can only be squeezed, misinformed, or used once before the word gets out.

Builders who have been doing the same or similar type of projects and construction for years have their latest project's costs on each phase. The annual rate of inflation and additional costs of labor and material are computed and they then know beforehand at what each trade or material item should be bid. They use this knowledge as their negotiating tool.

If a building company was costing out a new type of construction, operating in an unfamiliar area, or starting out new, they would have to cultivate new bidders, check their references, and ask for competitive bids with possibly an informal bid opening. In checking references, they should use the same criteria listed above and they should only accept bids from those to whom they would give the work if their bids were successful.

It is customary at this stage to inform the successful bidder that he has the job if the project goes ahead. He is told approximately when the job will start so that he can protect his material prices and reserve his manpower. There are a number of things that must happen before entering into a formal contract with the subcontractor or supplier and they depend on the type of project and position the company requesting bids is in.

## GENERAL CONTRACTOR

If the company is a contracting firm which is bidding on a project itself, then, obviously, they cannot enter into a contract with a subcontractor until they have been awarded the master contract. A word of caution here—some subcontractors have a habit of protecting themselves and the time that it took to prepare their bid by calling all the general contracting firms bidding the project and giving them their prices. They figure that this way, if they are low bidders in their phase, they have a good chance of getting the subcontract no matter which general contractor is awarded the job. Unfortunately, the practice does happen; and if it is carried to ridiculous extremes, all bidders would be using the same low subcontractors and the bid would go to the general contractor with the lowest overhead and/or the one willing to work for the least profit and/or the one who made the biggest mistake on his bid. The importance of choosing reputable, dependable, and honorable people cannot be overemphasized.

### BUILDER/DEVELOPER

If the company bidding the job is a builder/developer who is checking the economic feasibility of a project, then he will not enter into a subcontract until he has assured himself that the final cost and profit analysis is positive. He must also have his final maps and all government approvals and permits. His financing must be completed and, in most cases, the loan recorded. Then, and only then, can the builder/developer, in all fairness to himself and the subcontractor, enter into a binding formal subcontract agreement.

### THE SUBCONTRACT AGREEMENT

The Contract Checklist and Subcontract Agreement Forms are presented later in this book and at the time and place they need to be executed.

## ACCOUNTING

Your accountant is probably one of the most important subcontractors that you have. There are many kinds of people in the business world that can provide you with accounting-type services. There are bookkeeping services and there are people who use the guise of investment and bookkeeping services. There are Public Accountants (PA's), which is a phase of the profession for which there no longer is a license issued in some states, and Certified Public Accountants (CPA's).

### CHOOSING YOUR ACCOUNTANT

How do you find an accountant or accounting service that will serve your needs? Check with the people that you are working with, the people in the industry. Who do your competitors use? Bankers will refer people they know who are technically qualified. And last, but not least, find out who in your community can supply the services you need.

The questions that you should ask about a prospective accountant or accounting service are:

1. Are they professionally qualified?
2. Do they do work for other contractors?
3. Do they have the staff to get the work done?
4. And, can they get the work done in a reasonable time period?

Often people will tell you they can get it done, but your financial statement will arrive months later. By then, that job is done and two more are started, and suddenly you have a $75,000 income and you don't know what to do with it. So you must keep up on it.

**Interest and Communication.** You must be sure that whoever is doing your work takes an interest in *you*. Can you communicate with him or her? Do you know what is in your financial statement? Do you know how your profit and loss statements were derived? Do you know if you should buy or lease your next car or piece of equipment? You have to be able to sit down with your accountant and discuss these things.

Your accountant is just as important as a roofer and a concrete man. That accountant, whether he is a CPA or a bookkeeping service must be able to help you get to the bottom line. And, the bottom line is what counts.

**Fees.** When you are looking for a firm to do your work, find out what the fees are. One thing that you should take into consideration is that the quality and not the price is probably most important. It is not a question of whether you can get it done for $75 instead of $400. Perhaps the person charging $75 has not given you any help; all he has done is close your ledger. So when you are looking in this direction there are a lot of ways that you can find out who can do a particular job. If you do not have the people in-house, then get outside help to get you to the point where you have statements, to help you understand what you are doing financially, to help you with tax problems, and to help you with costing your next job.

When people go to an outside service, an accountant, bookkeeper, CPA, PA, or whatever it may be, a lot of them say, "Here's all my work, do it." There is no detailed agreement made beforehand. And when the first bill arrives, they say, "Wait a minute, this is not what we wanted." Well, it is the fault of the accountant and also the fault of the client because they have not communicated what they want. Suddenly you find that the accountant is doing bank reconciliations and other bookkeeping and filing jobs.

**In-House Help.** The majority of builders have staffs of less than two or three, and it is really to your advantage to train some of these people in bookkeeping. First, the more you use your staff, the more control you will have. And second, their services will be cheaper than going outside. There are a lot of firms, especially accounting firms, that do not want to reconcile bank statements or schedules. If you can do that work inside, then you are going to save yourself money and, at the same time, you are going to be up on things.

When you are out there pounding nails and making money and getting everything done, you can forget that you have to take care of having an account of the records. There are so many things that you can get someone in-house to do. You can, for instance, hire a bookkeeper with a little bit of strength. You may have to pay her a little bit more money—perhaps

$800 or $900 or even $1,000 a month, depending on your requirements and the work load—but if she is worth her salt, she will pay for herself. She can cut a lot of time previously needed from the outside services and at the same time keep a handle on inside things for you. The other advantage to having your own people is that you can train them the way you want them to do the job.

**Good Records.** How you keep your records is a pretty good indication of how well you are going to operate. We all want to get the project started, finished, solved; we want to realize the profit, but we have to account for everything through paperwork and reports. If you have a good clerical staff and you have your records in order, then the rest of your job becomes easier. Take a look at payroll reporting. How many times has a contractor missed the timely deposit on a payroll tax and later had a penalty of underpayment of Federal taxes? These taxes are *very* stiff. The same thing applies to payroll reports and union reports; they need to be done properly and on time.

Last but not least, you have to consider the subcontractor's insurance liability. The field inspector from your workmens' compensation or liability insurance company could come to your office and go through your records for about a day and a half trying to find out who the subcontractors are. Perhaps you do not have insurance certificates or ID numbers from subcontractors. You can get those insurance inspectors out much quicker and cheaper if your records are in order.

## FINANCIAL STATEMENTS

One of the most important items is the financial statement. Banks like to see financial statements that come from a third party, not from in-house. Bankers, particularly those concerned with the construction business, get anything from numbers written on pieces of paper to audited financial statements. An audited financial statement prepared by a bookkeeper is questionable. Normally, audited financial statements are prepared by certified public accountants. What they are doing in essence is attesting to the fairness of the report. The fee for an audited financial statement normally is four to six times the fee for an unaudited financial statement.

There are occasions when the lender, unless he knows you, will not give you the loan if he does not have an audited financial statement. What is the difference? Basically, the difference is the time involved. More additional tests and operations have to be run—such as checking, internal control, verifying receivables—to make sure that in essence the financial statement represents what the business actually is.

You may get by with an unaudited financial statement. The majority of the banks will accept it, particularly in the small- to medium-level project. The banker should be able to pick up the report and easily read the statements. There should be footnotes, even on the back, for disclosure so that he doe not have to make four or five phone calls to find out what it means. The financial statement, even though unaudited, should be able to stand by itself. Most importantly, the financial statement should be used as a tool to inform you of your financial standing. Assets and liabilities should be clearly stated, broken down between current assets and current liabilities.

**Get on a Timely Basis.** It is important that you, and whoever is doing your work, go over what has been done so you understand it. You might think that you are so sound in your cash flow that you do not need a financial statement to get a loan from your bank. Six months later you may need one. What do you do? You can call the accountant, telling him you need a financial statement through June. He may tell you he has a trip already planned to Alaska for six weeks. He cannot get your work started until September, which means you will get your statement by the end of October. By that time you've lost the job. What's the secret to that? The secret is to get on a timely basis with whomever you are doing work.

When financial statements are done, give them to your banker. Keep them in the bank's portfolio under your name. When you need a job or when you need some money, you can call the banker and tell him you need money. He will have your financial statement; at least, the latest. It may be a quarterly, six-month, or monthly statement. He cannot tell you he will not give you the loan because he does not have a current statement on you. When a bank has your file in a portfolio—and all banks have the required information there when you call—you will not have to go through a tedious process to obtain a loan, whether it is long-term or short-term.

**Historical Cost.** Good financial data can also provide you with a good history of costs for the purposes of cost evaluation. In an inflationary period, it is absurd trying to go back in six months, three months or even one month, to price anything, but at least you have some data with which to start. You may have a better understanding of costs because you are on top of it. It is the unknown costs that may introduce sudden problems into your budget when you start to evaluate what you are going to make on your project. The project may be four times the cost of the last one.

Another reason for good documentation and good records is that it is going to protect you when you have future losses or litigation, and we are all vulnerable to this issue.

**Reporting to the Government.** Good records are extremely important in government reporting. Perhaps you have personal property taxes, inventory, or fixed assets to report. After you are through accounting for a particular period of time (fiscal year, short year, or calendar year) for everyone—individuals, corporations, partnerships, and joint ventures—there comes that time when you have to file a report, whether you have taxable income or not. The cleaner your records are, the quicker you are going to get those year-end things closed.

Keep your files up to date. Keep your records orderly. You are going to have a lot of expenses if you have poor records. If an auditor from one of the government, union, or workmens' compensation agencies arrives and discovers that you have inadequate records, he may make a career out of your books. He probably could be out of your office in a day and a half, but if your records are bad he will have to stay for three or four weeks, and he will do it. It is extremely difficult and time consuming to substantiate claims that are several months old and, in many cases, two or three years old. This can be and must be avoided. It is easy to do it right and completely in the beginning.

## RECORDS AS A MANAGEMENT TOOL

The most primary objective of reports, compliances, etc., is not the reporting to all of the agencies, it is the available data that can be used as a management tool. That point is so often overlooked. It's great to get all of the agencies and insurance forms and other compliances taken care of, but in those filing drawers, you have the knowledge and material that can help you so much in planning your business, moving ahead and getting to that bottom line.

**Is the Job Really Profitable?** Some contractors do not know if they have made a profit until after all the data have been accumulated and after the job is completed. The tragedy is that so many contractors are in this position. They say they have been in the business for 15 years and they know what their costs are. They know that they made this dollar amount on a particular job because they have been doing it all these years. Their records are bad. They do not know how to account for a job. Then they begin to analyze it. They look at each item to determine their costs, cost and profit analysis, budget, etc. They start listing the categories on how the job was bid and then apply the costs as they really occurred. As they go down the list and start highlighting those items, they wonder how they could lose money on that job. It can be a shock. This shock can be relieved or avoided if you develop a system that can let you know how you stand as you are progressing. You do not have to wait until the job is completely finished and sold to know what your profits are. You will be able to tell from month to month.

There are systems that can be even more current, so that when you are down to that bottom line, there are no surprises. Perhaps the shock has been brought along each month as you realized how you missed a cost here and a cost there. One contractor missed a category by 70 percent and another by 30 percent, but when he got to the bottom line, it was right on target. Fantastic? No, lucky. It could have been the other way. The data are there. You have it when you write a check or when you receive your payables. You have the basic data for costing to find out where you stand on a particular job.

If you prepare a proper budget, it is definitely going to help you in cash flow. You certainly know what your requirements are, especially if you have two or three units going. If you are in a bind and you have a construction loan on one and you do not have one on another, you can go to the bank and tell them you want a loan because you know where you stand.

**Corrective Action Possible.** Budgets allow you to take corrective action before you get to the point when it is too late to do something to keep costs from going completely out of line—get rid of some of the glamour items because they are unprofitable, change materials, fixtures, etc. The budget should be reviewed regularly. If you can review it monthly, or even weekly, it is better than at the end of the job. You can be the most sophisticated builder in the world, but if you cannot look at your costs in relation to the total project, you are going to have some surprises.

## ACCOUNTING SYSTEMS

What kind of system do you need? Every firm is different. It depends on what kind of staff that you have, how accurate your records are, and how much data you require.

In the old bookkeeping system, for example, which employed the executive checkbook, you write a check and fill out the stub. At the end of the month, with the information on the stubs, you list all of the cash dispersed and all of the dates. You put them in a summary of accounts, go through the journal, put them in a chart, and summarize the journal. You may have 100 and you cannot get the journal to balance. If you do get it to balance, you take the journal and post the checks in the general ledger. You still do not have anything yet.

**Simplified Systems.** Some systems have job cost cards, but there are systems in which cost cards are not needed. One efficient way of doing it is to use three or four columns on a ledger sheet for House No. 6 and perhaps the next three or four columns for House No. 9. In those three or four columns you can quote your *labor*, your *direct costs*, and your *subcontractors*. You can total your sheet and, at the end of the month, post this to the general ledger. At the same time, post it to the cost analysis ledger by category so you know where you are year to date. It is much better to have someone who is clerically inclined do that to help you get the cost analysis data than to have her code checks, put them in the cash disbursement journal, post them into the general ledger, and then miss the most important thing—the cost breakdown.

**Safeguard System.** There are many other types of systems. Safeguard has a system that is even simpler than the one above, and it does not have job cards. You simply take the cost from the cost and profit analysis and put it on worksheets. This give you all of your categories. You will know what your bid was, and you will know what your budget is on that particular job. And, you will have a comparative month-to-date cost as you do the job.

Whatever the system is, it has to allow you the opportunity to summarize the data and get you through those month-end closings. The system may have to be modified. It has to be designed for you and your needs, i.e., you will not need a $700 system, when perhaps all you require is a $100 or $200 system.

Many people will overkill on accounting systems. Data processing is a fantastic tool and it can give you the data you want. But many people really do not need data processing. They can use service bureaus, have banks write their checks, or get an in-house computer. You have to look at all these avenues to cut costs. There are also service bureaus that could help you gather this particular data. Most importantly you must know when you need the data.

## BANKERS

The next area that is really important is bankers. Much consideration should be given in the selection of your banker. Unfortunately, with large banks, if you get a good branch manager who is there for three or four years, and you form a good relationship with him, he is apt to be transferred to a better job. His replacement may not be able to make any decisions. He may tell you, for example, that he will check your loan request and will give you a call next week. If you need the loan sooner, you may have to go to another place to try to get credit.

You have to choose your banker with the utmost care. Check with your peers. Talk to the bank manager and keep him informed. Tell him about your good jobs along with the bad ones. Once you begin communicating with him, he will be communicating with you too. He may tell you that you should not be in that job, but you are the person who must make that decision. You might start respecting him and find out that he is not, after all, as conservative as you thought he was.

Smaller banks are undoubtedly nicer to work with. They do not, perhaps, have to go through loan approval, but they are also limited in the amount of funds that they can lend to you.

**Put Financial Statement on File.** Give the banker a copy of your present financial statement. Let him keep it. You may not need a loan, you may have enough funds or you may have that construction loan when it comes out and you won't need that 30-, 60-, 90-day credit to get you over.

But when you have a statement done, even if it is only for internal use, give it to him. It will be on file so you don't have to call someone on a Friday afternoon at 6 P.M. to get those statements. That person may have to spend all weekend preparing the statement so that on Monday morning you can get that line of credit. When a statement is done, give it to your banker, talk about it, and tell him what you have.

Let him know what you are doing now and what your future jobs are. Provide him with your short-term and long-term commitments. If in six months you intend to buy some vehicles, let him know ahead of time. Don't tell him at the last moment—you might end up buying only half a fleet. You have to keep him interested. About a month or two later he may ask you when you are coming in to buy those vehicles. He'll help you —if you have a good record.

**Negotiate.** When you work out the payment schedule, make it reasonable. If you know you cannot pay it in 30 days, say so. There is nothing worse than asking for an extension. Try to get it for as long as you need it and be realistic about it. Your projections may be such that you think you do not need it, but give yourself some leeway. It makes for a little more comfortable position.

Discuss the interest rate with your banker. Not everyone is going to pay the same interest rate. Depending on the job, in many situations the prime rate is definitely going to have a factor on it. There are always certain conditions in risk jobs. If he tells you that you are going to pay prime plus-4, point out your record and ask for a lower rate. Discuss it with him. In many cases, bankers' decisions to approve or disapprove your line of credit or, for that matter, your construction loan, can be negotiated. Work with him. Don't get excited because he is charging you an extra one-quarter of one percent on a short-term transaction. Don't go to another bank, particularly if you have a good rapport with him, because, needless to say, there are other things that bankers can do for you.

Let the banker know what activity you are going to put through that bank—a general account, a payroll account, a commercial account, credit cards, or, after the house is sold, CD's. Let him know what activity you are going to give him. He will be a little more interested in you than if you have, for instance, a payroll account in one place, a savings account in another, and so forth. Bankers like to have everything under one roof.

But it does not hurt to keep a minor account in another bank; it can provide a good alternative just in case your bank turns down your loan application.

It also helps when your bank changes policy and personnel. A new bank manager may come in when you have *everything* established there. Suddenly, you have nothing. If you have a good record, you can just pick up your portfolio and go to another bank.

## CASH MANAGEMENT

Another vital concern of cash flow is the cash management of your funds, particularly when you have to draw on the construction loans coming in and, especially, when you get a large loan before you have to use it. Put it into a cash mover account for four or five days. Get that little bit of interest. It may be just 5 percent but it is a lot better than letting it sit in a commercial account and having to pay interest on it.

If you have funds that you won't be needing for 3 to 9 months, put them into Treasury bills. You know you are getting 12 percent interest and it's better than the 5 percent you would get in a savings account. Also, it is much better than looking solvent in your commercial account, which is not going to do anything for you. Put these funds into Treasury bills or other high-yield bills and keep them working. You can get a loan against them if you need the funds before maturity, but make your cash work for you.

## SUBCONTRACTOR/EMPLOYEE TAXES

In the construction industry, particular attention must be paid to taxes in relation to subcontractors. It is quite a shock if you are audited by the Internal Revenue Service and they declare that certain subcontractors are "employees." You cannot prove they are subcontractors because you don't have an invoice with the contractor's license number on it. The IRS has gotten very strict on this particular issue. They will go through your check register and look for all the proper names and ask if they are really contractors. They will demand about 35 percent of those wages—for the FICA that you should have withheld from the wages, for the state unemployment insurance on it, for the Federal unemployment insurance on it, and for the state and Federal income taxes. You may have a minor dollar amount in question, but suddenly, at 35 percent, you have a $25,000 lien. It happens, and it's frightening. The IRS says they will allow you to retrieve all of this money when your employees file W2 forms and they amend their tax return. It is, however, difficult to tell an employee who receives cash wages that you are going to amend his tax return.

**How Do You Protect Yourself?** Make sure that everyone who can be classified as an employee is covered. Be aware that the contractor is the person held responsible for any discrepancies. In some states, the contractor's license boards require that all contractors and subcontractors have insurance and that they use their license numbers on any advertising or contract forms. The law defines the difference between contractors and employees, methods of payments, extent of supervision, and communication. Follow the procedures. If you have backup documentation, you will be covered.

Insurance companies can present another problem. An insurance agent will ask if a subcontractor has signed his release, which says that he is paying the wages and has the workmens' compensation and everything else. Whenever you are working with subcontractors, have them sign a release. If the subcontractor won't sign, he has a reason. He usually isn't covered. Check with the insurance company that carries your workmens' compensation and liability insurance. They will tell you that in the subcontractor's agreement it must be spelled out that the subcontractor must give you a copy of the insurance forms and name you as additional insured. You should make this a requisite for payment to that subcontractor as part of your contract with him.

# FINANCE

The image that a builder should present to everyone, and especially a lender, is one of professionalism and credibility.

The lender is one of the major figures in the operation. You can have the best program imaginable, but if you do not have financing, both construction and take-out, at a tolerable rate, you do not have a project.

And what does your lender look at? He looks at the market, at the project, and at the program, and he looks at the borrower—you.

## THE MARKET

The lender and his loan committee are extremely cognizant of what shape the present market is in. They have economic forecasts of the future market. They know the existing inventory. They know how many projects are in the pipeline and they have some knowledge of how many projects are in the planning or incubation stage.

The lender knows their exposure pertaining to area and use, and it will be their determination as to whether they want to extend themselves further.

## THE PROJECT

The lender will be looking at every item on your site study and feasibility study. It would be to your advantage to supply him with your own study to be assured that he sees it as you do and that your case is presented in the best possible light. He will be primarily concerned with return on the investment, duration of the loan, and solidity.

## THE BORROWER

To the lender, there is no substitute for the borrower's experience and a good "track record." If the lender does not know you, he will be looking at your financial statement and profit and loss statements. He will evaluate your experience rating for the same type of project for which you are applying. He will check your reputation as a businessman, with major emphasis on whether you can get the job done and get it done for the amount budgeted.

**Shopping the Money Market.** You can shop for rates, points, terms, and amounts. You can move from one lender to another and, in good times, you will most certainly save money. But what about the bad times? And what about the future? There are two schools of thought on shopping the money market, and the decision lies with the individual. You can shop and change lenders as need be, or you can build a strong, firm, lasting relationship with a good lender of predictable policy and both of you can prosper in good times and in bad times.

**How To Be in Control.** In the financing stage, as well as in all other stages of the construction process, it is important to be in control of the situation. Know what you need and what you want. Know what you should be paying for it and the options that are open to you.

## FEASIBILITY STUDY FOR FINANCING—
## FORMS 360 AND 370

Finance feasibility is a study of the amount of funds needed and available for the project. It also relates to the cost of money through land acquisition to the final cost of take-out commitments and FHA/VA fees, if applicable. The study is a tabulated form of what money costs, where to get it, timing, and types available. It is presented in Form 360.

Lenders as well as projects vary as far as requirements or information needed at the time of loan application.

Your purpose, at this time, is to present the project in the best light possible, and do it in a concise, understandable, and professional way. But it is also important to tell the lender what you know about the project. If it is not a good project for him, it is possible that it will not be a good project for you either.

Form 370 is a checklist of items that most lenders need or prefer in the initial loan application package. The variables are: the complexity or simplicity of the project, the present availability of money, and the borrower's experience or relationship with the lender.

# FINANCIAL FEASIBILITY STUDY

**360**

A. **Amount of financing needed for development**

    1.   Land Purchase: Land Cost $_____
           Loan Amount $_____ x
           Time _____ months, x interest rate _____ % = $_____
           Loan Fee _____ Points & other fees       = $_____

    2.   Land Development: Cost $_____
           Loan Amount $_____ x
           Time _____ months, x interest rate _____ % = $_____
           Loan fee _____ points & other fees       = $_____

    3.   Construction: Cost $_____
           Loan Amount $_____ x
           Time _____ months, x interest rate _____ % = $_____
           Loan fee _____ points & other fees       = $_____

B. **Amount of financing needed for takeout**

    1.   Sales Price Avg. $_____
           Loan commitment fee _____ points     = $_____

    2.   FHA - VA commitment fee
           Points _____                                     $_____

C. **Total amount of financing**   $_____

D. **Total Cost of financing**                       $_____

E. **Timing**

    1.   Possible change in fees or interest rates
           _____

    2.   Optimum timing - project starting date relative to weather, possible strikes, material or labor shortage delays.
           _____

    3.   Phasing of project to save interest charges
           _____

F. **Types of financing available**

    1.   Banks _____
    2.   Savings and Loan _____
    3.   Insurance companies _____
    4.   Union _____
    5.   Pension Funds _____
    6.   Investors _____
    7.   Other _____

NOTES

# FINANCE PACKAGE CHECKLIST

**The Request**

    Cover letter including: borrower's name and address, project location, amount of loan requested, time, rate and loan fee. _____ ☐

**The Program**

    Site study _____ ☐

    Market survey _____ ☐

    Market study conclusion _____ ☐

    Projected unit distribution, sales price _____ ☐

    Schedule relative to absorption rate _____ ☐

    Pictures of site _____ ☐

    Renderings or publicity relative to the program _____ ☐

**The Project**

    Preliminary title report _____ ☐

    Land acquisition agreement _____ ☐

    EIR or negative declaration _____ ☐

    Land survey and topo map _____ ☐

    Soils and geological reports _____ ☐

    Site map _____ ☐

    Plans and specification _____ ☐

    Cost and profit analysis _____ ☐

**The Builder**

    List of present work on hand _____ ☐

    List of past projects and references _____ ☐

    Profit and loss statements _____ ☐

    Financial statements _____ ☐

## MONEY MANAGEMENT

Using other people's money is a science. We take out construction loans. We buy or lease our equipment on time. We may at one time or another take out short-term business loans. We use credit cards and installment buying both for record keeping and deferred payment, and in doing this we are using other people's money. This is also called leverage, and we pay for this privilege in finance charges.

### CASH FLOW CYCLE

There are other ways of using other people's money that are a little less obvious. This method is based on money management. It is the art or science of shortening the receivable cycle, by fast collection of money due, and increasing the payable cycle, by holding back payments on bills owed to the maximum time allowed by contract agreements. (We are not recommending delayed payments—just discussing it.)

We are using other people's money whenever we are ahead of them in work or material received in relation to money paid out.

We are ahead of workmen and office personnel if we pay them once a week. We stay ahead of them if we use a cutoff date two days before payday. This is common practice to allow time for accounting.

We are ahead of our suppliers and subcontractors if we have a billing cutoff date of the 25th of the month with payments on the 10th of the following month. The billing of all work or materials performed or delivered on the 26th carries to the 25th of the next month and would not be paid until the 10th of the month after that, which is 45 days. The least you can be ahead, for items performed and billed prior to the 25th, is 16 days.

Thirty-day invoices could be for items as much as 30 days old for a total of 60 days of free use. But is it free? Of course not. Financing is, or should be, part of the markup that is passed on to the contractor. It is usually passed on as overhead, whether earned or not.

**Optimize Payment Timing.** It is necessary to optimize; pay bills on time, but determine the cost of paying them ahead of time. The actual amount realized from a two-percent discount for paying a bill within ten days of receipt depends directly on what you value your liquid cash at, or what you are paying for borrowed money. We are in no way advocating cheating anyone, or poor or unethical business practices.

**Prompt Payment Beneficial.** Prompt payment of bills gives you a good credit rating. It may help you obtain lower bids. It may give you preferential scheduling. Promptness is a virtue and it is usually rewarded. We pay our bills twice a month. Bills in by the 1st are paid by the 15th. Bills in by the 15th are paid by the 1st. The benefits have been many-fold—excellent relations, scheduling, and assistance.

**Borrow Sufficient Amount.** The science of good money management starts with borrowing or funding the maximum possible for a project and tailoring the draws so that you can either get ahead or stay even with the cash flow. For instance, an equitable disbursement on a five-draw progress schedule would be 30 percent on the first draw and 10 percent on the last draw, which is usually paid 35 days after notice of completion is recorded. This allows the borrower a slight cushion at the start to help defray start-up costs and alleviate the tight financial situation caused by the differential cash needed for land purchase, loan service, and escrow fees.

**Correlate Cash Flow.** The optimum use of other people's money is achieved when a cash flow schedule is correlated with a building schedule, i.e., you build and schedule to the cash allotment draws and, further, to the billing cutoff dates. This is especially true in townhouses and subdivision work.

Here is an example: The project: 30 townhouses in northern California. Time: the winter of 1977-78. The problem: rain, stucco material, and labor shortage. In January, the project was just past the framing stage with most buildings complete and lathed, some with the stucco scratch coat on and into the drywall stages. Stucco material was scarce and the labor to put it on was in heavy demand. To compound the situation, it was the middle of a particularly rainy winter. The decision was made to continue the scheduling of other phases. At one time there were buildings ready for third and even fourth construction draws on the inside that could not qualify for a second draw because the second coat of stucco was not on. Cash flow was stretched to the limit, bills were in for drywall, doors, cabinets, finish labor, etc. There were no progress payments to cover them.

This builder happened to have a very understanding lender. He also had sufficient cash reserves to be able to get away with this sort of action. But not everyone can do this and survive. You can see the problem and the potential danger.

Cash flow balance is the goal of money management, and you achieve this by:

1. Borrowing sufficient amounts to be able to finish the project.
2. Negotiating a favorable disbursement schedule.
3. Building and scheduling with consideration for progress draws.
4. Filing the notice of completion as soon as you qualify for it.

# 4
# Cost and Profit

## COST AND PROFIT ANALYSIS

The single most important function in the building process is for each builder to know his costs. More mistakes are made by incorrect assumptions than any other item. Far too often we have heard horror stories of houses being sold before the final costs were in, before they were bid out, and even before the land had closed escrow on the original purchase.

The forms of the Cost and Profit Analysis are the type used and the information needed to make a clear and concise study of the actual costs of any given project. This format can be used for 1 or 500 houses. It can be adapted to commercial and industrial projects as well.

The Cost and Profit Analysis consists of a package of six forms: **Form 400**—Cost and Profit Analysis (Face Sheet); **Form 410**—Work in Process Budget (Indirect); **Form 420**—Work in Process Budget (Direct); **Form 430**—Product Line Detail Support (Work Sheet); **Form 440**—Financing/Tax Budget; and **Form 450**—Model Excess Budget.

If you fill out this package in full and completely understand the various items, you will have a bottom-line figure that will at least approximate your profits or losses. This can also be used as a tool for purchasing land. If filled out in its entirety, at best a one- or two-day job, the final decision to purchase can be made based on bottom-line numbers. When you tie up a piece of land contingent upon economic, engineering, and government studies, this is the point in process and the forms that will help you determine the economic feasibility of your project.

## FORM 400—COST AND PROFIT ANALYSIS (FACE SHEET)

Starting with the face sheet of the Cost and Profit form:

**Item 1, Land and Allocations** covers the cost of the land and includes all costs attributable to land acquisition.

**Item 2, Improvements.** There would be very little to fill out if you were buying improved lots from developers, as is done in the Chicago area. However, if you are a developer who is buying raw land, you would have this entire section to fill out. Your estimate of direct costs could come from your engineers; the indirect, such as gas and electric, could also come from your engineers. We break this into two areas: *direct*, which is going to be spent on the land, and *indirect*, which are those dollars spent in fees, but not used in the field. The *Interim Interest* and *Loan Points/Fees* are those monies that we are going to take from the direct and indirect item developed in Form 440, Financing/Tax Budget. These are the interim interest and loan point fees that you would need strictly for the improvements to the land. The *Recreation* item is for townhouses or P.U.D., where you might have a pool, tennis courts, landscaping, or other amenities added to the project. This total would give you a *Developed Lot Cost*.

**Item 3, Construction.** The *direct costs* come from your bidding, which is your actual per-foot cost, or an estimate based on a per-foot cost that you have developed. If you have built before, you have a good idea of what your actual per-foot cost is with a percentage added for each year since the time of your empirical study. The *indirect costs* come from Form 410, Work in Process Budget—Indirect. The *Interim Interest* and *Loan Points/Fees—Miscellaneous* are worked out in Form 440, Financing/Tax Budget. The addition of the above now gives you your *Total Cost of Sales*, and if you wish to compute it, your **Gross Margin, Item 4.**

**Item 5, Direct Selling Costs,** is self-explanatory. *Commissions* may result from sales conducted out-of-house or in-house. Much success is being experienced by builders in both areas. We use both systems, but we recommend that the builder delegate the criteria or use both as the situation dictates.

The *Model* under Item 5 comes from Form 450, Model Excess Budget. The *Takeout and Loan Points/Fees* can be broken out of the Model Excess Budget or left as a model expense. *Title Costs* are based on a unit of sale basis. *Taxes/Insurance* are computed, based on a usage of money and time basis. *Escrow Fees* are again one item that is self-explanatory. We have always kept *Advertising* as a direct-selling cost. Depending upon the size of the tract, the quality of the product, and the number of units; advertising can be budgeted at anywhere from ¼ to 1 percent of cost of sales.

**Item 6, Overhead**, is again self-explanatory to a point. Under *Marketing*, if we feel our advertising will be successful, we set the budget at ¼ percent. The *General/Administrative* covers office and bookkeeping expenses. These are not attributable directly to a job and vary with volume of work and expenses. If you are reporting to a parent entity, your parent will designate a specific amount of money for administrative expenses. A single builder might not carry an administrative expense, most of his overhead being an indirect cost charged under Improvements and Construction, Items 2 and 3. He could feel that his own time was relatively free and would include any general expenses in gross profits. *Corporate* is a very specific item and your corporate or parent will tell you, as most do, what percentage on each sale should be reimbursed back to the parent for their use.

**Items 7, 8, and 9, Total Costs, Profit, and Selling Price** are below this.

**Item 10, Includes Premiums of.** This item pertains to premiums charged on lots that have views, are in cul-de-sacs, are larger, or have some other sales advantage.

The vertical columns for *Total Dollars* is self-explanatory. The *Percent of Sales*, using "ball park" figures, gives us our land-developed cost which is generally underlined and runs to about 25 percent of our sales price. Condominium projects, single-family home projects, different areas of the country, different counties, or other factors can adjust this figure and change it. We suggest that you form your own percentage comments. If you get them from empirical studies, it is good to know what percent of sales you use for land, profit, etc. It makes you cognizant of what you are doing.

The item **Per Unit Fixed** is used by some major corporations. If they prefer a per unit dollar cost, the form is made flexible so that the per unit fixed can be the total per unit.

## FORM 410—WORK IN PROCESS BUDGET (INDIRECT)

The next sheet is the Work in Process Budget—Indirect. We have gone into great detail on these sheets and have spelled them out for easy reading. You will note that they are self-descriptive. So many times builders underestimate the cost of temporary toilets, temporary power, common labor, blueprinting, and other indirect charges caused by improper projections and analyses. Other items can be added to this form to cover various areas of the country. This form filled out completely carries the majority of the costs that you will encounter in what we call Construction—Indirect. After the form is filled out completely, the total is carried forward to the face sheet of Form 400 under Item 3, Construction—Indirect.

## FORM 420—WORK IN PROCESS BUDGET (DIRECT)

Form 420 has many versatile uses. It can be extended as a cost sheet, a running budget or, as you will note, it has been coded to be used on a computerized system. These are not complete sheets. As we have found in the past, each area of a state, county, or municipality has completely different fees and terms.

This form is presented for your review and to act as a model to aid you in designing a specific form that will be used by you and your firm.

Some of you may be able to use it as is; others may need changes. There are many methods and styles of tabulating construction costs. The information gathered is the same, the order in which it is recorded is all that varies.

Form 420 is an adaptation of the Construction Specifications Institute's numerical 16 item format and is adaptable to all construction types—residential, commercial, and industrial.

Form 425 is in, more or less, chronological order to be more consistent with scheduling and cash flow analysis. The form as presented is specifically for residential construction (single and multiple). It can be changed for other types of construction. Both types are presented as a comparison and to point out the existence of two of the many methods.

## FORM 430—PRODUCT LINE DETAIL SUPPORT (WORK SHEET)

The Product Line Detail Support work sheet is set up to get a close estimate on the construction price, a per-unit cost and a total sales price. This is strictly a work sheet to enable you to fill out the Cost and Profit Analysis form. For instance, if you know your house cannot sell for under $79,500 and after filling out the balance of the Cost and Profit Analysis form you see you do not have a profit, it is pretty obvious that this particular project should be scrapped. The work sheet is just that—the totals are carried forward to Form 400.

## FORM 440—FINANCING TAX BUDGET

Needless to say, you not only need to know the amount of money you are borrowing, but once you determine the amount you feel you will have to borrow, you must assume how much you will pay for the money and for how long. If you are building 100 homes, it can be assumed that you will be borrowing 50 percent of your money outstanding at any one time. But, it is also axiomatic that a particularly rainy season in the West or heavy snows in the East can put a crimp in your normal schedule, and you could end up paying an additional six- or eight-months' interest above budget unless you made that assumption. Form 440 is only an assumption sheet, and to fill out your Cost and Profit Analysis form (under Construction, Items 3 and 4: Interim Interest and Loan Points/Fees—Misc.), it is necessary that a hard look be given to this item.

As an added benefit of Form 440, it is generally helpful with a wise builder that his lending institution is made aware of his asumptions, because many institutions require an impounding of an amount of money for interest and point payments. If the bank and the builder do not agree with the assumptions, then this is another area in which you should clarify the issues and make sure the Cost and Profit Analysis form reflects these changes.

## FORM 450—MODEL EXCESS BUDGET

In tract and townhouse projects, the builder will usually set up model home complexes. In boom sales years for smaller projects, this was not done. In difficult sales years, even the smaller tracts have some kind of model display. In California, model homes are used extensively.

The Model Excess Budget takes into account dollars per unit for furnishings, decorator fees, air-conditioning costs (which are singular for models and may not be in the full program), decking and patios, landscaping, floodlighting, and fencing. The budget form also takes into account signs, both interior and exterior, which definitely constitute a cost. Taxes are handled on an individual basis and separately inasmuch as the models will be built first and sold last. We also treat model home financing as a separate item because the normal financing assumptions cannot be derived in the same fashion as the field program.

Model maintenance is also treated specifically, as far too many times builders forget to assign the costs of maintaining their models in a clean and orderly fashion. Utilities are included, as these are often overlooked.

There is a section for the sales area. A parking lot has to be built, and special structures and improvements will be needed for the sales area. In this form we feel we are a little more specific by having a restoration item. Most builders forget that after a model is built, it has to be restored back to its original shape for final sale. In the next section, sales office, we consider design, construction, furnishings, exhibits, and restoration.

Further down our sheet we have insurance, vandalism/theft, and contingencies. These are very important items and they need to be considered in the cost process at this point.

This form, filled out properly and completely, will give you a true picture of your model budget. Take the bottom-line cost and carry it to the face sheet of Form 400, under Direct Selling Costs, Item 2: Model.

# COST AND PROFIT ANALYSIS

400

Division _____    Product Feasibility _____
Project _____     Preliminary _____
Acres____ Density____ Units_____    Final _____
Location of Property _____    Update Revision _____

| | | Schedule Reference | Total Dollars | Percent of Sales | ASSUMPTIONS Per Unit Fixed | Comments |
|---|---|---|---|---|---|---|
| 1. | LAND & ALLOCATIONS | | | | | |
| 2. | IMPROVEMENTS | | | | | |
| | Direct | | | | | |
| | Indirect | | | | | |
| | Interim Interest | | | | | |
| | Loan Points/Fees-Misc. | | | | | |
| | Recreation | | | | | |
| | TOTAL | | | | | |
| | DEVELOPED LOT COSTS | | | | | |
| 3. | CONSTRUCTION | | | | | |
| | Direct | | | | | |
| | Indirect | | | | | |
| | Interim Interest | | | | | |
| | Loan Points/Fees-Misc. | | | | | |
| | TOTAL | | | | | |
| | TOTAL COST OF SALES | | | | | |
| 4. | GROSS MARGIN | | | | | |
| 5. | DIRECT SELLING COSTS | | | | | |
| | Commissions | | | | | |
| | Model | | | | | |
| | Takeout Loan Points/Fees | | | | | |
| | Title Costs | | | | | |
| | Taxes/Insurance | | | | | |
| | Escrow Fees | | | | | |
| | Advertising | | | | | |
| | TOTAL | | | | | |
| 6. | OVERHEAD | | | | | |
| | Marketing | | | | | |
| | General/Administrative | | | | | |
| | Corporate | | | | | |
| | TOTAL | | | | | |
| 7. | TOTAL COSTS | | | ✕ | | Amount |
| 8. | PROFIT | | | | → | |
| 9. | SELLING PRICE | | | ✕ | | |
| 10. | INCLUDES PREMIUMS OF: | | | | → | |

410

## WORK IN PROCESS BUDGET - INDIRECT

Division Name _____  Date _____

Originator _____

Project _____

Description                                                                 BUDGET

1. **SUPERVISION** (Include 10% Benefits)

    A. Manager:          $_____/month x _____ months _____
    B. Superintendent:   $_____/month x _____ months _____
    C. Asst. Supt.:      $_____/month x _____ months _____  _____

2. **COMMON LABOR** (Include Benefits)

                         $_____/month x _____ months _____  _____

3. **AUTOMOBILE BUSINESS EXPENSE:**

                         $_____/month x _____ months _____  _____

4. **TEMPORARY FACILITIES:**

    A. Trailer:          $_____/month x _____ months _____
    B. Chemical Toilets: $_____/month x _____ months _____
    C. Temporary Power (Lump Sum)                            _____
    D. Storage Shed (Lump Sum)                               _____
    E. Utilities:
        1. Electricity:  $_____/month x _____ months _____
        2. Water:        $_____/month x _____ months _____
        3. Gas:          $_____/month x _____ months _____
        4. Telephone:    $_____/month x _____ months _____

    F. Safety Equipment and Signs (Lump Sum)         _____  _____

5. **ARCHITECTURAL FEES:**

                         $_____/unit x _____ units    _____  _____

129

**WORK IN PROCESS BUDGET - INDIRECT (Continued)**

                                                                                            **BUDGET**

6. **LAND PLANNING:**     $_____/unit x _____ units     _____ _____

7. **BLUEPRINTING:**     $_____/unit x _____ units     _____ _____

8. **OFFICE EXPENSES:** (Lump Sum)     _____ _____

9. **EQUIPMENT RENTAL / SMALL TOOLS:** (Lump Sum)     _____ _____

10. **MAINTENANCE EXPENSE:** (Lump Sum)     _____ _____

11. **WAREHOUSE EXPENSE:** (Lump Sum)     _____ _____

12. **SECURITY:**     $_____/month x _____ months     _____ _____

13. **WARRANTY EXPENSE:** $_____/unit x _____ units     _____ _____

14. **BOND PREMIUMS:** (Lump Sum)     _____ _____

15. **FILING FEES:** (Lump Sum)     _____ _____

16. **PARK FEES:**     $_____/unit x _____ units     _____ _____

17. **SCHOOL FEES:**     $_____/unit x _____ units     _____ _____

18. **INSURANCE:** (Lump Sum)     _____ _____

19. **LEGAL:** (Lump Sum)     _____ _____

20. **CONTINGENCY:**     $_____/unit x _____ units     _____ _____

21. _____ _____ _____
22. _____ _____ _____
23. _____ _____ _____
24. _____ _____ _____
25. _____ _____ _____
26. _____ _____ _____
27. _____ _____ _____
28. _____ _____ _____
29. _____ _____ _____
30. _____ _____ _____

                                                     TOTAL     _____

420

## WORK IN PROCESS BUDGET
## REC./COMMON MAINT. DIRECT

Division Name _____    Division _____

Originator _____    General Ledger Account _____

Project Name _____    Charge No./Phase _____

Date _____

| CODE | DESCRIPTION | BUDGET |
|------|-------------|--------|
| | **GENERAL REQUIREMENTS** | |
| 0141 | Rough Cleanup | |
| 0142 | Finish Cleanup | |
| 0180 | Building Permits/Fees | |
| 0185 | Sewer/Water Connection Fee | |
| 0190 | Equipment Rental | |
| 0192 | Direct Materials | |
| | **SITE WORK** | |
| 0205 | Trenching | |
| 0221 | Site Grading | |
| 0231 | Foundation Drilling | |
| 0255 | Site Utilities - Plumbing | |
| 0256 | Site Utilities - Electric | |
| 0257 | Reimbursable Electric | |
| 0258 | Site Utilities - Gas | |
| 0259 | Reimbursable Gas | |
| 0261 | Paving | |
| 0271 | Fences | |
| 0274 | Irrigation System | |
| 0275 | Yard Improvements | |
| | **CONCRETE** | |
| 0301 | Slab - Liveable Area | |
| 0303 | Footing/Foundation Walls | |
| 0304 | Lightweight Concrete | |
| 0305 | Termite Control | |
| 0306 | Specially Placed Concrete | |
| | **MASONRY** | |
| 0420 | Unit Masonry - Walls | |
| 0426 | Pavers - Entry | |
| 0431 | Fireplace | |
| | **METALS** | |
| 0550 | Miscellaneous Metals | |
| 0570 | Ornamental Metal | |
| | **CARPENTRY** | |
| 0610 | Rough Carpentry - Labor | |
| 0611 | Framing - Material | |
| 0613 | Trusses | |

**WORK IN PROCESS BUDGET**
**REC./COMMON MAINT. DIRECT (Continued)**

| CODE | DESCRIPTION | BUDGET |
|---|---|---|
| | **CARPENTRY (Continued)** | |
| 0614 | Roof Sheathing | |
| 0620 | Finish Carpentry - Labor | |
| 0621 | Wood Trim | |
| 0622 | Millwork - Material | |
| 0623 | Wood Siding | |
| 0641 | Cabinetwork | |
| | **MOISTURE PROTECTION** | |
| 0720 | Building Insulation | |
| 0721 | Rat Proofing | |
| 0722 | Weatherstripping | |
| 0730 | Shingles/Roof Tile | |
| 0750 | Membrane Roof | |
| 0760 | Sheetmetal Work | |
| 0763 | Gutters/Downspouts | |
| | **DOORS, WINDOWS & GLASS** | |
| 0837 | Sliding Glass Doors | |
| 0852 | Aluminum Windows | |
| 0870 | Finish Hardware - Materials | |
| 0885 | Glass & Glazing | |
| | **FINISHES** | |
| 0910 | Lath & Plaster | |
| 0925 | Gypsum Drywall | |
| 0930 | Ceramic Tile | |
| 0935 | Synthetic Marble Tops | |
| 0965 | Resilient Flooring | |
| 0969 | Particle Board Flooring | |
| 0990 | Painting | |
| 0995 | Wallpaper | |
| | **SPECIALTIES** | |
| 1025 | Firefighting Devices | |
| 1062 | Folding Partitions | |
| 1081 | Shower Doors/Enclosures | |
| 1082 | Mirrors | |
| 1085 | Decking | |
| 1095 | Waste Disposal Units | |
| | **EQUIPMENT** | |
| 1192 | Kitchen/Lav Counter Top | |
| 1193 | Kitchen Equipment | |
| 1194 | Laundry Equipment | |
| | **FURNISHINGS** | |
| 1240 | Carpets & Pads | |
| 1250 | Drapery & Curtains | |

WORK IN PROCESS BUDGET
REC./COMMON MAINT. DIRECT (Continued)

| CODE | DESCRIPTION | BUDGET |
|------|-------------|--------|
|      | **SPECIAL CONSTRUCTION** | |
| 1301 | Mechanical Cores | |
| 1305 | Panel Construction | |
| 1386 | Saunas | |
|      | **MECHANICAL** | |
| 1517 | Plumbing System | |
| 1530 | Plumbing Fixtures/Trim | |
| 1531 | Fiberglass Tubs/Showers | |
| 1580 | Air Tempering System | |
|      | **ELECTRICAL** | |
| 1630 | Electrical System – All | |
| 1640 | Lighting Fixtures | |
| 1643 | Luminous Ceilings | |
| 1656 | Alarm Detection System | |
| 1659 | Television | |
| 1680 | Electric Heat System | |
| 1900 | **CONTINGENCY** | |
|      | **REC.** | |
| 2801 | Swimming Pool | |
| 2802 | Playground Equipment | |
| 2804 | Landscaping | |
| 2805 | Fences | |
| 2806 | Flatwork | |
| 2808 | Furn/Equipment | |

TOTAL

COST PER SQUARE FOOT

# NOTES

# PRODUCT LINE DETAIL SUPPORT

(Work Sheet)

Division _____    Date _____

Originator _____    _____

Project _____    _____

| Model No. | BR | B | GR | Square Footage 1 FL | Square Footage 2 FL | Square Footage Tot. | $/Sq. Ft. | Cost/ Unit | Units | Total Direct Const. | Base Price/ Unit | Total Sales |
|---|---|---|---|---|---|---|---|---|---|---|---|---|
| | | | | | | | | | | | | |
| | | | | | | | | | | | | |
| | | | | | | | | | | | | |
| | | | | | | | | | | | | |
| | | | | | | | | | | | | |
| | | | | | | | | | | | | |
| | | | | | | | | | | | | |
| | | | | | | | | | | | | |
| | | | | | | | | | | | | |
| | | | | | | | | | | | | |
| | | | | | | | | | | | | |
| | | | | | | | | | | | | |
| | | | | | | | | | | | | |
| | | | | | | | | | | | | |
| | | | | | | | | | | | | |
| | | | | | | | | | | | | |
| | | | | | | | | | | | | |
| | | | | | | | | | | | | |
| | | | | | | | | | | | | |
| | | | | | | | | | | | | |

430

# NOTES

# FINANCING/TAX BUDGET

440

Division _____   Date _____

Originator _____

Project _____

---

**LAND/IMPROVEMENT FINANCING ASSUMPTIONS:**




---

**CONSTRUCTION FINANCING ASSUMPTIONS:**

Interim Interest:

    Loan at _____% of Sales Price

    Interest Rate of _____%

    Average Funds Borrowed at _____% of Total Loan

    Loan Outstanding for Average of _____ Months

    Sales Price x _____% (% of sales borrowed) x _____ (interest rate)

    x _____ ( $\frac{\text{usage in months}}{12}$ ) = Budget

Loan Points/Fee:

    _____% of _____% of Sales Price = Budget

Miscellaneous Loan Costs:

    $_____/unit x _____ units = $ _____
                                                          Budget

---

**TAX ASSUMPTIONS:**

## NOTES

# MODEL EXCESS BUDGET           450

Division Name _____     Date _____

Originator _____

Project _____

| Description | Budget |
|---|---|

Furnishings: $_____ /model for _____ models _____  _____

Furniture/Accessories: $_____ /model for _____ models _____  _____

Decorator Fees: $_____ /model for _____ models _____  _____

Air Conditioning: $_____ /model for _____ models _____  _____

Decking and Patios: _____

Landscaping: $_____ /model for _____ models _____  _____

Floodlighting _____  _____

Fencing _____  _____

Signs (Interior, Exterior Model ID) _____  _____

Taxes _____  _____

Financing: $_____ Loan x _____ % Loan x

          _____ % Interest Rate x _____ Months _____  _____

Model Maintenance & Landscape Maintenance: $_____ /model

          for _____ models for _____ months _____  _____

Utilities: $_____ /model for _____ models for _____ months ___  _____

Sales Area:
    Parking Lot _____    _____
    Special Structures _____    _____
    Improvements _____    _____
    Restoration _____    _____
                            Total $ _____    _____

Sales Office:
    Design (Architect - Engineer) _____    _____
    Construction _____    _____
    Furnishings _____    _____
    Furniture _____    _____
    Exhibits _____    _____
    Restoration _____    _____
                            Total $ _____    _____

Insurance: _____  _____

Vandalism/Theft: _____  _____

Contingencies: _____  _____

                                       TOTAL  _____

## NOTES

# 5

# Construction

## MOBILIZATION

The Cost and Profit Analysis of the preceding chapter should provide the information needed to make a financial feasibility determination. If the decision is to proceed, then there are certain items that usually must be completed before the actual construction can begin.

## DOCUMENTS AND PERMITS

If a lender is involved he will insist that the construction loan be recorded before any construction begins or material deliveries are made to the site. He will require that the title company assure him that his loan is in first place ahead of any mechanic's liens or other encumbrances. And most title companies—if they do not know you too well—will not allow any site disturbance prior to recordation; they may even send out inspectors with cameras to document their findings the morning of recordation. Some title companies, for their larger, well-established clients, if they have a continuing guaranty document on file, will sometimes relax this rule.

All government permits, building permits, encroachment permits, and all utility fees need to either be in your hand or ready to be picked up. On most projects, when a lender is involved, these permits are prerequisite to funding and closing of escrow.

**Final Land Acquisition and Title Transfer.** Before the final loan is recorded, the most important consideration is allowing enough time for the title company, and any other agency or entity that is involved, to get proper signatures and documentation in order. There may be a time coordination problem if there is a need for all of these things to happen at the same time. On large projects it may be necessary to tie the construction loan, land improvement loan, land purchase loan, and funding for the building permits all out of the same escrow—and this all takes lead time.

## CONTRACTS

Once the project documents have been signed and escrow has closed, it is time to sign the construction contracts and the subcontractors' and suppliers' agreements. These documents are usually consummated by the principal, or the contract and purchasing department. They are very seldom handled by the construction department. It will, however, be the field superintendent's job to oversee the terms of the contract; therefore, it is imperative that he know what is in the contract. If he does not, he might ask a subcontractor to clean up his debris and find out that it is not included in the subcontractor's agreement. Or he might even find himself asking one subcontractor to do something that is in another man's contract—and try to straighten that mess out, with deducts, add-ons, and even contract default—if it gets that far.

If it is the policy of upper management not to disseminate the final subcontractor's agreement to the field, for whatever reason, then a copy of the portion that covers what the work agreement includes or excludes is the least that can be given to the field. Your field personnel may not need to know the final money amount of the contract, but they certainly need to know their legal limits and know the parameters of time, work to be done, payment terms, and quality or types of material or product.

### FORMS

There are certain forms that you *must* have. If you are the general contractor, you have to have a contract for your subcontractors. If you are the owner, you have to have a contract with your general contractor. There are a wide variety of forms that you can use. Most people tend to use the American Institute of Architecture (AIA) form; they are generally accepted throughout the industry. There are a number of different initial pages, depending upon which form you want to use. The AIA can supply you with a series of contracts between owner and architect, owner and engineer, owner and contractor, and one between contractor and subcontractor, and on down the list.

One of the things you don't want to forget or lose sight of is that these forms tend to be brief, they tend to have large blank spaces to be filled in, and most of them incorporate a set of general provisions, which is very lengthy and has a lot of fine print in it, and which very few people read.

Sometimes people do not attach it. Sometimes you will see AIA contracts that refer to the general conditions as being incorporated; no one has ever seen them, let alone attached them to the agreement. And yet, the agreement says these are incorporated and are part of the agreement.

**Prepare Your Own Contracts.** Do not sign a contract that someone else has produced if you do not know what is in it or you have not read it. If you do not have the time to read it and understand it, give to your attorney and let him do it for you. Otherwise, you may be wasting your money because you are letting the other person dictate the terms of the contract. Chances are he may not have read it either, so you are both gambling on what is in there. If he has read it and he knows what is in there and you do not, he is ahead of you, and you do not want to be in that position.

## CONTRACT REMEDIES

If you run into a problem with your subcontractor, what should you do? Let's say you are the owner and you have a contract with a general contractor who is developing a subdivision for you. One of the provisions in your contract says that he is supposed to perform a job by a certain date and that date has come and gone. The best thing to do is to write him a letter telling him he is in default and spell out how he's in default, referring to the specific provision in the contract. Tell him you will give him a period of time—24 hours, one week, ten days, etc.—to perform, and if he hasn't done so in that period, you will hire someone else to do the job, with the additional costs charged to him. Send him the letter and make sure he gets it, even if you have to hand deliver it or send it certified mail. If the established period of time has gone by and he hasn't done anything, hire someone else. But, before you hire another general contractor, give your original contractor one last chance. When you find out what the new costs will be, send him another letter, telling him that you *have* hired someone else and state the starting date and the amount it will cost him if he does not begin the job immediately. Now you've covered your bases and you have "papered your file," as they say. You are ready to hire another contractor and let him do the job. Meanwhile, you hold back, of course, on any further payments to the contractor who has defaulted and, later, when you have the job done, you have to settle up. You have to pay the person who did the job. You have to work out how much more than the contract price it cost you to get the job done. You have to offset any money you owe him, for work that he had done up to the point of default against the final cost. It may turn out that you owe him a small amount of money. It may turn out that he owes you a lot of money because you were not that far ahead of him and it cost you a lot more to get the job done by somebody else.

Arbitration. One way to settle these matters is to go into court, but there are other ways, of course. Most of the AIA contract provisions call for arbitration. They usually designate someone as an initial arbitrator, such as an architect or an engineer, and if there is a disagreement, the architect or the engineer will be the arbitrator and his decision is final on both parties; so, they may or may not be helpful. If there is a technical dispute about something—about whether the work was done properly in accordance with the specifications and/or within certain tolerances—frequently, an arbitration clause will give an architect or an engineer authority to make a decision which is binding on both parties and you can go on with the contract.

If everything breaks down and you have your choice between arbitration and litigation, what do you do? Some contracts will have binding arbitration; others will have it worded in such a way that it is optional. Do you want arbitration or do you want to go to court? That all depends on how good your case is. If your attorney tells you you've got a "dead-bang" winner in the law, the last thing you want is arbitration because arbitrators tend to be compromisers. No matter how strong one side is and how weak the other, they tend to split things down the middle because compromise is the essence of arbitration. So, if you have a strong case, do not go to arbitration—go to court. If you have a weak case, go to arbitration and make the best argument that you can.

Types of Arbitration. There are many different kinds of arbitration. Most people go with the American Arbitration Assocation (AAA) rules. They have people in, or related to, the industry—builders, contractors, architects, attorneys—serve on panels. The cost is minimal. You get a high degree of expertise. The rules are well-defined, they are easy to follow, and it is a fairly good system. If your contract doesn't specify AAA, you can use your state arbitration act. It sets forth the procedures of arbitration. It is somewhat similar to the AAA. Many contracts are drawn up with a special arbitration clause and it will have a simple system. It may state agreement on a common arbitrator and allow him to decide. Or another may state that each will select an arbitrator and the two of them will select a third, and that panel will decide. These are some of many variations. AAA is used in many contracts because most people are familiar with them and with what they do; they are effective and not too expensive.

## LIEN PROBLEMS

Lien problems, especially *mechanic's lien*, are something you may have to deal with when you are working with general contractors, subcontractors, material men, or laborers. If you are the owner, you have a direct relationship with the general contractor and an indirect relationship with the subcontractors and the material men. If you are the owner, and the subcontractor and material men want to file a mechanic's lien against your property, they have to give you a preliminary notice. And that means that within 20 days of the time that they do some work on your project they have to send you a notice and tell you that they are supplying concrete, labor, equipment, or something on the job. If they do not do that, they cannot file a lien on your job later on. The first thing to do when you get a lien notice from someone you do not know is to find out if he ever sent you a 20-day notice; if he has not done so, he cannot make a claim.

You cut off lien problems, of course, by filing a notice of completion. Once you've filed that notice, it starts a time clock running and they have either 30 days or 60 days to get their liens on file, depending upon whether they have a direct or indirect relationship with you. If they do not get their liens on file, the matter is closed. But, if they do file, another time clock starts running, and from that time, they have 180 days to file a suit on their lien. If the 180 days passes and they have not filed their suit they are without recourse.

**Stock Notices and Bond Notices.** The mechanic's liens are only one of three weapons that these people have. There are two other things—*stock notices* and *bond notices*. If you have a construction lender, they can file a stock notice with your lender without filing a mechanic's lien claim. They can say that they haven't been paid and ask that payment on the construction loan be stopped until they are paid. Then the construction lender will stop the payment. So even though you do not have the 20-day notice, someone with whom you do not have a direct relationship and you do not know, can file a stop notice with your lender if he is not paid.

Bond notices are similar. If you have a big bond up on an off-site improvement job in a tract and someone you don't know has not been paid, he can file a bond notice with the bonding company. The bonding company can then make you pay.

**Lien Releases.** What do you do to avoid lien problems? There are a couple of very simple things which most people do. One is to get releases from everybody. In order to get releases, however, you have to know who they are. And you *should* know who the people are. If you do not have a direct relationship with someone, the material man, for example, you want to find out who he is, you want to know who is supplying concrete to your job, and your want to be sure that he is getting paid. When you pay the contractor and the subcontractor you want to be sure that the material man is getting paid. It is a good idea to get a release from him each time you pay so you can say to the subcontractor: "Give me a release from them and then I'll give you your check. Here's a list of the material men and the subs that you are dealing with." That is somewhat cumbersome, but sometimes you have to do it.

**Joint Checks.** Joint checks are another method. Make your check payable jointly to a series of people and place a statement on the back saying that anyone who endorses the check releases and waives all lien claims. Then anyone who signs the check has a hurdle to overcome if he claims later that he was not paid.

**Builder's Control.** There are other ways to handle this problem. Builder's control is one. This is used when there is a problem with the project. They control the disbursements very tightly. They make sure they know everyone who is working on the tract, they make sure that every dime that is paid out goes to everyone who is supposed to get it, and they make sure that when someone gets some money, he does not pay someone else.

**Retentions.** Retentions are another way you can stay ahead of the subcontractor or, if you are the owner, the general contractor. You can hold back a retention from his payment until after the lien period has run out. In some forms, this is included. And for some companies, retentions are standard procedure.

## CONSTRUCTION CONTRACT CHECKLIST—FORM 500

As stated in the preceding pages, there are standard contract forms for subcontractors and material suppliers. You may sometimes sign forms provided by others or you may rewrite or review your contracts and tailor them to each project.

The nature of the building business is such, that even though buildings and building types are relatively complex and varied, the actual building procedure is, for the most part, the same. And so it is with legal contracts. The basic format and process followed are quite similar. It is the work to be done and the inclusions or exclusions that vary. If the specific inclusions and exclusions are set up to float free in an addendum to the basic contract, in an exhibit, then the contract form becomes quite versatile. Form 500 is a checklist of the more important items to be included in a contract form for housing tracts. It can be adapted for single homes, townhouses, and small commercial or industrial buildings. And because it is possible to add a variable Exhibit "A", it can be used for all subcontractors' and material suppliers' contracts. Review it well with your legal counsel, as we did; change it, adapt it, but use it at your own risk.

# CONSTRUCTION CONTRACT
## CHECKLIST
### For Subcontracts and Material Supply Contracts

500

1. Prime contractor or owner named and identified. _____ ☐
2. Subcontractor, supplier or other party named and identified, and contractors license number, if applicable. _____ ☐
3. Date contract initiated. _____ ☐
4. What constitutes contract document.
    a. Exhibits, material and labor breakdown, bid proposal. _____ ☐
    b. Construction plans and specifications. _____ ☐
    c. Other work itemized in contract or addenda. _____ ☐
    d. Work implied - work to comply with all codes, laws, safety regulations, and that which is customary whether documented or not. ____ ☐
5. Project Location - address, lot, block, tract number. _____ ☐
6. Total cost of work to be performed. _____ ☐
7. Scope of work.
    a. Reference to item 4, a through d. _____ ☐
    b. Change orders - deduct or add on cost - how handled. _____ ☐
    c. Start of work and notice to commence. _____ ☐
    d. Completion of work and penalties for delay. _____ ☐
8. Additional drawings to be furnished by _____ .
    a. Shop or fabrication drawings. _____ ☐
    b. As built revised drawings. _____ ☐
9. Lien release for labor and/or material. _____ ☐
10. Union agreement - if applicable. _____ ☐
11. Insurance - certification and approval.
    a. Workers' compensation. _____ ☐
    b. Comprehensive general liability. _____ ☐
    c. Property damage and protective liability. _____ ☐
    d. Comprehensive automobile liability of property damage. _____ ☐
    e. Contractor named as additional insured on liability policy. ____ ☐
    f. Other. _____ ☐
12. Payment schedule and statement of qualification. _____ ☐
13. Damage or destruction of material provision. _____ ☐
14. Clean-up and haul off excess material. _____ ☐
15. Warrantee clearly defined and time clarified. _____ ☐
16. Breach of contract - what constitutes and penalties. _____ ☐
17. Termination of contract provision. _____ ☐
18. Attorney's fees to be paid by: _____ ☐
19. Signatures, license numbers, titles, addresses. _____ ☐
20. Date signed. _____ ☐

## NOTES

## SUBCONTRACT AGREEMENT—FORM 510

It is beyond the scope of this book to provide legal advice or to discuss at any length the actual wording of contracts. Form 510 is presented as a *sample guide*. The important thing is that the contract have sufficient detail to be completely understood by all parties involved and that it is specific enough to cover the particular job for which it is intended. Know what the contract says. There must be a reason for every word and phrase and it must be relevant to the particular project. Keep it in plain language. Keep it "simple." Review the so-called "standard fine print" usually found on the back and, above all, make sure there is nothing in the contract you can not live with or that gives the other party an unnecessary advantage.

## SUBCONTRACT AGREEMENT

510

THIS AGREEMENT made this _____ day of _____, 19__ by and between _____ hereinafter referred to as Contractor, and _____
hereinafter referred to as Subcontractor,

### WITNESSETH:

The Subcontractor, for the total sum as outlined in Exhibit A, hereby agrees to furnish all material, labor, tools, appliances, permits and certificates and to complete in a workmanlike manner to the satisfaction of the Contractor, and in accordance with the Plans and Specifications, General and Special Conditions and Requirements, Supplements and Addenda prepared therefor by _____

for the construction of _____
_____

**Work Included**

Whether or not shown by the plans or mentioned in the specifications, the work includes the following:

(a)  Any item of labor, service and/or material reasonably inferred by the plans and/or specifications or customarily furnished by subcontractor performing work in this line.

(b)  Any item of labor, service or material required to complete the work in compliance with any applicable law, ordinance or regulation, or necessary to obtain any inspection approvals being obtained by Contractor.

**Commencement Time**

The Subcontractor further agrees to commence the above work within _____ days after notice by the Contractor, and to prosecute the same diligently and continuously to completion. Should the Subcontractor for any reason fail to proceed diligently with the above work, then the Contractor may terminate this subcontract, take charge of said work and the men employed thereon and the materials, tools, and appliances of the Subcontractor and complete the work provided for in this contract, and any extra cost thereof shall be a charge against the Subcontractor, together with any damage for unjustifiable delay or defective work of the Subcontractor. Contractor shall give the Subcontractor 24 hours notice by telegraph or personal service of intended cancellation of contract.

**Plan Changes**

The Subcontractor further agrees not to deviate from the plans, specifications and details of the above contract, except on written order of the Contractor, and that he will be responsible to the Contractor for any damage, inconvenience or increase of cost arising directly or indirectly from failure on his part to observe the same. But the Contractor shall have the right to make changes in the Plans, Specifications and details, and the Subcontractor, on notice thereof, shall be governed thereby. Allowances for extra work and deductions for omissions shall be by mutual agreement between the Contractor and the Subcontractor, but must be fixed in writing in advance, and in the manner provided in the Specifications for like claims by the Contractor upon the Owner.

If a dispute arises between Contractor and the Subcontractor concerning the amount to be charged for extra work or to be credited for omissions, the Subcontractor shall nevertheless proceed in accordance with the change order, and the dispute shall, if not settled within a reasonable time, be submitted to the Architect-Engineer for final decision.

**Lien Releases**

The Subcontractor further agrees to hold the Contractor harmless against any and all liens and claims of persons for labor or materials or appliances furnished under the subcontract. Upon the assertion or filing of any such claim, the Contractor may retain out of any monies due or to become due the Subcontractor, an amount sufficient to cover such lien or claim, plus the cost of litigation and attorneys' fees, until the same shall be satisfied or discharged. The Contractor, as a prerequisite to making any payment, may demand satisfactory evidence that the Subcontractor has paid the cost of the work and material for which such payment is to be made.

**Insurance**

Subcontractor agrees that he shall provide and maintain for the duration of this subcontract, insurance with insurors satisfactory to the contractor, as follows:

(a) Statutory Workmen's Compensation endorsed for Executive Officers and Employer's Liability Insurance, with minimum limits of $500,000.00.

(b) Comprehensive General Liability Insurance with minimum Bodily Injury Limits of $500,000.00 for each person and $1,000,000.00 for each accident, and Property Damage Insurance with minimum limits of $100,000.00 for each accident and $300,000.00 aggregate. The policy shall include Contractor's Protective Liability Insurance with the same minimum limits.

(c) Comprehensive Automobile Liability Insurance for all owned, non-owned and hired vehicles with minimum limits for Bodily Injury of $200,000.00 for each person and $500,000.00 for each accident, and Property Damage minimum limits of $100,000.00.

(d) Owner and Contractor, shall be named as additional insured as respects Liability insurance required above, and this shall be stated on the certificates of insurance required below.

(e) Subcontractor shall not commence work at the site under this subcontract until he has obtained all required insurance, and until such insurance has been approved by the Contractor. Approval of the insurance by the Contractor shall not relieve or decrease the liability of the Subcontractor hereunder. Certificates of insurance shall be filed by Subcontractor prior to commencing work. Such certificates shall show that the insured are protected from claims for damages because of bodily injury, including death, to the Subcontractor's employees and all others; and from claims for damages to property—any or all of which may arise out of or result from the Subcontractor's operations under the contract, whether such operations be by himself or by any subcontractor or anyone directly or indirectly employed by either of them.

(f) The required insurance must be written by a company licensed to do business in the state in which the work is located, at the time the policy is issued. In addition, the company must be acceptable to the owner.

(g) The Subcontractor shall not cause any insurance to be cancelled nor permit any insurance to lapse. All insurance policies shall include a clause to the effect that the policy shall not be cancelled or reduced, restricted or limited until ten (10) days after the Contractor has received written notice as evidenced by return receipt of registered or certified letter. Certificates of insurance shall contain transcripts from the proper office of the insurer, evidencing in particular those insured, the extent of the insurance, the location and the operations to which the insurance applies, the expiration date, and the above-mentioned cancellation clause.

**Damages - Subcontractor**

Subcontractor does expressly assume, to the extent of the work covered by this agreement, all of the indemnification provisions and guarantees imposed on the Contractor by the construction contract between the Contractor and the Owner, and agrees to hold harmless the Contractor and Owner against claims for injury to or death of any person and damage to or destruction of the property of any person caused in any way whatsoever by the Subcontrctor, its employees or its agents, or by the employees or the agents of any Subcontractors of the Subcontractor. Subcontractor further agrees to perform his work so that construction will not be delayed through his failure to perform at the proper time. Attention is specifically called to any specifications relating to time limit and damages (if any). If the Contractor is required to pay any penalty or damages because of failure to complete within the specified time and said failure to complete is the result of the Subcontractor's failure to perform his contract promptly and expeditiously, then the Subcontractor will reimburse the Contractor for any penalty and/or damages so assessed and paid by the Contractor.

**Payment**

The Contractor, for the consideration hereinabove set forth, promises and agrees to pay the Subcontractor for the above work as outlined in Exhibit A.

Contractor agrees to pay the Subcontractor according to the terms and conditions as set forth in this subcontract with the understanding that: (a) The payments to the Subcontractor are subject to the condition precedent that Contractor receives payment from the Owner for such work covered by the Subcontractor's billing; and that any payments may be made, at the option of the Contractor, by joint checks to Subcontractor and his materialmen, subcontractors, and suppliers; (b) That said work must comply with all laws or regulations, so that payment will be made only if the Subcontractor has furnished the Contractor satisfactory evidence of freedom from liens for each progressive work stage from his subcontractors, materialmen and suppliers; (c) Before retention or final payment is released, Subcontractor employing union men must present written evidence to the Contractor from the appropriate fund offices for its trade or craft that all fringe benefits have been paid for their labor on this project. (These offices include Health, Welfare and Vacation, Pension and Apprenticeship Fund Offices.) Payments to Subcontractor shall not imply acceptance of the work.

**Damages - Contractor**

The parties hereto have further agreed that in case of damage or destruction which the Contractor could not reasonably have foreseen and guarded against, the loss to be borne by the Contractor shall be the amount of all payments made or due by him to the Subcontractor at the time of the loss, and the Subcontractor shall bear the loss on all other materials and work.

**Clean-Up**

All debris and materials from this work are to be disposed of and/or removed from the job site at the expense of the Subcontractor.

**Attorney's Fees**

In the event of breach of this contract by Subcontractor, Subcontractor agrees to pay to Contractor a reasonable attorneys' fee to be fixed by the Court determining such breach.

**Termination of Contract**

If the Contract between the Owner and Contractor is terminated during the course of the work, and notice thereof is given to the Subcontractor, this contract shall likewise be terminated as of the date of said notice. Subcontractor shall be paid for all materials and labor incorporated in the work to such date, together with his pro-rata overhead and profit attributable thereto.

IN WITNESS WHEREOF, the parties hereby have executed this agreement the day and year first above written.

_____
                        Subcontractor                  License No.

By: _____
                                                           Title

_____
                     Subcontractor's Address

_____

_____
                          Contractor

By: _____
                                                           Title

_____
                      Contractor's Address

_____

# CONSTRUCTION FORMS

In the construction business you make your profit in many ways. You make it by buying the right piece of property for the right price. You make it by designing and marketing the right product for that property in the right way, and you make it by building that product within the allotted budget, on schedule, and with sufficient quality to minimize call-backs and legal problems.

How do you do all this, along with setting up the next project, so you can keep everything going after the project you are currently working on is done? If you are a one-man operation, it is not easy. You probably work 16 hours a day, 6 days a week, and long for the day that you can slow down enough to train someone to help you. If you are a large company with good organization, you do it with ease, whether you are doing one tract or twenty. A well-organized construction company, especially the field operation, is a predictable, efficient, finely tuned machine with built-in tolerances for deviation and with realistic goals and dependable accuracy of projected profits for all concerned.

The purpose of this section is to present some of the forms and procedures used by large companies. Most of these forms are presented with relatively little discussion. They are straightforward, to the point, and the type of forms that construction people are used to seeing. The great difference in this particular set of forms is the amount of detail and the thoroughness of the approach.

The amount of information that each individual desires and the complexity of each project is a variable that can cause inclusions or exclusions from the forms. And the personal desires and level of experience of those using the forms will have a great effect on the way these forms are used. In general, the more experienced a field superintendent or a general contractor becomes, the more he relies on forms for record keeping, counter-checks, and for the everyday scheduling and running of his business operations.

The forms used in the construction phase are, by necessity, few and relatively simple. They are: **Form 520**—Subdivision Schedule; **Form 530**—Weekly Construction Schedule; **Form 540**—Quality Control (Outline Form); **Form 550**—Quality Control (Itemized Form); **Form 560/680**—Field-Color Schedule Card.

There are other forms if you run your own construction crews, such as: **Form 570**—Employee Record Card; **Form 580**—Timecard; **Form 590**—Job Summary.

If you have your own crews, you will be involved with some warranty work. And if you subcontract everything out, you may have a warranty or customer service department separate from your construction operation, or you may handle your warranty coordination through your construction department. In any case, Chapter 6 of this book covers warranty and the warranty forms. These forms may or may not be added, as the case may be, to the field construction form dossier.

## SUBDIVISION SCHEDULE—FORM 520

The subdivision construction schedule is an extremely simple form, and simplicity is the key to the successful running of a subdivision. Many firms use PERT charts, graphs, and other very complicated forms of visual communication. This is not necessary. Most subdivision tracts will fit our simple form with a few minor modifications. For example, in the San Jose, California, area, the water would be installed ahead of the storm and sanitary, as this is a requirement of the San Jose Water Department.

With a few minor changes, this form will take you through the intricacies of a subdivision. If you follow the various stages closely and communicate with the superintendent, you will have a successful tract.

Many large builders have found, to their chagrin, that when their building superintendent was placed in charge of dirt moving and land development, a great deal of confusion ensued. Most superintendents treat subdivision work as if it is a necessary evil. It is very simple and usually you will have less quality problems than you will encounter in the buildings themselves.

The secret to subdivision work is the scheduling of the necessary staking by the engineers for the various components to do their work. You cannot expect the sanitary to be installed on a Tuesday when you have not called for the staking until late Monday afternoon. At that time you will find your work crews three days away; thus, your installation will be four days away.

Many large builders set up a very complicated work schedule. One department is kept busy altering that schedule on a weekly basis because very seldom has the schedule ever been met. Schedules of this type can change by several months from original conception to completion, due to the availability of men, equipment, material, strikes, and unforeseen physical complications. By knowing the tract, studying the respective form and arranging the staking properly, you will get a job that you can be proud of and one that will be done with good timing.

## SUBDIVISION SCHEDULE

520

Location _____

Tract _____  Soil Engineer _____

No. of Lots _____  Civil Engineer _____

| Item No. | Operation | Sub-Contractor | Variance Days | Days Allowed | Schedule Dates Orig. Start/Comp. | Rev. Start/Comp. | Rev. Start/Comp. | Rev. Start/Comp. | Rev. Start/Comp. | Days Actual Start/Comp. |
|---|---|---|---|---|---|---|---|---|---|---|
| | Clearing | | | | | | | | | |
| | Remove Irrigation Lines | | | | | | | | | |
| | Stake Pad & Streets | | | | | | | | | |
| | Round Grade | | | | | | | | | |
| | Stake Storm | | | | | | | | | |
| | Install Storm | | | | | | | | | |
| | Stake Sanitary | | | | | | | | | |
| | Install Sanitary | | | | | | | | | |
| | Stake Water | | | | | | | | | |
| | Install Water | | | | | | | | | |
| | Install Joint Trench | | | | | | | | | |
| | Stake Curb & Gutter | | | | | | | | | |
| | Grade Curb and Gutter | | | | | | | | | |
| | Install Curb & Gutter | | | | | | | | | |

| Item No. | Operation | Sub-Contractor | Variance Days | Days Allowed | Schedule Dates | | | | | | | | | | Days Actual | |
|---|---|---|---|---|---|---|---|---|---|---|---|---|---|---|---|---|
| | | | | | Orig. | | Rev. | | Rev. | | Rev. | | Rev. | | | |
| | | | | | Start | Comp. | Start | Comp. | Start | Comp. | Start | Comp. | Start | Comp. | Start | Comp. |
| | Make Sub-Grade | | | | | | | | | | | | | | | |
| | Place Rock | | | | | | | | | | | | | | | |
| | Test Water | | | | | | | | | | | | | | | |
| | Oil | | | | | | | | | | | | | | | |
| | Pave | | | | | | | | | | | | | | | |
| | Fog Seal | | | | | | | | | | | | | | | |
| | Raise Manholes | | | | | | | | | | | | | | | |
| | Stake Monuments | | | | | | | | | | | | | | | |
| | Install Monuments | | | | | | | | | | | | | | | |
| | Patch Pave | | | | | | | | | | | | | | | |
| | Punch List | | | | | | | | | | | | | | | |
| | City Acceptance | | | | | | | | | | | | | | | |
| | Comments: | | | | | | | | | | | | | | | |

# WEEKLY CONSTRUCTION SCHEDULE—FORM 530

Construction schedules are always laid out in chronological order. They can be very simple with as few as 26 major operations, or they can be all inclusive with over 100 operations, including material scheduling and delivery notations. Each superintendent has his own way of scheduling and his own preference concerning the amount of detail he wants in his form. From a contractor's point of view, there should be sufficient detail to insure that proper lead time is given for scheduling materials and labor. The schedule can act as a reminder and check for the many small, but extremely important, functions that constitute the chain of events that must be completed before the next phase is started or scheduled.

The most effective schedules are set up on a weekly or two-week basis. They are set up this way to minimize changes that would be needed due to delays caused by weather, manpower, or material problems. It is the contractor's job to notify subcontractors as to when he wants them on the job. Jobs in which the subcontractors schedule themselves—even though they have crews on the job every day—tend to favor the subcontractor and not the project. The contractor needs to retain control of this very important function. Who is in control if you have to ask someone when he is going to complete a certain job?

Be realistic with your schedules; leave some latitude for error or change. And stay on top of what is happening in the field. There is nothing worse than to have men standing around waiting for materials to be delivered or to have a trade pulled off the job because you were not really ready for them. There is more to be lost here than time or money, and that is your credibility and reputation. Scheduling is where you make or break your field operation.

Form 530 is set up with five columns as a weekly schedule. If you are scheduling for a large project you will use several pages of this form or you can put it on a spread sheet and add more columns. If you have a 30-unit townhouse project, you would need 30 squares in order to show the entire project on one sheet, or six 8½"-x-11" pages such as Form 530.

The form is set up with overlap in which several functions happen on the same day. These functions will vary with the size of the project and the size and detailing of the individual units. The schedule must be tailored to each project and each company's mode of operation.

## WEEKLY CONSTRUCTION SCHEDULE

530

Project _____

| Construction Phase                                                              Job # → | | Date | | | |
|---|---|---|---|---|---|
| 1. Layout & trench | | | | | |
| 2. Layout & drill, clean piers & tamp | | | | | |
| 3. **Inspect** pier holes & pour | | | | | |
| 4. Set forms & steel | | | | | |
| 5. **Inspect** forms | | | | | |
| 6. Pour foundation, set anchor bolts | | | | | |
| 7. Strip forms & clean up | | | | | |
| 8. Mudsill, termite flash, girders | | | | | |
| 9. Floor joists 1st floor | | | | | |
| 10. Rough plumbing & sewer hook up | | | | | |
| 11. **Inspect** underfloor | | | | | |
| 12. Sub floor - 1st floor | | | | | |
| 13. Frame complete | | | | | |
| 14. Floor joists - 2nd floor | | | | | |
| 15. Sub floor - 2nd floor | | | | | |
| 16. Frame complete, stairs | | | | | |
| 17. Roof trusses complete | | | | | |
| 18. Roof sheathing, fascia, verge | | | | | |
| 19. Plumbing 2nd floor & top out | | | | | |
| 20. Gutters, sheetmetal, windows, exterior doors | | | | | |
| 21. Frame pickup | | | | | |
| 22. Roof, heating rough, start exterior trim | | | | | |
| 23. Stucco lath, electric rough | | | | | |
| 24. Exterior trim complete, sweep-up | | | | | |
| 25. **Inspect** frame, plumbing, electric, heating | | | | | |
| 26. Insulation | | | | | |
| 27. Sheetrock hung | | | | | |
| 28. **Inspect** sheetrock, nailing | | | | | |
| 29. Stucco scratch, tape sheetrock | | | | | |
| 30. Top sheetrock | | | | | |
| 31. Stucco - brown | | | | | |
| 32. Sheetrock texture, paint exterior trim | | | | | |
| 33. Sheetrock scrap, scrape & sweep | | | | | |
| 34. Interior doors & trim, underlay | | | | | |
| 35. Undercoat kitchen & baths | | | | | |
| 36. Kitchen cabinets, stair rails | | | | | |
| 37. Stucco color, prime interior trim | | | | | |
| 38. Enamel kitchen & baths | | | | | |
| 39. Paint flat walls | | | | | |
| 40. Tile baths, exterior clean up, finish grade | | | | | |
| 41. Kitchen & vanity tops, fences | | | | | |
| 42. Linoleum | | | | | |
| 43. Plumbing finish (disposal & DW) | | | | | |
| 44. Electric finish (range & fixtures), heating finish | | | | | |
| 45. Enamel trim, start landscape | | | | | |
| 46. Shower doors & mirrors, trim cabinets | | | | | |
| 47. Wash windows, clean-up | | | | | |
| 48. Install base, pad, carpet | | | | | |
| 49. Finish hardware, final clean, paint touch-up | | | | | |
| 50. **Inspection** Final - planning dept., bldg. dept., public works, fire dept., Notice of Completion | | | | | |

# WEEKLY CONSTRUCTION SCHEDULE

Project _____

| Construction Phase        Job # → | | Date | | | | |
|---|---|---|---|---|---|---|
| 1. Layout & trench | | | | | | |
| 2. Layout & drill, clean piers & tamp | | | | | | |
| 3. **Inspect** pier holes & pour | | | | | | |
| 4. Set forms & steel | | | | | | |
| 5. **Inspect** forms | | | | | | |
| 6. Pour foundation, set anchor bolts | | | | | | |
| 7. Strip forms & clean up | | | | | | |
| 8. Mudsill, termite flash, girders | | | | | | |
| 9. Floor joists 1st floor | | | | | | |
| 10. Rough plumbing & sewer hook up | | | | | | |
| 11. **Inspect** underfloor | | | | | | |
| 12. Sub floor - 1st floor | | | | | | |
| 13. Frame complete | | | | | | |
| 14. Floor joists - 2nd floor | | | | | | |
| 15. Sub floor - 2nd floor | | | | | | |
| 16. Frame complete, stairs | | | | | | |
| 17. Roof trusses complete | | | | | | |
| 18. Roof sheathing, fascia, verge | | | | | | |
| 19. Plumbing 2nd floor & top out | | | | | | |
| 20. Gutters, sheetmetal, windows, exterior doors | | | | | | |
| 21. Frame pickup | | | | | | |
| 22. Roof, heating rough, start exterior trim | | | | | | |
| 23. Stucco lath, electric rough | | | | | | |
| 24. Exterior trim complete, sweep-up | | | | | | |
| 25. **Inspect** frame, plumbing, electric, heating | | | | | | |
| 26. Insulation | | | | | | |
| 27. Sheetrock hung | | | | | | |
| 28. **Inspect** sheetrock, nailing | | | | | | |
| 29. Stucco scratch, tape sheetrock | | | | | | |
| 30. Top sheetrock | | | | | | |
| 31. Stucco - brown | | | | | | |
| 32. Sheetrock texture, paint exterior trim | | | | | | |
| 33. Sheetrock scrap, scrape & sweep | | | | | | |
| 34. Interior doors & trim, underlay | | | | | | |
| 35. Undercoat kitchen & baths | | | | | | |
| 36. Kitchen cabinets, stair rails | | | | | | |
| 37. Stucco color, prime interior trim | | | | | | |
| 38. Enamel kitchen & baths | | | | | | |
| 39. Paint flat walls | | | | | | |
| 40. Tile baths, exterior clean up, finish grade | | | | | | |
| 41. Kitchen & vanity tops, fences | | | | | | |
| 42. Linoleum | | | | | | |
| 43. Plumbing finish (disposal & DW) | | | | | | |
| 44. Electric finish (range & fixtures), heating finish | | | | | | |
| 45. Enamel trim, start landscape | | | | | | |
| 46. Shower doors & mirrors, trim cabinets | | | | | | |
| 47. Wash windows, clean-up | | | | | | |
| 48. Install base, pad, carpet | | | | | | |
| 49. Finish hardware, final clean, paint touch-up | | | | | | |
| 50. **Inspection** Final - planning dept., bldg. dept., public works, fire dept., Notice of Completion | | | | | | |

# QUALITY CONTROL—FORMS 540 AND 550

Quality control of the construction process begins on day one. It starts with the first stake driven and the first blade of grass touched. It is ongoing throughout the construction phase. The phrase "if anything can go wrong, it will go wrong" should be the watchword of the builder and his construction team if errors are to be caught and costly, time-consuming mistakes minimized.

## CONTROL OF WORKMANSHIP

There is no acceptable excuse for shoddy or mediocre workmanship, yet we have all experienced it and paid for it. We have all heard excuses such as: "I can't hire good people anymore." "The preceding trade created the problem." "You didn't tell me you wanted it that way." "I knew the material was bad, but I nailed it up anyway because that's all that I had and I thought the painter could patch it." "It isn't my fault, it's nobody's fault, it just happened." And, of course, the worst one of all, "I didn't have enough time to do it the way I knew it should have been done." There are ways of stopping this, just good common sense, but they are worth reviewing. They are: (1) selectivity, (2) communication, (3) supervision, (4) checks and controls, and (5) a systematized quality control form and punch list.

**Selectivity.** Select only the people who are capable of doing the quality of work you require. Select the people who will stand behind their work and realize their responsibilities.

**Communication.** Make sure that your people know what you want. Review the plans and specifications with them. Direct them, define their areas of responsibility and, where possible, confirm the directions in writing. Keep the avenues of communication open and be available.

**Supervision.** Provide adequate and constant supervision. There is no job or no phase of operation so small that does not warrant direct attention. Quality control is an eight-hour-a-day job and, unless you have proper supervision, you, and only you, the builder, are at the mercy of the most inept man on the job.

**Checks and Controls.** Construction quality control goes beyond building to the regulations of government agencies. Quality control is regulated by the builder, and he sets the limits that are acceptable to himself and the type of product with which he wants to be associated. Some builders have reputations for mediocre work, others for high quality. The difference is that the one builder sets a higher standard of excellence. The facts are that the higher standard does *not* cost more. In the end, it will actually cost less because the quality control inspections by field personnel, the punch lists, the buyers' walk-through, the follow-through with tradesmen during construction, subcontractors, and suppliers are far less costly than warrantee calls after move-in, the related inspections, checks and counter-checks, and sign-offs. Even if the builder or his workmen do not have to do the work, it still costs in time and energy, not to mention reputation. Nobody wants to be in the warranty business.

**Quality Control Forms and Punch List.** The most effective method of quality inspection is to follow a systematized form in which important items are specifically listed, with space for comments, inspector initial, and date of inspection. This provides a record and a reference for follow-up and reinspection.

The form can be just as complete as you want to make it. They can contain 30 items or, conceivably, 300. The general consensus among large builders is to list items that are most vulnerable to error, and things that have been problems in the past.

The experience level of the quality inspector greatly determines the number of items on the list. There are those who start with a blank sheet of paper and list items as they see them. There is too much room for omission in this case. If an item is not noted, it is assumed correct. On the other hand, if the list is too complex, the usefulness of the document is greatly diminished by unnecessary work. Keep it simple, but be thorough.

The best way to list items is in chronological order and by trade. To do it completely and correctly, there are no shortcuts. Memory and personal opinion should be eliminated. The standards should be set and adhered to. For example, interior doors/warped, 3/8" or more, are replaced. Or is your policy ¼" or ½"? This is the responsibility of the company's chief policymaker.

The important thing that we are covering here is the method and general form to follow in the quality inspections. It will be up to the individual to adapt and change the items in the list to suit the construction method used and type of project being built.

**Format.** The format of Form 540 is used for many large multi-home tract operations. It is in outline form, listing general categories to be inspected. It serves as a reminder and a record for what, when, and who.

The long list of items in Form 550 follows the general construction procedure step by step. There is little room for error or omission. The form is filled out day by day and job by job. It is an invaluable tool to quality control and efficiency.

## QUALITY CONTROL - OUTLINE FORM

540

Job # _____  Lot # _____  Tract # _____

Plan # _____  Elev. _____  Address _____

| | Quality Inspection | | Correction Needed | | | Corrected | |
|---|---|---|---|---|---|---|---|
| # | Item | OK | Comments | Date | Insp. | Date | Insp. |
| 1 | Lot Layout | | | | | | |
| 2 | Services Located | | | | | | |
| 3 | Grading - Rough | | | | | | |
| 4 | House Layout | | | | | | |
| 5 | Trenching & Piers | | | | | | |
| 6 | Temporary Utilities | | | | | | |
| 7 | Foundation Forms | | | | | | |
| 8 | Foundation Concrete | | | | | | |
| 9 | Concrete Floor & Garage Slab | | | | | | |
| 10 | Lumber | | | | | | |
| 11 | Framing (crawl space) | | | | | | |
| 12 | Plumbing - Rough-in | | | | | | |
| 13 | Sewer Hook-up | | | | | | |
| 14 | Water Hook-up | | | | | | |
| 15 | Gas Ordered | | | | | | |
| 16 | Electric Ordered | | | | | | |
| 17 | TV Ordered | | | | | | |
| 18 | Heating - Rough-in | | | | | | |
| 19 | Framing - Subfloor | | | | | | |
| 20 | Framing - Walls | | | | | | |
| | | | | | | | |
| | | | | | | | |

| # | Quality Inspection Item | OK | Correction Needed Comments | Date | Insp. | Corrected Date | Insp. |
|---|---|---|---|---|---|---|---|
| 21 | Framing – Second Floor | | | | | | |
| 22 | Roof Framing | | | | | | |
| 23 | Plumbing – Top Out | | | | | | |
| 24 | Sheetmetal | | | | | | |
| 25 | Roofing | | | | | | |
| 26 | Windows | | | | | | |
| 27 | Exterior Doors & Garage Door | | | | | | |
| 28 | Exterior Wall Cover | | | | | | |
| 29 | Heating – Rough | | | | | | |
| 30 | Electrical – Rough | | | | | | |
| 31 | Sweep Out | | | | | | |
| 32 | Inspections – Frame | | | | | | |
| 33 | Exterior Finish & Trim | | | | | | |
| 34 | Insulation | | | | | | |
| 35 | Extras Prior to Wall Close-in | | | | | | |
| 36 | Interior Wallboard (Sheet rock) | | | | | | |
| 37 | Utility Check | | | | | | |
| 38 | Grading | | | | | | |
| 39 | Concrete Drive & Walks | | | | | | |
| 40 | Paint Exterior & Interior Prime | | | | | | |
| 41 | Doors & Trim | | | | | | |
| 42 | Paint Cabinets & Int. Prime | | | | | | |
| 43 | Tile | | | | | | |
| 44 | Sweep Out | | | | | | |
| 45 | Paint Interior | | | | | | |
| 46 | Counter Tops | | | | | | |
| 47 | Floor Covering – Resilient | | | | | | |

| # | Quality Inspection Item | OK | Correction Needed Comments | Date | Insp. | Corrected Date | Insp. |
|---|---|---|---|---|---|---|---|
| 48 | Finish Hardware | | | | | | |
| 49 | Appliances | | | | | | |
| 50 | Grading - Final | | | | | | |
| 51 | Heating & A/C | | | | | | |
| 52 | Plumbing - Finish | | | | | | |
| 53 | Electrician - Finish | | | | | | |
| 54 | Clean-up - Final | | | | | | |
| 55 | Floor Covering - Carpets | | | | | | |
| 56 | Paint Touch-up | | | | | | |
| 57 | Inspections - Final | | | | | | |
| 58 | Move-in | | | | | | |
| 59 | Other | | | | | | |
| 60 | | | | | | | |

| # | Item | OK | Comments | Date | Insp. | Date | Insp. |
|---|------|----|---------|------|-------|------|-------|
| | | | Quality Inspection | Correction Needed | | Corrected | |

Warrantee Record

# QUALITY CONTROL - ITEMIZED FORM

**550**

Job # _____  Lot # _____  Tract # _____

Plan # _____  Elev. _____  Address _____

| # | Item | OK | Comments | Date | Insp. | Date | Insp. |
|---|------|----|---------|----|------|----|------|
| | | | **Quality Inspection / Correction Needed / Corrected** | | | | |
| 1 | **Lot Layout** | | | | | | |
| .1 | Lot corners verified | | | | | | |
| .2 | Grading stakes checked | | | | | | |
| .3 | | | | | | | |
| 2 | **Services Located** | | | | | | |
| .1 | Gas | | | | | | |
| .2 | Electric | | | | | | |
| .3 | Cable TV | | | | | | |
| .4 | Water | | | | | | |
| .5 | Sewer | | | | | | |
| .6 | | | | | | | |
| 3 | **Grading - Rough** | | | | | | |
| .1 | Rough pad to elev. | | | | | | |
| .2 | Rough drainage established | | | | | | |
| .3 | | | | | | | |
| 4 | **House Layout** | | | | | | |
| .1 | Side yard setbacks | | | | | | |
| .2 | Front yard setback | | | | | | |
| .3 | Rear yard set back | | | | | | |
| .4 | Dimensions correct | | | | | | |
| .5 | Building square | | | | | | |
| .6 | | | | | | | |

| # | Quality Inspection Item | OK | Correction Needed Comments | Date | Insp. | Corrected Date | Insp. |
|---|---|---|---|---|---|---|---|
| 5 | **Trenching & Piers** | | | | | | |
| .1 | Depth correct | | | | | | |
| .2 | Width correct | | | | | | |
| .3 | Location & completeness | | | | | | |
| .4 | Bottoms cleaned or tamped | | | | | | |
| .5 | Utility lines dug | | | | | | |
| .6 | | | | | | | |
| 6 | **Temporary Utilities** | | | | | | |
| .1 | Electric | | | | | | |
| .2 | Water | | | | | | |
| .3 | | | | | | | |
| 7 | **Foundation Forms** | | | | | | |
| .1 | Level | | | | | | |
| .2 | Thickness correct | | | | | | |
| .3 | Shut offs | | | | | | |
| .4 | Steel amount and spacing | | | | | | |
| .5 | Steel not touching ground | | | | | | |
| .6 | Ties and supports | | | | | | |
| .7 | Utility provisions | | | | | | |
| .8 | Crawl space drains | | | | | | |
| .9 | Can outs | | | | | | |
| .10 | Access holes | | | | | | |
| .11 | Heat run provisions | | | | | | |
| .12 | Ventilation | | | | | | |
| .13 | Governmental inspection | | | | | | |
| .14 | | | | | | | |

| # | Quality Inspection Item | OK | Correction Needed Comments | Date | Insp. | Corrected Date | Insp. |
|---|---|---|---|---|---|---|---|
| 8 | **Foundation Concrete** | | | | | | |
| .1 | Strength & slump | | | | | | |
| .2 | Aggitate & rod | | | | | | |
| .3 | Anchor bolt placement | | | | | | |
| .4 | Clean up | | | | | | |
| .5 | | | | | | | |
| 9 | **Lumber** | | | | | | |
| .1 | Designate drop site | | | | | | |
| .2 | Check order of stacking | | | | | | |
| .3 | Verify quantity | | | | | | |
| .4 | Verify grade stamp | | | | | | |
| .5 | | | | | | | |
| 10 | **Framing (crawl space)** | | | | | | |
| .1 | Termite flashing | | | | | | |
| .2 | Anchor bolts - nuts tight | | | | | | |
| .3 | Verify grade stamp | | | | | | |
| .4 | Girders, piers - straight/level | | | | | | |
| .5 | Ground clearance | | | | | | |
| .6 | Floor joist spacing & blocking | | | | | | |
| .7 | Ground clearance | | | | | | |
| .8 | Foundation vents | | | | | | |
| .9 | | | | | | | |
| 11 | **Concrete Floor & Garage Slab** | | | | | | |
| .1 | Utility provisions | | | | | | |
| .2 | Plumbing in & tested | | | | | | |
| .3 | Plumbing inspected | | | | | | |
| .4 | Can outs | | | | | | |
| .5 | Sand, gravel | | | | | | |

| # | Quality Inspection<br>Item | OK | Correction Needed<br>Comments | Date | Insp. | Corrected<br>Date | Insp. |
|---|---|---|---|---|---|---|---|
| .6 | Vapor barrier | | | | | | |
| .7 | Mesh or steel spacing & ties | | | | | | |
| .8 | Ground clearance | | | | | | |
| .9 | Governmental inspection | | | | | | |
| .10 | Concrete strength & slump | | | | | | |
| .11 | Aggitate & rod | | | | | | |
| .12 | Anchor bolt placement | | | | | | |
| .13 | Finish & surface concrete | | | | | | |
| .14 | Clean up | | | | | | |
| .15 | | | | | | | |
| **12** | **Plumbing (crawl space)** | | | | | | |
| .1 | Location correct | | | | | | |
| .2 | Fall (drainage) | | | | | | |
| .3 | Test | | | | | | |
| .4 | A/C condensate line | | | | | | |
| .5 | Gas service location | | | | | | |
| .6 | Gas line in & tested | | | | | | |
| .7 | Gas log starter rough-in | | | | | | |
| .8 | Ice-maker water line rough-in | | | | | | |
| .9 | Governmental inspection | | | | | | |
| .10 | Clean up | | | | | | |
| .11 | | | | | | | |
| **13** | **Sewer Hook-up** | | | | | | |
| .1 | Location | | | | | | |
| .2 | Fall | | | | | | |
| .3 | Test | | | | | | |
| .4 | Governmental inspection | | | | | | |
| .5 | | | | | | | |

| # | Quality Inspection<br>Item | OK | Correction Needed<br>Comments | Date | Insp. | Corrected<br>Date | Insp. |
|---|---|---|---|---|---|---|---|
| 14 | **Water Hook-up** | | | | | | |
| .1 | Location | | | | | | |
| .2 | Test | | | | | | |
| .3 | | | | | | | |
| 15 | **Gas Ordered** | | | | | | |
| .1 | Schedule underground | | | | | | |
| .2 | Location | | | | | | |
| .3 | | | | | | | |
| 16 | **Electric Ordered** | | | | | | |
| .1 | Schedule underground | | | | | | |
| .2 | Location | | | | | | |
| .3 | | | | | | | |
| 17 | **TV Ordered** | | | | | | |
| .1 | Schedule underground | | | | | | |
| .2 | Location | | | | | | |
| .3 | | | | | | | |
| 18 | **Heating (crawl space)** | | | | | | |
| .1 | Ground clearance | | | | | | |
| .2 | Verify size and runs | | | | | | |
| .3 | Insulation | | | | | | |
| .4 | Run A/C lines | | | | | | |
| .5 | Governmental inspection | | | | | | |
| .6 | Vandal protection | | | | | | |
| .7 | Clean up | | | | | | |
| .8 | | | | | | | |

| # | Quality Inspection | OK | Correction Needed | | | Corrected | |
|---|---|---|---|---|---|---|---|
| | Item | | Comments | Date | Insp. | Date | Insp. |
| 19 | Framing - Subfloor | | | | | | |
| .1 | Clear crawl space debris | | | | | | |
| .2 | Verify grade stamp | | | | | | |
| .3 | Check building square | | | | | | |
| .4 | Glue | | | | | | |
| .5 | Nailing schedule | | | | | | |
| .6 | | | | | | | |
| 20 | Framing - Walls | | | | | | |
| .1 | Verify grade stamp | | | | | | |
| .2 | Check layout | | | | | | |
| .3 | Check openings | | | | | | |
| .4 | Bracing & blocking | | | | | | |
| .5 | Backing - tub, shower, cab. | | | | | | |
| .6 | Walls plumb | | | | | | |
| .7 | Nailing | | | | | | |
| .8 | | | | | | | |
| 21 | Framing-Second Floor | | | | | | |
| .1 | Verify grade stamp | | | | | | |
| .2 | Floor joist spacing & blocking | | | | | | |
| .3 | Dbl joists under bearing walls | | | | | | |
| .4 | Plumbing & heating provisions | | | | | | |
| .5 | Subfloor glue & nailing | | | | | | |
| .6 | Layout | | | | | | |
| .7 | Check openings | | | | | | |
| .8 | Bracing & blocking | | | | | | |

| # | Quality Inspection Item | OK | Correction Needed Comments | Date | Insp. | Corrected Date | Insp. |
|---|---|---|---|---|---|---|---|
| .9 | Backing - tub, shower, cab. | | | | | | |
| .10 | Walls plumb | | | | | | |
| .11 | Nailing | | | | | | |
| .12 | | | | | | | |
| 22 | **Roof Framing** | | | | | | |
| .1 | Verify grade stamp | | | | | | |
| .2 | Trusses - design compliance | | | | | | |
| .3 | Trusses - connectors, splices | | | | | | |
| .4 | Layout | | | | | | |
| .5 | Blocking & head offs | | | | | | |
| .6 | Fireplace provision | | | | | | |
| .7 | Eave & gable vents | | | | | | |
| .8 | Sheathing - grade | | | | | | |
| .9 | Nailing | | | | | | |
| .10 | | | | | | | |
| 23 | **Windows** | | | | | | |
| .1 | Check openings | | | | | | |
| .2 | Check flashing | | | | | | |
| .3 | Check set & square | | | | | | |
| .4 | Check operation | | | | | | |
| .5 | | | | | | | |
| 24 | **Exterior Doors & Garage Door** | | | | | | |
| .1 | Check openings | | | | | | |
| .2 | Check set, square & swing | | | | | | |
| .3 | Check shims & stability | | | | | | |
| .4 | Garage door - design | | | | | | |
| .5 | Garage door installation | | | | | | |
| .6 | | | | | | | |

| # | Quality Inspection | OK | Correction Needed | | | Corrected | |
|---|---|---|---|---|---|---|---|
| | Item | | Comments | Date | Insp. | Date | Insp. |
| 25 | Plumbing - Top Out | | | | | | |
| .1 | Set trees & vents | | | | | | |
| .2 | Provide roof vents | | | | | | |
| .3 | Set tub | | | | | | |
| .4 | Set shower plan | | | | | | |
| .5 | Water test | | | | | | |
| .6 | Gas test | | | | | | |
| .7 | | | | | | | |
| 26 | Sheet Metal | | | | | | |
| .1 | Gutter joints | | | | | | |
| .2 | Gutter fall (drainage) | | | | | | |
| .3 | Downspout location | | | | | | |
| .4 | Roof metal | | | | | | |
| .5 | Fireplace saddle | | | | | | |
| .6 | | | | | | | |
| 27 | Exterior Wall Cover | | | | | | |
| .1 | Sheathing or plywood grade | | | | | | |
| .2 | Sheathing or plywood nailing | | | | | | |
| .3 | Scaffolding | | | | | | |
| .4 | Stucco lath lap & coverage | | | | | | |
| .5 | Lath nailing & tightness | | | | | | |
| .6 | | | | | | | |
| 28 | Fireplace | | | | | | |
| .1 | In-progress inspection | | | | | | |
| .2 | Reinforcing in | | | | | | |
| .3 | Ties in | | | | | | |
| .4 | Firebox depth | | | | | | |
| .5 | Flue size & height | | | | | | |

| | Quality Inspection | | OK | Correction Needed | | | Corrected | |
|---|---|---|---|---|---|---|---|---|
| # | Item | | | Comments | Date | Insp. | Date | Insp. |
| | .6 | Damper working | | | | | | |
| | .7 | Clearance | | | | | | |
| | .8 | Flashing & saddle | | | | | | |
| | .9 | Workmanship | | | | | | |
| | .10 | Clean up | | | | | | |
| | .11 | | | | | | | |
| 29 | Roofing | | | | | | | |
| | .1 | Stocking provisions | | | | | | |
| | .2 | Verify grade | | | | | | |
| | .3 | Nailing | | | | | | |
| | .4 | Moisture barrier (paper) | | | | | | |
| | .5 | Roof metal placement | | | | | | |
| | .6 | Ridge & valleys, edges | | | | | | |
| | .7 | Vents & saddle placement | | | | | | |
| | .8 | Damage to gutters | | | | | | |
| | .9 | Clean up | | | | | | |
| | .10 | | | | | | | |
| 30 | Heating - Rough | | | | | | | |
| | .1 | Layout registers | | | | | | |
| | .2 | Backing & blocking | | | | | | |
| | .3 | C.A.R. location | | | | | | |
| | .4 | Vents & fans | | | | | | |
| | .5 | Thermostat wire | | | | | | |
| | .6 | | | | | | | |
| 31 | Electrical - Rough | | | | | | | |
| | .1 | Service location | | | | | | |
| | .2 | Fixture and plug locations | | | | | | |
| | .3 | Wire size | | | | | | |

| # | Quality Inspection | | Correction Needed | | | Corrected | |
|---|---|---|---|---|---|---|---|
| | Item | OK | Comments | Date | Insp. | Date | Insp. |
| .4 | Circuit distribution | | | | | | |
| .5 | A/C provisions | | | | | | |
| .6 | Extras | | | | | | |
| .7 | | | | | | | |
| 32 | Sweep Out | | | | | | |
| .1 | Clean interior | | | | | | |
| .2 | Clear exterior | | | | | | |
| .3 | Haul debris | | | | | | |
| .4 | | | | | | | |
| 33 | Inspections – Frame | | | | | | |
| .1 | Foreman | | | | | | |
| .2 | Supervisor or contractor | | | | | | |
| .3 | Punch list corrections | | | | | | |
| .4 | Governmental inspection | | | | | | |
| .5 | Gas test sign off | | | | | | |
| .6 | Punch list corrections | | | | | | |
| .7 | Governmental reinspect | | | | | | |
| .8 | | | | | | | |
| 34 | Insulation | | | | | | |
| .1 | Check specs | | | | | | |
| .2 | Check installation | | | | | | |
| .3 | Eave vent blocking | | | | | | |
| .4 | Post signed cards | | | | | | |
| .5 | Governmental inspection | | | | | | |
| .6 | | | | | | | |
| 35 | Extras Prior to Wall Close-in | | | | | | |
| .1 | Intercom – rough | | | | | | |
| .2 | Hi-Fi | | | | | | |

| # | Quality Inspection Item | OK | Correction Needed Comments | Date | Insp. | Corrected Date | Insp. |
|---|---|---|---|---|---|---|---|
| .3 | Central vacuum - rough | | | | | | |
| .4 | | | | | | | |
| 36 | **Interior Wallboard (sheet rock)** | | | | | | |
| .1 | Stocking provisions | | | | | | |
| .2 | Stocking damage - windows, doors | | | | | | |
| .3 | Hanging gaps, breaks, mars | | | | | | |
| .4 | Nailing | | | | | | |
| .5 | Openings & jambs | | | | | | |
| .6 | Corner beads | | | | | | |
| .7 | Cut-outs (electrical, heating) | | | | | | |
| .8 | Clean up - haul debris | | | | | | |
| .9 | Taping | | | | | | |
| .10 | Top | | | | | | |
| .11 | Skim | | | | | | |
| .12 | Mark walls for wallpaper | | | | | | |
| .13 | Texture and acoustic | | | | | | |
| .14 | Sand & finish | | | | | | |
| .15 | Clean up, haul debris | | | | | | |
| .16 | | | | | | | |
| 37 | **Utility Check** | | | | | | |
| .1 | Underground svc. lines to house | | | | | | |
| .2 | Trenches jetted | | | | | | |
| .3 | | | | | | | |
| 38 | **Stucco** | | | | | | |
| .1 | Scaffolding provision | | | | | | |
| .2 | Stucco scratch | | | | | | |
| .3 | Stucco brown (3 days) | | | | | | |
| .4 | Verify stucco color | | | | | | |

| # | Quality Inspection Item | OK | Correction Needed Comments | Date | Insp. | Corrected Date | Insp. |
|---|---|---|---|---|---|---|---|
| .5 | Stucco color (7 days) | | | | | | |
| .6 | Clean up | | | | | | |
| .7 | | | | | | | |
| 39 | **Paint Exterior & Interior Prime** | | | | | | |
| .1 | Eaves, facias, gutters | | | | | | |
| .2 | Exterior walls | | | | | | |
| .3 | Exterior trim and doors | | | | | | |
| .4 | Interior undercoat - cabinets | | | | | | |
| .5 | | | | | | | |
| 40 | **Carpentry - Finish** | | | | | | |
| .1 | Cabinets square, plumb, firm | | | | | | |
| .2 | Cabinet - mars | | | | | | |
| .3 | Doors - mars | | | | | | |
| .4 | Doors square, plumb, operation | | | | | | |
| .5 | Doors casing & jambs joints | | | | | | |
| .6 | Windows - sills, aprons | | | | | | |
| .7 | Closet - shelf & pole | | | | | | |
| .8 | Bookcases | | | | | | |
| .9 | Special cabinetry | | | | | | |
| .10 | Wall moldings | | | | | | |
| .11 | Special trim | | | | | | |
| .12 | | | | | | | |
| 41 | **Stairs & Rails** | | | | | | |
| .1 | Check risers for height | | | | | | |
| .2 | Head clearance | | | | | | |
| .3 | Railing spacings | | | | | | |
| .4 | Workmanship | | | | | | |
| .5 | | | | | | | |

| # | Quality Inspection | | Correction Needed | | | Corrected | |
|---|---|---|---|---|---|---|---|
| | Item | OK | Comments | Date | Insp. | Date | Insp. |
| 42 | **Masonry Veneer** | | | | | | |
| .1 | Fireplace face-material verify | | | | | | |
| .2 | Grout color | | | | | | |
| .3 | Workmanship | | | | | | |
| .4 | Clean up | | | | | | |
| .5 | Exterior veneer-material verify | | | | | | |
| .6 | Grout color | | | | | | |
| .7 | Workmanship | | | | | | |
| .8 | Clean up | | | | | | |
| .9 | | | | | | | |
| 43 | **Paint Cabinets & Int. Prime** | | | | | | |
| .1 | Check color | | | | | | |
| .2 | Sanding & finish | | | | | | |
| .3 | Prime doors, jambs, casing | | | | | | |
| .4 | Clean up | | | | | | |
| .5 | | | | | | | |
| 44 | **Grading** | | | | | | |
| .1 | Mark utility lines | | | | | | |
| .2 | Shoot grades | | | | | | |
| .3 | Swales | | | | | | |
| .4 | Drain away from house | | | | | | |
| .5 | Dirt to wood clearance | | | | | | |
| .6 | | | | | | | |
| 45 | **Concrete Drive, Porch, Walks** | | | | | | |
| .1 | Provide for sprinklers, lights | | | | | | |
| .2 | Recheck grades and drainage | | | | | | |
| .3 | Subbase | | | | | | |
| .4 | Reinforcing | | | | | | |

| # | Quality Inspection Item | OK | Correction Needed Comments | Date | Insp. | Corrected Date | Insp. |
|---|---|---|---|---|---|---|---|
| .5 | Layout | | | | | | |
| .6 | Governmental inspection | | | | | | |
| .7 | Concrete specs | | | | | | |
| .8 | Surface finish & score | | | | | | |
| .9 | Retardant | | | | | | |
| .10 | Clean up | | | | | | |
| .11 | | | | | | | |
| 46 | **Tile** | | | | | | |
| .1 | Subsurfaces clean, level, sturdy | | | | | | |
| .2 | Check color, style | | | | | | |
| .3 | Check tile quality, consistency | | | | | | |
| .4 | Workmanship | | | | | | |
| .5 | Joints | | | | | | |
| .6 | Dressing | | | | | | |
| .7 | Clean up | | | | | | |
| .8 | | | | | | | |
| 47 | **Sweep Out** | | | | | | |
| .1 | Clean interior | | | | | | |
| .2 | Clean exterior | | | | | | |
| .3 | Haul debris | | | | | | |
| .4 | | | | | | | |
| 48 | **Paint Interior** | | | | | | |
| .1 | Walls | | | | | | |
| .2 | Doors | | | | | | |
| .3 | Trim | | | | | | |
| .4 | Clean up | | | | | | |
| .5 | | | | | | | |

| # | Quality Inspection Item | OK | Correction Needed Comments | Date | Insp. | Corrected Date | Insp. |
|---|---|---|---|---|---|---|---|
| 49 | **Counter Tops** | | | | | | |
| .1 | Color selection | | | | | | |
| .2 | Mars | | | | | | |
| .3 | Joints | | | | | | |
| .4 | Installation, level | | | | | | |
| .5 | | | | | | | |
| 50 | **Shower Door** | | | | | | |
| .1 | Square | | | | | | |
| .2 | Operation | | | | | | |
| .3 | Mars | | | | | | |
| .4 | | | | | | | |
| 51 | **Down Spouts** | | | | | | |
| .1 | Placement | | | | | | |
| .2 | Ground clearance | | | | | | |
| .3 | | | | | | | |
| 52 | **Floor Covering - Resilient** | | | | | | |
| .1 | Underlay nailing | | | | | | |
| .2 | Color selection | | | | | | |
| .3 | Floor covering grade | | | | | | |
| .4 | Mars | | | | | | |
| .5 | Coving - trim | | | | | | |
| .6 | Clean up | | | | | | |
| .7 | | | | | | | |
| 53 | **Finish Hardware** | | | | | | |
| .1 | Towel bars, paper holders | | | | | | |
| .2 | Locks, pulls | | | | | | |
| .3 | Medicine cabinets | | | | | | |
| .4 | Mirrors | | | | | | |

| # | Quality Inspection<br>Item | OK | Correction Needed<br>Comments | Date | Insp. | Corrected<br>Date | Insp. |
|---|---|---|---|---|---|---|---|
| .5 | | | | | | | |
| 54 | **Appliances** | | | | | | |
| .1 | Diswasher ready to set | | | | | | |
| .2 | Range-oven ready to set | | | | | | |
| .3 | Extras | | | | | | |
| .4 | | | | | | | |
| 55 | **Grading - Final** | | | | | | |
| .1 | Swales finished | | | | | | |
| .2 | Clearance dirt to wood | | | | | | |
| .3 | Clods and debris removed | | | | | | |
| .4 | | | | | | | |
| 56 | **Heating & A/C** | | | | | | |
| .1 | Set furnace | | | | | | |
| .2 | Hook up furnace flue | | | | | | |
| .3 | Set registers | | | | | | |
| .4 | Install thermostat | | | | | | |
| .5 | Install hood vents | | | | | | |
| .6 | Install ventilation fans | | | | | | |
| .7 | A/C | | | | | | |
| .8 | Provide water heater flue | | | | | | |
| .9 | Clean up | | | | | | |
| .10 | | | | | | | |
| 57 | **Plumbing - Finish** | | | | | | |
| .1 | Set disposal | | | | | | |
| .2 | Hook up dishwasher | | | | | | |
| .3 | Set finish | | | | | | |
| .4 | Set water heater | | | | | | |

| # | Quality Inspection Item | OK | Correction Needed Comments | Date | Insp. | Corrected Date | Insp. |
|---|---|---|---|---|---|---|---|
| .5 | Hook up W/H gas & overflow | | | | | | |
| .6 | Install W/H flue | | | | | | |
| .7 | Hook up gas to furnace | | | | | | |
| .8 | Hook up condensate line | | | | | | |
| .9 | Clean up | | | | | | |
| .10 | | | | | | | |
| 58 | **Electrician - Finish** | | | | | | |
| .1 | Trim | | | | | | |
| .2 | Hook up appliances | | | | | | |
| .3 | Check service panel | | | | | | |
| .4 | Label service panel | | | | | | |
| .5 | Hang fixtures | | | | | | |
| .6 | Bulb | | | | | | |
| .7 | Clean up | | | | | | |
| .8 | | | | | | | |
| 59 | **Clean-up - Final** | | | | | | |
| .1 | Wash windows | | | | | | |
| .2 | Window tracks | | | | | | |
| .3 | Tubs | | | | | | |
| .4 | Showers | | | | | | |
| .5 | Sinks, vanities | | | | | | |
| .6 | Clean walls | | | | | | |
| .7 | Clean floors | | | | | | |
| .8 | Clean counter tops | | | | | | |
| .9 | Exterior clean up | | | | | | |
| .10 | Garage | | | | | | |
| .11 | | | | | | | |

| # | Quality Inspection Item | OK | Correction Needed Comments | Date | Insp. | Corrected Date | Insp. |
|---|---|---|---|---|---|---|---|
| **60** | **Floor Covering - Carpets** | | | | | | |
| .1 | Floors clean & ready | | | | | | |
| .2 | Base | | | | | | |
| .3 | Pad - check quality & weight | | | | | | |
| .4 | Carpet - check color selections | | | | | | |
| .5 | Seams, edges | | | | | | |
| .6 | Replace registers | | | | | | |
| .7 | Replace doors - check mars | | | | | | |
| .8 | Vacuum | | | | | | |
| .9 | Clean up | | | | | | |
| .10 | | | | | | | |
| **61** | **Paint Touch-up** | | | | | | |
| .1 | Walls | | | | | | |
| .2 | Doors | | | | | | |
| .3 | Cabinets | | | | | | |
| .4 | | | | | | | |
| **62** | **Inspections - Final** | | | | | | |
| .1 | Foreman | | | | | | |
| .2 | Superintendent - contractor | | | | | | |
| .3 | Service manager | | | | | | |
| .4 | Correct punch list | | | | | | |
| .5 | Governmental | | | | | | |
| .6 | Correct punch list | | | | | | |
| .7 | Governmental reinspect | | | | | | |
| .8 | Service manager | | | | | | |
| .9 | Buyer's walk-through | | | | | | |
| .10 | Sign Compliance Inspection Form | | | | | | |
| .11 | Appliance and fixture warrantee cards delivered | | | | | | |

| # | Quality Inspection Item | OK | Correction Needed Comments | Date | Insp. | Corrected Date | Insp. |
|---|---|---|---|---|---|---|---|
| .12 | All deficiences corrected | | | | | | |
| .13 | Service manager | | | | | | |
| .14 | | | | | | | |
| 63 | Move-in | | | | | | |
| .1 | Power turned on | | | | | | |
| .2 | Check electrical | | | | | | |
| .3 | Check appliances | | | | | | |
| .4 | Check furnace | | | | | | |
| .5 | Check water heater | | | | | | |
| .6 | | | | | | | |
| 64 | Other | | | | | | |
| | | | | | | | |
| | | | | | | | |
| | | | | | | | |
| | | | | | | | |
| | | | | | | | |
| | | | | | | | |
| | | | | | | | |
| | | | | | | | |
| | | | | | | | |
| | | | | | | | |
| | | | | | | | |
| | | | | | | | |
| | | | | | | | |
| | | | | | | | |
| | | | | | | | |
| | | | | | | | |

| # | Item | OK | Comments | Date | Insp. | Date | Insp. |
|---|------|----|----|------|-------|------|-------|
| | | | Quality Inspection / Correction Needed / Corrected | | | | |
| 65 | Warrantee Record | | | | | | |
| | | | | | | | |

## NOTES

## FIELD-COLOR SCHEDULE CARD—FORM 560/680

The color schedule card that goes to the field is compiled from the buyer's color-selection schedules by someone other than the field superintendent. The information is originally gathered by the sales department, if a buyer is involved, or the architectural decorating consultant, or the owner, or the person or department in the company from which these kinds of decisions are delegated. In most cases, the people in the field are not part of the color-selection process.

The field cards must be in the superintendent's possession by a certain cutoff date. This date varies by project and the lead time required for ordering. The field cards must be correct and there must be a control on them that insures that no changes are made once the cards are in the field. (In practical application, there should be no changes after a certain date; however, this is sometimes relaxed depending upon the circumstances.)

The Field-Color Schedule Card 560/680 is presented in both Chapter 5, Construction, and Chapter 6, Marketing and Sales, because it is used by both departments. It originates in one and is administered by the other. This particular form, like many others used in construction, is, to a certain extent and up to a certain point, ongoing and subject to revision. Hopefully, the cutoff date for change will come before the card is sent to the field. However, there should be an understanding and provision for updating these cards and a method of knowing which card is current and correct. The date at the top of the card is very important. It is also necessary to destroy or void all obsolete cards.

Form 560/680, as it is shown, can be used for most custom residences and some higher priced tracts. Forms for low-cost tract homes and condominiums or townhouses will not need the breakdown of rooms for interior paint and flooring because they are usually painted one color throughout and only one type and color of carpet is used throughout. This form is presented as a model, to be adapted and changed to fit a specific project or mode of operation.

## FIELD–COLOR SCHEDULE CARD

560/680

| Tract Name & Number | Lot No. | Plan No. | Elev. |
|---|---|---|---|
|  |  |  |  |

### INTERIOR COLOR SCHEDULE

| Room | Walls | Ceilg. | Trim | Floors | Room | Walls | Ceilg. | Trim | Floors |
|---|---|---|---|---|---|---|---|---|---|
| Living |  |  |  |  | Bdrm. 1 |  |  |  |  |
| Halls |  |  |  |  | Bdrm. 2 |  |  |  |  |
| Entry |  |  |  |  | Bdrm. 3 |  |  |  |  |
| Dining |  |  |  |  | Bdrm. 4 |  |  |  |  |
| Family |  |  |  |  | Bdrm. 5 |  |  |  |  |
| Den |  |  |  |  | Bath #1 |  |  |  |  |
| Kitchen |  |  |  |  | Bath #2 |  |  |  |  |
| Nook |  |  |  |  | Bath #3 |  |  |  |  |
| Garage |  |  |  |  | Laundry |  |  |  |  |

Doors: Int. _____ Front _____ Other Int. _____ Gar. _____ Ext. _____
Cabinets: Kit. _____ Bath _____ Bars _____ Other _____
Counter Tops: Kit. _____ Bath 1 _____ Bath 2 _____ Bath 3 _____ Other _____
Appliances: _____
Hardware: _____
Light Fixtures: _____

### EXTERIOR COLOR SCHEDULE

Exterior Color: Body _____ Trim _____ Gar Dr _____ Front Dr _____ Ext Dr _____
Stucco # _____ Masonry Veneer _____ Fireplace Style _____

### OPTIONAL ITEMS TO BE ADDED

| Extra | Yes | No | Extra | Yes | No |
|---|---|---|---|---|---|
| Air Conditioning |  |  |  |  |  |
| Mirrored Ward. Doors |  |  |  |  |  |
| Wet Bar |  |  |  |  |  |

# NOTES

## OTHER FIELD CARDS—FORMS 570, 580, AND 590

Construction companies that have their own field crews need forms to help regulate and keep track of the work in progress. Depending on the amount of detail required, this information can be anything from a blank sheet with the employee's name and weekly hours written on it, to a comprehensive study of what each man did each day, with a weekly summary to help determine the productivity of each man, crew, or phase, along with their past performance, estimated time, budgeted time, and actual time.

The field cards, by necessity, must be simple and easy to fill out. The sample cards that follow—**Employee Record Card, Timecard,** and **Job Summary**—correlate by category and item, one to the other. This means that the items on the Timecard must be the same as the column heading on the Job Summary sheet.

These cards are for internal company use only. It is entirely up to the head of the company as to what, if any, information is desired. The project or particular type of operation will greatly dictate the method of cataloguing this information. The forms presented are samples that can be altered to apply to specific projects and company requirements.

# 570

## EMPLOYEE RECORD CARD

Name _____

Address _____

Phone Number _____ Social Security Number _____

Marital Status _____ Number of Exemptions _____

## JOB RECORD

Date Started _____ Date Left _____

| Job Classification | Date From – To | Wage From – To | Comments |
|---|---|---|---|
|  |  |  |  |
|  |  |  |  |
|  |  |  |  |
|  |  |  |  |
|  |  |  |  |

## REFERENCES

| Previous Employers | Date From – To | Job Description | Reason for Leaving |
|---|---|---|---|
|  |  |  |  |
|  |  |  |  |
|  |  |  |  |
|  |  |  |  |

## COMMENTS

_____

_____

_____

_____

## TIMECARD 580

EMPLOYEE _____

CLASSIFICATION _____

|  | Date ___ | | Date ___ | | Date ___ | | Date ___ | | Date ___ | |
|---|---|---|---|---|---|---|---|---|---|---|
|  | Job | Hrs. | Job | Hrs. | Job | Hrs. | Job | Hrs. | Job | Hrs. |
| Material Handling | | | | | | | | | | |
| Girders, Underpin, Joists | | | | | | | | | | |
| Subfloor | | | | | | | | | | |
| Layout | | | | | | | | | | |
| Frame | | | | | | | | | | |
| Stairs | | | | | | | | | | |
| Trusses, Joists, Rafters | | | | | | | | | | |
| Roof Sheathing | | | | | | | | | | |
| Windows, Exterior Doors | | | | | | | | | | |
| Exterior Sheathing Rustic, Trim | | | | | | | | | | |
| Pick-up | | | | | | | | | | |
| Interior Trim | | | | | | | | | | |
| Hardware | | | | | | | | | | |
| Clean Up | | | | | | | | | | |
| TOTAL HOURS | | | | | | | | | | |

TOTAL HOURS _____ WEEK ENDING _____ _____ HRS.

COMMENTS _____

JOB SUMMARY  590

JOB _____  ADDRESS _____

| | TOTAL HOURS WEEK ENDING | | | | | | | | TOTAL |
|---|---|---|---|---|---|---|---|---|---|
| | | | | | | | | | |
| Material Handling | | | | | | | | | |
| Girders, Underpin, Joists | | | | | | | | | |
| Subfloor | | | | | | | | | |
| Layout | | | | | | | | | |
| Frame | | | | | | | | | |
| Stairs | | | | | | | | | |
| Trusses, Joists, Rafters | | | | | | | | | |
| Roof Sheathing | | | | | | | | | |
| Windows, Exterior Doors | | | | | | | | | |
| Exterior Sheathing Rustic, Trim | | | | | | | | | |
| Pick-up | | | | | | | | | |
| Interior Trim | | | | | | | | | |
| Hardware | | | | | | | | | |
| Clean Up | | | | | | | | | |
| | | | | | | | | | |
| TOTAL HOURS | | | | | | | | | |

COMMENTS _____
_____
_____

# 6

# Marketing and Sales

## MARKETING

Marketing is not sales, and sales is not marketing. Marketing and sales and their interrelationship can be compared with the execution of a play. Marketing is the writing of the play, the casting of the play, the production of the play, and the promotion of the play through the media—sales is the performance, the presentation of the overall plan. Thus, in this phase of construction, we will be discussing marketing as the general plan and sales as the presentation of that plan.

## CONDITIONS

In real estate today we are working in the midst of an ever-changing political, social, and economic arena. A brief period of calm is coupled with turmoil; a robust time is accompanied with strain and stress. And because the marketing production always takes place in this changing environment, it must be sturdy enough to withstand the changes. It cannot be stagnant.

This chapter will consider the means of making the important marketing and sales decisions in order to secure that these well-costed, well-constructed, and well-orchestrated building plans being put together will meet the market and will be accepted and be profitable.

## LOCATION AND THE BUYER

The two most essential things to consider are: first, locations, and second, the people who will buy them. We cannot tell you which is more important, because within every town, every time period, and every market, one can be more important than the other.

For purposes of presentation, we will assume that location may be the first thing with which you may become involved. It may be that you will secure, or intend to secure, a piece of land before you get into some of the other considerations. The most important aspects of choosing the right location are location, location, location—three of the most important rules of real estate. Real estate is not like a car. You cannot pick it up and take it home. You are not able to change the environment around the land, so choosing the right piece of land is always important.

Another thing to keep in mind is that we are living in an era of shortages. Shortages may be supply shortages, they may be material shortages, they may be government-imposed shortages. We are dealing with an economy in which a piece of land that was not worth anything yesterday can be worth quite a bit today due to some of these constraints. Changes in sewers, school districts, and other things can change the relative values of pieces of land. As you evaluate land you have to remember that you are evaluating it not in terms of its worth today but in terms of its worth at the time the product will be sold and when it is ready to be delivered. If things are going to change during that period, you have to incorporate that into your overall strategy.

## DEMAND

In every area there is always a basic demand for shelter. As marketers, you must address yourself to the specific issue of the demand in this area, the number of homes or condominiums per year that can be absorbed in this area, given the economic climate of today and given the economic climate that is likely to be present in the future.

Also in the selection of a site, you should take a very hard look inside a valuation at two important factors, one being the things that can change and the other being the things that cannot change.

**Things That Change.** What can change? You can buy a piece of land that is next to a beautiful field. This can change. That beautiful field could turn into a garbage dump or it could turn into an industrial plant. So as you look at sites, you have to be confident that the piece of land you are acquiring is not across from something that will change substantially to the worse. If it will change for the better, then pursue it.

You also have to understand that every town has a different economic base. It may be a well-diversified economic base or it may be a single economic base. For example, if you were building houses in Seattle in the mid-1960's and you became aware that Boeing was going to be rapidly cutting down their operation, this would have caused you to change your site selection and the kind of housing you planned. So you must consider the economic base and you must be comfortable that the economic base will support an absorption rate that fits your plan.

Another thing that can change is the growth trend in an area. Many times, due to municipal changes and the shortage of sewer taps, etc., the growth can jump from one side of town to the other side of town. San Jose, California, is a good example. For many, many years the east side of San Jose was a disaster and no one wanted to build houses there. As building sites became unavailable in the South Valley and as the Evergreen area became a less viable area, the east side became more desirable.

**Things That Do Not Change.** There are things in the marketplace that do not change. The proximity of a piece of land to a freeway is not going to change. The proximity of the land to major transportation is not going to change. The proximity to the ocean or major amenity, or the proximity to a large shopping center or major parks, all make a significant impact on value. These are the things that cannot change, so as you are making your evaluation, keep in mind that a beautiful tree-studded hillside may be completely removed tomorrow because it is zoned for a different kind of use.

## TARGET GROUPS

After we find a beautiful piece of land, one of the things we have to determine is: Who will buy it? This is called a target group. Our marketing consultant spends a lot of time and devotes a lot of energy to defining target groups for clients. They represent three of the largest building companies in Northern California. They have 27 other clients with whom they are working and, with all those clients, one of the best services that they can provide is to help them identify, before they begin a project, the kind of person who is likely to purchase. The more accurate the definition of that person or group, the better chance of success. Here is an example.

Most of real estate today is being influenced by two-income families, with both husband and wife working. Years ago this was not the case. With the passage of the Equal Credit Act in 1975, women's income could contribute to qualification for credit. This had a major influence on the sale of single-family detached homes. Prior to that time, it was becoming more and more difficult to get people qualified. The single-family detached customer has two children and a dog, if we want to follow the classic definition. They have certain wants and desires that must be included in your plans if you are going to be successful with that group.

In contrast to that, we also have seen a tremendous growth in families without children. For example, *Newsweek* magazine did a study not too long ago. They determined that there are 56.7 million family groups in the

United States (with a family group defined as a husband, wife, and, possibly, children). Of that number, 22.6 million had no children under 18, and 24.9 million had children under 18. So, probably 40 percent of the family households in the country have no children. This obviously has to have a major impact on how people are going to live. If you plan to get into housing that appeals to people with few or no children, consider their specific interests and desires apart from families with children. Your site selection and your architecture will be influenced by those you believe to be a portion of your customers.

**Future of Your Target Group.** The next consideration in defining your target groups is the expectation of the future of the target group. If you are dealing with people who assume that in three years their life is going to be better, you have a pretty good chance of selling them real property. If you are working with a group who is uncertain of what life is going to be like in two or three years, then "for sale" housing may not be the solution for them. Perhaps you should be looking at that land in terms of rental, with the possibility of conversion in the future. In other words, profit is not always in the building and selling of a single-family detached house on a lot. If you are in tune with the constraints of the neighborhood where you are working and the needs of the target group that you are after and the quantity of that target group in your market area, you may be forced into radically different conclusions, but those conclusions can make you money. It is not always necessary to build "for sale" housing. You can go into rental. You can perhaps mix commercial and residential on the same site. It is being done, and it is possible. These are all things that have to be fit into your overall strategy plan.

**Follow the Market.** It is also well-advised to be careful in your planning so that you are not trying to create a market. Many people in the real estate field thought they could create a market. If you are going to be successful, you should follow the market, but do not create it. Most of the new towns in the United States were created with the idea of bringing forth a new concept that everyone would want. They found they could not create a market. Real estate is different from consumer products. You cannot go on TV and tell people that their smile will be prettier if they move to a particular location. It has not worked, and I doubt that it will in the future. Many times architects will attempt to design a product for a new market. But as the consumer of those services, you must be sure that your architect is not getting carried away and that the solution he has proposed will fit the target group that you have defined.

## TYPES OF HOUSING

As you move from site selection, buyer's profile, and target group analysis, probably the next thing you will consider, outside of cost and profit analysis, will be the selection of the housing type. On most pieces of land you do not have a choice of high density or low density. The existing zoning is important. If you try to change the zoning, the chances are that you may not be able to do so. Something that you will also consider on most pieces of property that you acquire is this: What is the highest and best use of the property? You may be able to get 40 units to the acre, but if no one will buy them you will not make money. There is a trade-off between what you can do with the property and what people are likely to buy.

There are life-style decisions that are made whenever you select housing types. To give you an example: If your target group consists of older buyers, 40-60 years of age, the design of your home is going to have a very important influence upon your success. If the houses are beautiful, but they have stairs, you can cut your market 80 percent. Few architects really understand this. Years ago there was a widely held notion that everyone hated condominiums and apartments and that what they really wanted were stacked townhomes, with living on the ground floor, stairs, and living on the upper floors—no one above, no one below, only attached on the sides.

We have seen radical changes in the market since 1975. People who have discretionary income will walk up and down a flight of stairs to get to their home *once*, but they would prefer not to do it all day, every day. So the market has reverted to a lot of previously forbidden concepts such as flats—a flat meaning a unit that is all on one level; they may be stacked or they may be right on the ground. In terms of density analysis, if you have 2 two-story townhomes side by side, you consume the same amount of land if you take the same square footage and stack two units one over the other. So in terms of your ability to get density, whether you go townhomes or flats, you can reach pretty much the same density. Another thing to be considered is parking. You will have to decide if people are willing to park away from their homes. That is part of your target group data.

Another thing that has to be looked at is the location of the bathrooms in the house. How does the kitchen function? These are things that you understand or that you will understand about the importance of traffic flow and design.

The other consideration in regard to land planning is the impact of California's Proposition 13. The large parks and beautiful community facility of the past may be *in the past*. It may be that as developers we will get greater cooperation from the local government, be it city, county or state, if we build planned unit developments and we put in parks that are maintained by our associations because of the inability of the municipality to put in public facilities. We may be at the dawn of a tremendous surge of planned unit developments because city and county governments cannot provide parks and recreational facilities for people.

**Design with Inflation in Mind.** It is very critical, no matter if we are dealing with one house or a thousand houses, to design homes—be they condominium, town, or single-family detached—with inflation in mind. We all know that real estate is going up 12 to 18 percent per year, depending upon the area. We all know that costs seem to be following right behind. Today's fantastic buy at $55,000 may be tomorrow's disaster at $70,000 because we have left our target group behind.

Here is an example. We have designed a project that is set to sell for $55,000 in a remote rural area. We are going to build single-family detached homes stripped to the bone. We are going to do this as cheaply as we possibly can, as our target group are people who have relatively fixed incomes, because of the agricultural base, in the $20,000 range, husband and wife combined. Therefore, they cannot afford more than a $50,000 to $55,000 house. We have a magnificent piece of land, and we have developed a package.

Beware! The municipality at the drop of a hat can pass a $5,000 hookup fee. Your construction costs can start to soar. You can have some layoffs. There can be problems and suddenly that $55,000 "can't-miss" house is now $70,000. The target group for which it was designed no longer qualifies, so now we have to move up the economic ladder and we have to appeal to people that may get a combined income of $25,000 to $30,000. These people would not buy because you have designed in features that are absolutely unacceptable to the people in that market group. You have to design with inflation in mind. You have to be able to design a product that will weather a certain amount of inflation, because if you leave your target group behind, you move up to a category in which you must appeal to a more monied group. If there are things in those homes that they will not have, you can have a "white elephant" in the most robust of times.

**Selling Dissatisfaction.** Another thing that is critical in the design of a product is the concept of "selling dissatisfaction." Probably the most important thing that a developer of a new piece of real estate has to offer is something that will make people dissatisfied with their current living situations. If they are not dissatisfied, they will stay. So you have to take a hard look at the design elements.

The town of Pleasanton, California, can serve as an example. Pleasanton grew dramatically between 1965 and 1971–72. There was incredible growth. Thousands of homes were built. Then the market slowed down. Builders today are looking at Pleasanton again as a good housing market. What makes a difference is a large shopping center and a slight relaxation in the sewer problem. There is a *possibility* that growth will return to Pleasanton—we say possibility because you never know what the municipality is going to do.

How should we design for those people? One thing you can do is draw a five-mile circle around your project, and if it is well designed and well merchandized, 80 to 90 percent of your sales will come right out of that territory. It's very, very rare that you will get more than 50 percent of your buyers from more than five miles away. Generally, unless we are talking about a radical life-style change with people coming from single-family to condominium because the absence of children or change in income or change in expectations, they do not travel far. So you have to be careful with that "magic circle"—the five-mile circle.

In Pleasanton, within that five-mile circle, there are literally thousands of homes that were built with a particular square-footage range in mind with the same characteristics. The relationship of the kitchen and the family room is repeated the same way in thousands of homes in Pleasanton. The relationship of the master bath and the master bedroom is a certain way. The relationship or proportion of hall space to the overall floor plan is pretty much the same. If you are going to design for "dissatisfaction," you have to keep in mind those design issues. You have to come up with a better "mousetrap" in the important areas that are evaluated in a home: the elevation, the outside appearance, the flow of the floor plan, the relationship of the kitchen, the family, the living and the dining rooms, and the relationship of the bedrooms one to another, and the bathrooms to the bedrooms. These are critical areas in any design.

If we are going to design with dissatisfaction in mind, we have to know what kinds of houses exist. You should not design in a vacuum. Do not trust your architects to tell you. Go find out yourself. You can enlist the service of a local realtor at any time and look at 25 houses in one day in the town where you intend to build. This will give you a better education than all the meetings with all the architects in the world when it comes to knowing what is available.

**Demand Pockets.** If you're designing for a "demand pocket," it better be a deep one because you can get a *big* surprise if you design for a demand pocket that *is* satisfied. San Ramon, California, is a good example of this. Many real estate people who went into the San Ramon area in 1971 thought the market needed a little fancier version of what they already had. But they missed the market. They did not sell nearly as many houses as they should have. One particular builder had every market study that you could buy; the studies showed that what they were doing was absolutely wrong, that people would not pay 30 percent more for a home that was 30 percent bigger. All the market studies, however, were wrong. The vein was very deep and they were able to sell 300 to 400 very expensive homes in a market area where everyone said that they could not survive. The studies had shown that the market did not exist. But, one particular builder, through two large community-size subdivisions, was able to capture a brand new market. What they sold, essentially, was dissatisfaction. Their homes are big enough, fancy enough, etc., that the people are willing to say, "I've had it with this old place, I'm going to get the bigger one."

How did they know this when others didn't? At the time, other companies conducted surveys, and they proved conclusively that larger, more expensive homes would not work.

The surveys were basically prepared using "extrapolation." You take what everyone else is doing, examine their sales rate, and then insert a new project and compare its value with the value that is on the market and extrapolate their sales curve based upon what everyone else is doing. This system breaks down when you cannot find a like project to compare; that is an element of risk. Large companies can afford to take those kinds of risks. Small builders are generally more conservative. It depends on the time, it depends on the market you are in and who you are, and your ability to withstand a disaster if you want to go into an area that is heretofore untapped.

Much of the survey information came from door-to-door canvassing to find out what kinds of homes people were living in and what their expectations were in the future. The demand appeared to be there, but there was nothing in the marketplace that was there to pick up that demand. But it was something that was predictable.

When we talk about creating markets, we are talking about being the first company in your area to do a retirement community in a market area where one has never been done before. In San Ramon, they really were not creating a market for bigger, fancier houses. They were betting that the demand for bigger, better, fancier houses was there based upon the fact that people were crowded in the homes they were in. They had developed substantial equities and it was time to take that stagnant equity and move it into a bigger residence. And they were right.

## INVENTORYING LAND

Land inventory comes down to basic philosophy. The large builder, previously mentioned, when asked how he had come to have so much land, has always told this story: "You know, the greatest general in World War II was Rommel. How come he didn't win? Well, he ran out of gas." That builder never intends to run out of gas. As a builder you have to have land, so he has a philosophy and a conviction that land is a raw asset, has significant value, and he intends to have a lot of it. He is different from the typical builder because he ascribes no opportunity cost to the cash that is tied up in that land that could be into other ventures. Their company is not nearly as leveraged as the typical building company. They have a significant portion of their balance sheet in land, whereas most other builders have much less. It is obvious that if you are leveraged you are going to get a greater return than if you are not leveraged. That is a philosophical decision that each developer has to make. Where is the drawing line between leverage and a conservative growth goal? It varies with every builder.

## MARKET SURVEY

How much confidence should you have in market surveys? Surveys should make no pretensions about growth trends. But, if you want to verify that there were 25 houses sold at Las Laderas in Hercules, California, last week, you can get that information. Surveys can give very accurate counts on who is selling, where they are selling, and how many are sold. Surveys are probably valuable if you want to validate your own thinking.

The worst kind of survey you can buy is one from a local realtor who expects to get the sales contract. He will tell you anything you want to know, because whether you make money or not, he will. Also, these surveys tend to be less reliable than those that are commissioned as research.

As you are evaluating your marketing packages, you will know how your plans will be compared with others. What are people going to be thinking about when they go through your homes versus when they go through someone else's homes? Do not be deluded into thinking that people only look at new houses, and that if you have a new house and it is a better buy than one across the street, which is also new, you will do better. There is a second choice of an older resale house and a third alternative that is called "staying right where I am now." That makes more sales per year than all the new home subdivisions combined. That is a very viable alternative.

The market for new homes is getting increasingly difficult with the liberalization of credit requirements in the savings and loan associations and banks. Just about on your signature alone, you can now get a second loan for home improvement. And, you do not *have to* improve the home. You can go to the bank today, and you can tell the credit officer that you *intend* to improve your home and you want $10,000. If the equity is there, he will give you the $10,000. Previously, they gave you $500 at a time with paid receipts in your hand. Those days are gone, because banks found they can make a tremendous amount of money by increasing borrowing against real estate. So improving and changing houses is a very viable part of our economic picture. That is why dissatisfaction is even more important. You must offer housing and features that are better overall than what a buyer has now or he is very likely to stay right where he is.

**New Tax Effect on Market.** In California, the major impact of the Jarvis-Gann legislation has been to stimulate people who want to buy more housing. People can now buy 25 percent more because taxes are one-third of what they used to be. On a qualifying basis, they are able to buy 25 percent more for the same amount of money per month.

**Research Incongruities.** There are some incongruities in research, things you will want to watch out for. We have a philosophy about research, which is: Whatever the newspapers and magazines say, do exactly the opposite, because by the time they get to it, it is already over. As a small developer, you want to be sure you do not get caught on the bandwagon just as it starts to coast downhill.

Most land you will look at has a possibility of density higher than that of single-family detached. You will find surveys such as the one *Professional Builder* magazine put out in their Western survey in 1978. They found out that 93 percent of the people surveyed wanted single-family detached; 4 percent wanted townhouses; 3 percent wanted condominiums. Therefore, 93 percent of the people will be buying single-family detached homes. Wrong! Of the 100 percent surveyed, less than 25 percent of them *could* buy. That is a big difference. The research involved people who have bought or could buy. That is much more important than research concerning people who cannot buy, because, unfortunately, people who cannot buy, do not count. So, be careful as you evaluate trends and as you evaluate research regarding people who can afford to buy and people who could buy. Those are your clients. Those are the people for whom you are designing, defining, and marketing toward, not the people who cannot buy.

**Perceived Value.** *Perceived value* is another area of research that you must study carefully. This is especially true of the surveys of builder's magazines. They will do opinion surveys and tell you that people want fireplaces in their master bedroom, they want skylights in their bathroom, they want thermopane glass, and other elaborate items. These are all interesting items; however, you must balance that with what people will pay for them. This is called "perceived value." The perceived value of insulation, so far as we can determine, is about 300 percent of its cost. The perceived value of a fireplace in the master bedroom is about 20 percent of its cost. Therefore, if you're going to put in a master bedroom fireplace, do not expect to make a lot of money off that single investment, because people do not truly appreciate the master bedroom fireplace in most new housing series. In the luxury market ($150,000 or over), it becomes purely discretionary and that is a different set of circumstances.

What people want and what they will pay for are things that you, as developers, and your marketing team will have to determine. If you are dealing with a super-luxury home, $150,000 and up (or in your town it could be $100,000 and up), you have to make decisions on what you will include and what you will not include. Our recommendation is that if the perceived value of an item is greater than the cost, put it in. If the perceived value is less than the cost, be careful and make sure that there is something extra that will help sell dissatisfaction with what he has now.

## VALUE OF ENERGY CONSERVATION FEATURES

Energy conservation, with regard to the initial buying decision, does not really make a great impact because the kind of buyer who is really concerned about his utility cost is not in the frame of mind to buy. There are different ego states that we get into when we purchase something. Many psychologists have conducted studies on what ego state you are in when you make a decision.

There are various books on the topic of transactional analysis (we are not endorsing T.A.—just borrowing some of its words). The book *I'm O.K., You're O.K.* relates three principle ego states that we all have: the child, the parent, and the adult. In the child, you are in a happy, excitable frame of mind. In the parent, you are reserved; you are concerned about such things as energy and utility. In the adult, you are an authority figure; you make decisions, you move forward. Time and time again, studies which have been made on the buying decision show that when people are ready to buy, they are not in the parent, they are not in the adult—they are in the child state. One of the duties of sales is to move people around and get them excited, and utility bills do not excite people. There may be justification. After we make the decision to buy, we go through another state, and that is called, "Oh, oh! What do I do now?" If you have done a good sales job, then you have dealt with the utility cost issue, you have dealt with thermopane glass, you have dealt with the things that do come with the home and the things that do not. The buyer will go home justifying his decision. If there are gaps in your presentation, if he will be uncomfortable about energy, and if he is uncomfortable about the cost of ownership, he will "unbuy." So we have to understand what frame of mind we want the person to be in at the time we get his decision to buy.

Where does the utility cost figure in? It figures in very early in the presentation to justify the quality of the product with which we are dealing. If it is removed from your overall package, a high percentage of buyers would not fall out—except if you are dealing with fixed income, i.e., the older market. Then the utility cost situation is of major importance.

We live in a changing environment. You have to continuously watch the economic backdrop behind the real estate market as we make decisions as to what kind of home to build, who will buy it, and what the motivations of that person are.

## MARKETING STRATEGY

Once we have acquired the site, examined our buyer's profile, examined what motivates him, examined who he is and what his expectations are in the future, we design a product. Now it is time to take this production and put it into the public arena. So we must choose a marketing strategy. One of the most important things that you can do in creating this backdrop is to put together a "success atmosphere." No one wants to deal with an unsuccessful operation. There is one exception in that group. There are people in our economy who look for failures with the expressed purpose of picking up something at a "fire sale" and turning it into a profit. I am assuming that this is not our market. We are not destined to fail and, therefore, we are going to leave opportunists out.

**Create a Success Atmosphere.** We look for a success atmosphere in everything we do. How do you create a success atmosphere? There are some key concepts that remain true no matter what kind of housing you are in, no matter if it is for young people, old people, people with children, without children, rich, or poor. We must deal with a concept of *privacy and exclusivity*. People are motivated to purchase real estate for a lot of different motivations. Privacy and exclusivity rank number one because this is something that can be sold regardless of the price range. People want to be comfortable purchasing the project and they want to be comfortable with the land plan and the outside environment.

Borrowing from transactional analysis again, psychologists tell us that if the whole feels good, people will seek out that market. If the whole does not feel good, they cannot understand their part. So, in the complete marketing program, you are trying to gear people into making that important decision, which is to buy your project or your home, in order for you to make money. So you must deal with privacy and exclusivity from the moment they arrive.

Also, people will move from *general to specific*. As you articulate your marketing plan, you have elements that are outside the community, you have elements inside the community, and you have the specific elements inside your sales office and your model complex. As you move from general to specific, remember that people, as they make decisions, will move in that direction. They want to be comfortable with what they are doing before they buy.

**Articulate Prices Based on Worth.** Another concept that you have to deal with is this: How do I, on the last day of sales work, put together a strategy to sell the last piece of inventory and have it close on time at a profit? On every project, unless you're talking about a single house, there are homes or condominiums or locations that are better than others. It is your duty in marketing to deal with the worst part of your project and the best part of your project.

The mistake most frequently made by builders in marketing is the failure to understand the difference between the best and the worst. A lot of that is a product of the method in which we do our accounting. We do our accounting by plan and we do our accounting by elevation. Some of this is false teaching, because the way in which we put our numbers down are decisions that we make in allocation, but people do not buy based on that. People buy what they like, and they will pay exactly what it is worth. People are very smart. When you look at the sales of a project, you can see that the good homes sell fast and the bad ones lag. A lot of that is related to your pricing decision. You must articulate your prices because there will always be a best and a worst. As a developer, you had better know which is which, or you will have problems at the end of your project.

**Know the Odds of Success.** In your marketing strategy you must make a realistic estimate of your odds of success. Every day you go to work, every day you put together a package, every day you make a decision, you are making a bet. You need to know what your chances are of success. If you have a long shot, you had better know it. If you feel it is a relatively easy opportunity, you should know that too, because it is going to influence the way you operate.

One element that radically influences marketing plans is called the "already sold." This has defeated more builders than anything else in the industry. The "already sold" can be described this way: "Don't worry about that. Why? We've got them already sold." That happens one time in a million, and if it does, your prices are too low. They are never already sold because they come on the market at a specific time. If they are already sold, then there is no need to plan. They are not already sold because those people may get hit by a truck, they may move, they may lose their money. You never know what is going to happen. Forget about the "already sold" and design a package that makes sense for the market at the time in which you enter that market.

**Model Area Entrance.** Your entrance into the model area is important. If the sand piles are four feet high and you are asking people to drive through junk and across timbers to get to a nice model site, are they really going to appreciate it? Not likely. People discount. If they see things that lower their perception of value, they will lower it on the sales floor when it is time to make a sale. Your product will move a little slower. There is always a trade-off. Every project cannot have a yellow brick road that leads right up to the front door. There are decisions that you must make, but first take a look at your entrance. Have your friends (this is a very cheap thing) get in a car and drive out to your project while it is under construction and ask them for an opinion. How did they feel as they drove down the road? What concerned them most? Generally, you will be going from one neighborhood to get to another. How did they feel as they entered the neighborhood? This is all part of your mood setting.

## PRICING AND PROFIT

The finalizing item on the marketing list is pricing and profits. We want to make sure that in our pricing package, a profit is made. Many times you can make more profit by selling one house for a $5,000 profit and another for a $10,000 profit than if you sold each for a $5,000 profit. You have to be able to deal with what is going on in the marketplace, what people can afford, and their expectations. So, for profit per house, guard against pricing your product strictly based upon cost. You need to know what people will pay.

Here is an example. We have a subdivision of homes for which a market study was done. We are able to determine that people were paying approximately $55 per square foot for these homes and we tried to put together a pricing package that would make sense and make a profit. We found that very, very few subdivisions had a sufficient quantity of one-story homes and that there seemed to be quite a demand for them. We also found an abundance of another type—a basic four-bedroom, two-and-one-half bath, two-story, about 2500-square-foot home. Conventional wisdom would have said price them all at $55 per square foot. Instead, we priced the one-story at $75 per square foot and we priced the home which seemed to be in danger of the most competition at $50 per square foot, but we sold the one-stories too fast. Even at a radically different figure, we still sold the one-stories too fast. We thought we had covered ourselves with about a $20 premium per square foot but it still was not enough. And that was an error in our pricing strategy.

Pricing is something that should be examined no less frequently than once a week. You should take a look at it to make sure that it fits with your plans and strategy.

## ADVERTISING

Part of marketing is execution. One of the elements that we use in marketing to express our ideas is advertising. Many of you will not be dealing with large-space ads; you will be dealing with small-space ads. It does not matter whether it is large or small, the ad has to zero in on the target group. There are things to be learned in advertising. Advertising agencies are often able to articulate the ideas better than you can. There is no reason not to use one. It costs about $500 to $600 to produce an ad, and that may be the best $500 or $600 you ever invested.

Here are some examples of what not to do and what could work for you. Part of the selling strategy is withholding information. If you give all your information in the ad, you have lost. You have lost because what you need to do in your marketing is to create an interest that can only be filled by seeing the site. Very, very rarely do you sell a house over the telephone; the odds are one in a million. So your advertising must get people out to your site so you can deal with them there. This assumes that we are not talking about projects that are so small that they could possibly be handled in a local broker's office.

Generally, real estate is a tactile, immovable product and it can be best sold in the product because you have more to work with, you have more tools. Ads can include many elements. Some have headlines, some do not. Some have art, some do not. The decision a prospective buyer makes when going through a newspaper is whether or not to read an ad. Again, we are not concerned with the people who are not in the housing market. We are only concerned with people who could buy houses.

You may be tired of seeing your ad over and over and you may think you need a new one. But people come in and out of the housing market every 60 to 90 days. You could run an ad for two years and it would not matter because as people come into the market, they see it for the first time. So when you do find an ad that is very successful, do not think that you have to change ads every 90 days because you do not. If it is a successful ad you can alter it slightly, but the key to advertising is getting the people motivated to get into their car and drive out to your project so that they can be in an area where a decision can be made.

Generally, maps in ads are very important in real estate because you have to know how to get to the site. They must be accurate. On a proportions basis, it is better to have a big map and forget the art, because unless the people can find their way there, the art does not matter.

Another personal philosophy, which is not shared by some people in the real estate community, is that the services of the marketing agent are very important. The agent's function is not to develop future business for himself. His function is to sell homes for developers. So when you discuss this with the marketing agent, one of the decisions that you have to make is whose name goes in the ad? How many names can you get in the ad before it gets to be cluttered? The *only* reason for having a marketing agent's name in an ad is for him to get business in the future. There is no other reason to have his name in there because not one single individual would buy a home from you as a developer because your marketing agent was better known than you were.

It has been said that the intellect of the average TV viewer is 12. Well, in real estate, we are not much further ahead. We are impatient people. We cannot wait for our TVs to warm up. We live in an era of instant gratification. Know this as you are preparing your advertising. Advertising takes into account the fact that people really do not read; their attention span is short. That is why many companies are emphasizing headlines, minimum copy, maps, etc.

Ads featuring snob-appeal are not always the best. This is also true of financing ads. The best ad is an ad that people can read and understand, one that elicits a decision to get in a car and go and see. That is a successful ad. Of secondary importance is their qualification, but first you have to get them in the car.

The other thing which we think is very important in advertising is to let people know where you are located. Generally, when you are advertising in the newspaper, the newspaper blankets an area and you do not want someone to read the whole ad only to find out that it is outside of his area. Somewhere in your ad you should be forthright about where you homes are located.

Pioneering is part of new-homes marketing. People want to be pioneers or they would not be investing in new homes. The pioneer spirit does have something to do with what you are trying to accomplish. Nostalgia is another way of getting people interested. People assume that yesterday's quality is better than today's. That is not always right, but that is common assumption. If, in your advertising, you are able to communicate that you have modern conveniences with old world craftsmanship, generally speaking, it is a successful way of getting people motivated to come out to your site.

**Name of Project.** Name is another important selection. If the name on your project means nothing, then it is not working for you. If it means something, then you have an added mood-setting vehicle. Stay away from naming things for your children or for your favorite uncle because name is an important element of mood setting and value engineering that you are leaving out.

Here are some names that we can consider. "The Old Del Georgia Place." It provokes instant nostalgia. "Danville Mill." It tells you instantly that it is in Danville and, ironically enough, there is a windmill at the top of the hill. And, they have affixed their name to a geographical area, which may work for them. Sunset Ridge, Canyon Dale, Harbor Town, Marlboro Hills, Seascape, Oakknolls, Willowwood are also interesting.

**Plan for the Worst.** For model sales office and advertising we recommend that everyone, no matter what you do, have an "A" Plan and a "B" Plan. The "B" Plan can be used in case it rains everyday and things are really tough. In real estate, we are dealing in cycles—up, down, up, down. So, plan for the worst. If you have a fortunate occurrence and your homes sell quicker than you expected and the market conditions are not quite as disastrous as they might have been, then you can pull back. Maybe you furnish only one model instead of four. Maybe you do not use advertising at all. There are many alternatives. Those are adjustments to a plan. He who plans for a fast sellout and no problems in real estate is in for a big surprise. Generally, if houses are easy to sell, you should have priced them $10,000 more per house. You would have made more money. So you want to get prices up as fast as you can, which means you have to do an adequate production or you are going to leave a lot of money on the table.

**Homeowners' Associations.** Another important part of your execution is your homeowners' association. Many of you may already understand that in planned unit developments, condominium towns, there are homeowners' associations. Set them up wisely. There are consultants who can be retained. With an association you create a person; a legal person who can cause you a lot of problems.

"Square dealing" is very important with homeowners' associations. They will not simply go away. They will hound you. So if you do your homework, if you do a good job, if you are structured well, if you deal squarely, you will come out the winner. They are also good advertising when the job is done well.

## INVENTORY STRATEGY

You need an inventory strategy. If homes are not selling and you want them to sell, you have to do something. The first thing you should do is have a look at them, because adjusting prices is easier, but much more expensive in the long run, than cleaning up dirty houses. You must know what your inventory looks like. You should spend a little extra time and money to make sure that the appropriate subcontractor cleans up the houses for the weekend, which is still the time when the bulk of the traffic comes out.

**Model Home Trap Needed.** You should have some means of trapping people when they come to your site. We recommend a trap for a project no matter how small. If you give people the option of walking through the homes and leaving, they will. Unless you have an incredibly fleet-of-foot salesperson or marketing agency, a lot of your people will drive down the street. You have a tremendous investment in your endeavor. Do not shortchange yourself by allowing people to just walk out without ever being funneled through your sales office. Traps are important. Big builders do it. Small builders do it. Unsuccessful builders many times do not do it, figuring it will not matter. It does matter.

**Flow.** Your model site should flow right. There should be a reason why they see this one first, this one second, this one third, and this one last. Our recommendation is to finish on a "high note." The number one house should be a lot less important than the last house. Finish on a high note.

**Lighting.** Lighting is important, especially exterior lighting. If your project is lit up like a jewel box at night, the people in the neighborhood are going to want to know what is going on there. There will be conversation about it. There is a great fascination for things that are well-lighted. So consider lighting as an important part of your landscaping and model execution.

## FINANCING

Financing is a big area, and we are not going to go into a lot of details about it. As developers, you should spend time with a good savings and loan or mortgage company to find some means of acquiring financing. In Northern California, which is different from Southern California, probably 70 percent of your customers will go through your designated lender so long as your designated lender has attractive rates and fees. People in Northern California tend to be more sensitive about such terms as prepayment provisions, down payment provisions, and interest rates. On the other hand, 99 percent of Southern Californians will go through your lender. It is just customary. They are much more rate-conscious than terms-conscious. In Southern California, the typical savings and loan still gets a prepayment penalty most of the time. In Northern California, they do not. It is not all "up-front points." This is money out of your pocket and it is important, but in the long run it may be one of the least important things. For a slightly additional cost, you may be able to get a financing package that will help ease your product above that of another builder.

## SALES OPERATION

The last thing we are going to deal with is the sales operation. The sales operation is also a big area, and we will only be able to touch on a few points here. It is important for the actors who are in the play to be comfortable with what is supposed to happen here. When you orchestrate a play, it is important to have people understand what is going on so they can communicate the wisdom that has been put into the plan. We believe in something called *"full disclosure,"* because the truth always wins in the long run. If the truth is on your side, you will be more successful than people who attempt to get by with half truths.

The quality of the individual presentation of the salesperson on the site is important. The credibility of the salesperson is important. Do you believe him when he tells you something? That is a critical issue.

Demonstration is important. How does the salesperson demonstrate the house? Does he listen and not talk? To dispel a conventional fallacy, sales people who talk a lot are bad. If you hear a salesperson who is constantly talking and whacking people on the back, he is not creating interest. He is destroying it. The best salespeople talk 20 percent of the time and listen 80 percent of the time. If you are talking, you are not learning. A certain amount of talk is necessary in presentation because people have to understand what is being sold. But, after the presentation, you have to listen. You have to ask questions to find out why they came here, what they are interested in, where they live now, what their equity is, how much can they put down. Unless you know these things, you are not going to be in a position to close. A salesman needs to be a good listener. He also needs to be a good closer. People who are afraid to ask you to buy will not survive in real estate.

## MARKETING EVALUATION: ONE PROJECT

The following is a report prepared by our marketing consultant for a savings and loan association. They had a project that was virtually completed in Alamo, California, called Alamo Bridge, adjacent to the 680 Freeway. It was being marketed by a local realtor who in seven months sold only four houses. They were called in to take over the project and to recommend some changes. They did not reconstruct the houses; they reconstructed the atmosphere around them. Through a series of changes, they were able to sell the balance of the project, which was 83 homes, in a little under a year at a profit. The savings and loan was quite happy about that because they were carrying the project on their books at a substantial loss. The following is an analysis that we did for them. We include it here because it might be helpful to others.

## DESCRIPTION

Alamo Bridge is a condominium community of 87 attached homes arranged in 12 village clusters in Alamo, California. Each home features one or two stories with 1,200 to 1,900 square feet and two-car enclosed garage nearby.

Over 60 percent of the homes in this suburban Eastbay community face a busy freeway—Interstate 680. Although the homes are distinctive and the community outstanding, location and style failed to produce a winner.

At the time (March 1976) our firm was retained to revitalize the marketing of this project, all 87 homes had been finished. In fact, all the homes had been finished in September 1975 and only four had been sold after a massive advertising campaign.

The savings and loan, the owners of Alamo Bridge, wanted the project sold and off their books within one year. A possible deterioration in the price level was of critical concern. Our firm was given the responsibility and the authority to create the marketing programs and implement the conclusions in face-to-face selling opportunities.

## THE MARKETING PLAN

It is safe to say a number of problems were uncovered in our analysis. In the interest of time, the elements that needed immediate attention were: (1) perceived value, (2) the sales office, (3) advertising, (4) inventory management, (5) the model site, and (6) the project entrance.

**Perceived Value.** In spite of the project's location in the prestigious community of Alamo (average selling price, $105,000), the buying public did not agree with the project's marketing claims. The following points contributed to this problem:

    a. Competitive projects averaged $9 to $12 per square foot lower in sales price.
    b. The best and worst homes in the project were priced within 2 percent of each other.
    c. No concept of scarcity was obvious to the clients.
    d. The submarket financing offered by the savings and loan had the appearance of justifying inflated prices.
    e. The project appeared unsuccessful.

f. The freeway noise was a great distraction.
g. The project had a "ghost town" feeling.
h. Brokers in the community referred to the project as a "Big Loser" and waited for the inevitable death and concurrent "fire sale."
i. Weeds and broken windows had been tolerated for some months.
j. Weekly customer traffic to the project was at an all-time low in spite of large advertising campaigns over the previous seven months.

**Sales Office.** Prior to stimulating new customers, our top management team spent a week in the old complex and interviewed customers for their reactions. We compared field results with our in-house appraisal. The following steps were then taken:

a. The office was reorganized to include private conversation areas.
b. New furniture was ordered.
c. The good points of the freeway location were emphasized.
d. A "trap" was completed in the complex.
e. The displays were de-emphasized.
f. Plants were added to soften and subdue the harshness in the office decor.

**Advertising.** Prior to any advertising campaign, our firm recommended a pricing strategy that was designed to produce a sales volume in excess of the price level when we started (projected $5.87 million). With a coordinated attack, we produced a final sellout of $5.91 million without submarket interest rate loans from the savings and loan. To make the public aware of the new offering, the following strategies were employed:

a. When the project was new (September 1975), over 2,000 people saw Alamo Bridge on the first weekend. Few were interested in condominium homes. We reversed this trend by limiting advertising to publications with high-income demographics to reduce unqualified traffic.
b. Since most of the local people were influenced by the apparent lack of success (and broker "bad-mouthing"), our new focus was on success. Early low prices attracted quick sales. Brokers were excluded from the project marketing by removing the homes from the Multiple

Listing Service. The resale brokers were then educated on the merits of the project by our office and soon realized, by the educational process, that the project had outstanding qualities. The bad-mouthing continued for a while, but by excluding brokers from the cooperative sales process, buyers received better treatment. Few residential resale brokers understand condominiums.

c. New customers were attracted by ads that emphasized the word "Alamo" in the location. Five separate advertising campaigns were necessary in the ten-month sellout to sustain qualified traffic. With an average of 30 qualified people per week, we were able to maintain a good rate of sale.

d. Ads in local papers were dropped and classified ads were placed in the major San Francisco paper. Media cost per week was reduced and traffic quality and numbers improved.

e. The message in the ads was changed to attract likely condominium customers, not the single-family buyers. We expressed our townhome-condominium features prominently in the ads.

f. The brochures were altered slightly to emphasize the uniqueness of the villages.

g. All interaction with the resale brokers was reserved for our main business office. Brokers were allowed to buy homes, but not to "hang around" the sales office.

h. The freeway location was utilized to generate extra traffic through flag exposure. Easy commuting was highlighted.

i. Prices were quoted only to reflect the homes we wished to sell. As they were sold, more inventory were released.

j. A barrage of public relations stories written by our firm was released to the media emphasizing the significant "newsworthy" happenings at the project. These were supplemented with special events and charity functions to expose people to the true quality of the project. One of the qualities discovered by people attending our special functions was the relative calm and quiet in certain areas of the project. The freeway noises were not as bad as people had imagined prior to visiting Alamo Bridge.

**Inventory Management.** The look of a winner is clean and organized, a place where people take pride in their homes. Alamo Bridge had none of these things in March 1976. To achieve this look, the following items were analyzed and solutions developed:

a. Alamo, like so many other large projects, had the appearance of a large, monolithic mass. We had to break it down into meaningful marketing elements.
b. Inventory was cleaned up and lights were placed for night showing.
c. The word "SOLD" had to be communicated.
d. Each village had to be marketed as a unique place to live. The project was split into two halves, with one for sale and one held off the market until the first was sold out.
e. The noisiest villages were marketed first.
f. A directory was added to call attention to the unique villages.

**The Model Site.** The strongest part of the program when we started was the model presentation. All the homes were well-designed and colorful. Very little was done to change the model presentation. To capitalize on the good model site, we tried to reduce the physical and mental obstacles in getting to the models. The only significant model change involved one plan, and that represented 43 percent of the inventory. Here are the changes instituted at the model site:

a. To encourage more "double owner" buyers, we changed the master bedroom access to afford a twin master bedroom, which was set up upstairs in the high inventory plan.
b. The conversion price of the master bedroom access in this plan was quoted in the sales price to provide a savings opportunity for families that wished to take the home "as is."
c. Potential buyers for our problem properties were directed to only those properties, even when substitute properties were available.
d. Once the problem properties were sold and occupied, the other homes became immediately more attractive and their perceived value went up in the eyes of the public because of scarcity. We were then able to increase prices on a systematic basis.

**Project Entrance.** Two of the foremost obstacles to Alamo Bridge are its freeway frontage and obscure side street entrance. To turn these problems into assets, we concentrated on the following:

  a. All marketing energies were directed to make the project an island of calm against a noisy, busy backdrop.

  b. Good ads with maps, and signs and flags helped people find the project. A heavy public relations program had encouraged them to find out "where this Alamo Bridge is."

  c. To help "out-of-area" people overcome their shock at realizing the project was next to a freeway, we made the trip to the sales office an adventure. We landscaped the bridge and emphasized the signing along the winding approach to the sales office. The freeway noise was masked by installing flags along the drive, which created a pleasant distraction.

**Conclusion.** Working all the problems and solutions together in a well-orchestrated plan, Alamo Bridge was opened for sale in May 1976 at $50,850 to $70,000. We finished the sales program in February 1977 at $72,950 to $91,950, with a final sales volume of $5.91 million. The variety of approaches all worked for a short time, but it became necessary to restructure marketing programs as the inventory was reduced.

We are certain that, in a large measure, our expert staff made the difference between success and failure. In our opinion, a sales staff completely versed in the intricacies of the condomium marketing plan is a prerequisite for success. No amount of advertising or money expenditures for marketing can overcome ineffective sales practices. As in many businesses, it is the salesman who holds the product in his hand when the customer arrives. The more complicated the real estate offering, the more essential it becomes to have an expert sales organization communicating with the buying public.

# SALES AND MARKETING PLANNING CHECKLIST— FORM 600

The following marketing checklist is very long; it contains many different elements. It is important that each item be covered. We have tried to pinpoint responsibility. Who is responsible for commissioning the architects? When are they going to do it? Who is going to get it done?

We are always working under pressure and, generally, we are always behind. Thus, we have included columns for *actual* dates. When did we start it and when did we finish? We can easily make comparisons and track progress by looking at these entries.

## RESPONSIBILITY

Fixing responsibility is the key. As active consultants, because we do more than just define the marketing objectives, we staff the plant. We have about 50 salespeople right now. We believe in doing more than just telling you what to do and how to do it; we believe in proving it.

It is critical when affixing responsibility to have the responsibility in the right place. Just as you have heard a lot of talk about subcontractors, each subcontractor must know what he is supposed to do. If you are going to have in-house people working directly for you who are not responsible to any agency, you had better know more than they know or you are not going to be a good boss. Because if they know more than you know about how to do it, how are you going to lead them? They will lead you. We recommend that the person you are dealing with in marketing execute the plan. Guard against dealing with account representatives.

If you are dealing with a local realtor, make sure he understands the plan. Team selling rarely works, because in real estate most successful ads deal with credibility. People sometimes come back four times before they buy. If they see a different face every time they arrive, they will not conclude it is a successful operation. So, as you are affixing responsibility, you must define to the various marketing people what roles they are to play and when they work. And, hopefully, they will work together. Affixing responsibility is part of your duty as a developer.

## RETAIN MARKETING CONSULTANT EARLY

To define the overall thrust of the plan, you should retain your marketing consultant early. Why? Because marketing decisions have to be made early "in the game." It is generally unwise to find a piece of land, fit the land to a project, work out a design, and then go to a marketing representative and tell him what you have, because profits may come from things that today appear to be outlandish. The conversion field is one of them. Other fields that have come far and are just around the corner are condominium offices, condominium commercial, and condominium warehouses. There are many different things that are coming into the economy now. You should not be the first in your area to try it, but be ready. It is a way of making money. So, bring your marketing person or your marketing organization into your early planning in order to produce a better product—and stay flexible. *Don't be just in the building business; be in the profit business.*

# SALES AND MARKETING PLANNING CHECKLIST
## NEW HOMES PRE-OPENING

600

Community Development _____

Tract Number _____ Number of Lots _____ Number of Models _____

Sales Office Address _____

| Item | Respon-sibility | Basic Schedule Start or Submit | Basic Schedule Finish or Receive | Actual or Revised Dates Start or Submit | Actual or Revised Dates Finish or Receive |
|---|---|---|---|---|---|
| Complete sales contract | | | | | |
| Set architectural criteria | | | | | |
| Set architectural budget | | | | | |
| Commission architects | | | | | |
| Design landplan | | | | | |
| Draft floorplan | | | | | |
| Establish target prices | | | | | |
| Estimated start of models | | | | | |
| Estimated start of production | | | | | |

### 75 to 100 Days Before Grand Opening

| Item | | | | | |
|---|---|---|---|---|---|
| Set product theme | | | | | |
| Select community name | | | | | |
| Set advertising theme | | | | | |
| Start project graphics | | | | | |
| Projected buyer profile defined | | | | | |
| Select advertising agency and order rough program layout | | | | | |

| Item | Respon-sibility | Basic Schedule Start or Submit | Basic Schedule Finish or Receive | Actual or Revised Dates Start or Submit | Actual or Revised Dates Finish or Receive |
|---|---|---|---|---|---|
| Research and select media effectiveness | | | | | |
|     A. Newspaper | | | | | |
|     B. Radio | | | | | |
|     C. Magazines | | | | | |
|     D. Billboards | | | | | |
|     E. Direct mail | | | | | |
|     F. Other | | | | | |
| Set marketing budget | | | | | |
| Select billboard company | | | | | |
| Select layout and copy | | | | | |
| Select brochure format | | | | | |
| Establish PR thrust | | | | | |
| Tour site with executives | | | | | |
| Establish sales staff requirements | | | | | |
| Lay out landscaping plan | | | | | |
| Select interior decorator | | | | | |
| Design entrance site plan | | | | | |
| Order site sign for entrance | | | | | |
| Design entrance arrangement | | | | | |
| Design feature, directional model signs | | | | | |
| Select names for model homes | | | | | |
| Select sales office designer and decorator and order preliminary recommendation | | | | | |
| Arrange for samples of standard features | | | | | |

|  | | Basic Schedule | | Actual or Revised Dates | |
| Item | Respon-sibility | Start or Submit | Finish or Receive | Start or Submit | Finish or Receive |
|---|---|---|---|---|---|
| Design standard sales forms | | | | | |
| Complete CC&R's, By-Laws, Articles | | | | | |
| Select take-out lender | | | | | |
| Develop standard inclusions and options | | | | | |
| Set price estimates | | | | | |
| Select title company or escrow | | | | | |
| Define warranty and walk through procedures | | | | | |
| Select carpet company | | | | | |
| Define special conditions to be disclosed | | | | | |
| Order and file for commissioner's report | | | | | |
|    A.  Pink report | | | | | |
|    B.  Final white report | | | | | |
| **50-75 Days Before Grand Opening** | | | | | |
| Tour site with executives | | | | | |
| Set up temporary pre-sales office | | | | | |
|    A.  Rent large air-conditioned trailer | | | | | |
|    B.  Flags - temporary | | | | | |
|    C.  Set of floor plans and elevations (colored with see-through ink and displayed on wall | | | | | |
|    D.  Plot plan - temporary | | | | | |

| Item | Responsibility | Basic Schedule Start or Submit | Basic Schedule Finish or Receive | Actual or Revised Dates Start or Submit | Actual or Revised Dates Finish or Receive |
|---|---|---|---|---|---|
| E. Temporary brochures | _____ | _____ | _____ | _____ | _____ |
| F. Temporary price sheets | _____ | _____ | _____ | _____ | _____ |
| G. Order temporary toilet | _____ | _____ | _____ | _____ | _____ |
| H. Order phones | _____ | _____ | _____ | _____ | _____ |
| Approve decorator's model and furniture layout | _____ | _____ | _____ | _____ | _____ |
| Select model interior color schemes | _____ | _____ | _____ | _____ | _____ |
| Order interior color charts | _____ | _____ | _____ | _____ | _____ |
| Select model exterior color schemes | _____ | _____ | _____ | _____ | _____ |
| Approve and order final displays | _____ | _____ | _____ | _____ | _____ |
| A. Plot map | _____ | _____ | _____ | _____ | _____ |
| B. Neighborhood feature map | _____ | _____ | _____ | _____ | _____ |
| C. Area map | _____ | _____ | _____ | _____ | _____ |
| D. Elevations and renderings | _____ | _____ | _____ | _____ | _____ |
| Review and approve ad layouts with agency | _____ | _____ | _____ | _____ | _____ |
| Review model trap layout | _____ | _____ | _____ | _____ | _____ |
| Review and approve radio commercial copy | _____ | _____ | _____ | _____ | _____ |
| Design and order interior merchandising signs for models | _____ | _____ | _____ | _____ | _____ |
| Design and order designation signs | _____ | _____ | _____ | _____ | _____ |
| Seek advertising assistance | _____ | _____ | _____ | _____ | _____ |
| A. Suppliers | _____ | _____ | _____ | _____ | _____ |
| B. Title Company | _____ | _____ | _____ | _____ | _____ |

|  | | Basic Schedule | | Actual or Revised Dates | |
| --- | --- | --- | --- | --- | --- |
| Item | Responsibility | Start or Submit | Finish or Receive | Start or Submit | Finish or Receive |
| C. Utility companies | | | | | |
| D. Other | | | | | |
| Order offsite signs and billboards | | | | | |
| Order flags installed | | | | | |
| Order tot-lot equipment | | | | | |
| Set up complete | | | | | |
| A. Sales manual | | | | | |
| B. Policy manual | | | | | |
| C. Warranty manual | | | | | |
| Receive and review project's soil report | | | | | |
| Salesmen complete | | | | | |
| A. Competitive evaluation sheets | | | | | |
| B. Community fact sheets | | | | | |

**30-40 Days Before Grand Opening**

|  | | | | | |
| --- | --- | --- | --- | --- | --- |
| Plan and order exterior lighting for models | | | | | |
| Start landscaping | | | | | |
| Final check | | | | | |
| A. Newspaper copy | | | | | |
| B. Publicity schedule | | | | | |
| C. Final copy for first ad | | | | | |
| Establish | | | | | |
| A. Final advertising schedule | | | | | |

|  | | Basic Schedule | | Actual or Revised Dates | |
|---|---|---|---|---|---|
| Item | Respon-sibility | Start or Submit | Finish or Receive | Start or Submit | Finish or Receive |
| B. Confirm advertising schedule with newspaper | _____ | _____ | _____ | _____ | _____ |
| C. Confirm spots with radio | _____ | _____ | _____ | _____ | _____ |
| Plan a pre-opening party (catered) for press and VIPs | _____ | _____ | _____ | _____ | _____ |
| Order invitations printed for grand opening party | _____ | _____ | _____ | _____ | _____ |
| Order telephones installed | _____ | _____ | _____ | _____ | _____ |
| Arrange | _____ | _____ | _____ | _____ | _____ |
| A. Interior maintenance | _____ | _____ | _____ | _____ | _____ |
| B. Landscaping maintenance | _____ | _____ | _____ | _____ | _____ |
| Contact personnel managers of local companies | _____ | _____ | _____ | _____ | _____ |
| Order copy machine | _____ | _____ | _____ | _____ | _____ |
| Order installation of sales office merchandising | _____ | _____ | _____ | _____ | _____ |
| Order toilet covers | _____ | _____ | _____ | _____ | _____ |
| Install playground - tot lot | _____ | _____ | _____ | _____ | _____ |
| Hook up utilities in models | _____ | _____ | _____ | _____ | _____ |

**20 Days Before Grand Opening**

| | | | | | |
|---|---|---|---|---|---|
| Have invitation for pre-opening party mailed now for one week prior to grand opening party | _____ | _____ | _____ | _____ | _____ |
| Order "no smoking please" signs for "butt cans" | _____ | _____ | _____ | _____ | _____ |
| Finalize plans for pre-opening party | _____ | _____ | _____ | _____ | _____ |
| Set up bootleg sign program | _____ | _____ | _____ | _____ | _____ |
| A. Cardboard on stakes | _____ | _____ | _____ | _____ | _____ |
| B. Boat trailer or related | _____ | _____ | _____ | _____ | _____ |

|  | | Basic Schedule | | Actual or Revised Dates | |
|---|---|---|---|---|---|
| Item | Respon-sibility | Start or Submit | Finish or Receive | Start or Submit | Finish or Receive |
| Prepare press kits | | | | | |
| Install patios and patio covers | | | | | |
| Install drinking fountain | | | | | |
| Order music installed in sales office and models | | | | | |
| Salesmen are tested for | | | | | |
|    A. Product knowledge | | | | | |
|    B. Competitive knowledge | | | | | |
|    C. Community knowledge | | | | | |
| Prepare a list of all prospects (with addresses) from inquiries | | | | | |

**14 Days Before Grand Opening**

|  | | | | | |
|---|---|---|---|---|---|
| Install carpets, drapes, furniture and temporary carpet protection | | | | | |
| Order prospect cards | | | | | |
| Check sales office for proper set | | | | | |
|    A. Forms | | | | | |
|    B. Sales and policy manuals | | | | | |
|    C. Displays (plot, renderings color boards, map, story | | | | | |
|    D. Final touches on sales office merchandising | | | | | |
|    E. 1. Set up lot files with all necessary forms | | | | | |
|       2. Prepare files for pending deals | | | | | |
|       3. Prepare files for closed deals | | | | | |

| Item | Respon-sibility | Basic Schedule Start or Submit | Finish or Receive | Actual or Revised Dates Start or Submit | Finish or Receive |
|---|---|---|---|---|---|
| F. Finalize Clarification of Contract | | | | | |
| Receive production schedules | | | | | |
| Install model fencing, entry gates and related | | | | | |
| Arrange for hostesses for press party and grand opening | | | | | |
| Distribute grand opening brochures and announcements to | | | | | |
|    A. Local chambers of commerce | | | | | |
|    B. Local business establishments | | | | | |
| Place pre-opening sneak preview ad in newspaper | | | | | |
| Send PR releases to newspaper for grand opening | | | | | |
| Secure office and model keys | | | | | |
| Arrange for photographer for | | | | | |
|    A. Pre-opening party | | | | | |
|    B. Grand opening | | | | | |
| Final clean - models | | | | | |
| Final check for grand opening | | | | | |
| Mail grand opening letter or postcard to all prospects | | | | | |
| Arrange interior option display feature and included signs in models | | | | | |
| Distribute press kits at pre-opening party | | | | | |
| Install all permanent flags and pennants | | | | | |

| Item | Respon-sibility | Basic Schedule Start or Submit | Finish or Receive | Actual or Revised Dates Start or Submit | Finish or Receive |
|---|---|---|---|---|---|
| **3 Days Before Grand Opening** | | | | | |
| Team dinner sales meeting with builder for motivation and last minute "charge" pep talk and discuss grand opening day procedure | ———— | ———— | ———— | ———— | ———— |

## AGREEMENT FOR SALE OF REAL ESTATE— FORM 650

Real estate forms are important. You should have a supply of your own forms. There are many different types available. Most builders who do a certain amount of volume will have their own forms printed and have them drafted by their own attorney. Some of the smaller builders will use a form from a title company or broker's office; others will use whatever form a broker gives him. You do not want to let the broker dictate to you which form you use. It is your contract, your project, and you should know what is in that form. If a broker tries to enforce the use of his form because he feels it has no sales risks and knows he can make a lot more sales with it, the pressure is on you to accept it. You do not have to do that, because you are paying him to do a job. You can tell him what form to use. Tell him that if he is a good salesman, he can sell your product with any form. Make him use one with which you are comfortable.

There has never been a form that cannot be improved. Form 650 is presented as an example of one of the many different sales forms.

### COMPONENTS

In *paragraph one*, be sure that there is an adequate description of what is being built, with an accurate reference to plans and specifications. Problems can arise if the actual house varies from the model. If you are selling unbuilt houses, to be patterned after a model, you have to be sure that what you sell will be an exact duplicate of that model, unless you have a provision in the contract which says that it does not have to be like that model. You will not find such contracts—unless you draft them yourself. So, be sure that there is a proper description, a proper reference to the plans, that the plans are current, and that the plans are, in effect, incorporated by the appropriate governments.

Time Limit.  A portion of *paragraph one* says that the structure must be completed within one year from the date of this agreement; if not so completed, the buyer may terminate by written notice and get his deposit back. You have to have some kind of a termination date. Some forms will not have a set date; they will stipulate completion within a reasonable time, which is to your benefit, if you can manage that. In an up market, that is not a problem. In recent years, because of inflation, it has been financially advantageous to have a buyer back out of an agreement by the time you get through building it because the house will probably be worth $5,000 or $10,000 more than when you signed up. So, that does not become a problem. But when things level off, or if they start going the other way, you want to be careful. The clause that gives you the most flexibility is "complete in a reasonable time." However, there is a weakness in that, because what may be reasonable for one person, may not be reasonable for another, and this is the kind of thing that can lead to some litigation. No one can give you an exact definition of reasonable.

**Price and Options.** In *paragraph three*, fill in your price and your optional items. You may run into a problem here because you do not know what all the items are at the beginning and changes will be made. But, you should do the best you can, initially, to complete it as accurately as possible. The other breakdowns—cash deposits, remainder of purchase price, and cash proceeds—depend, of course, on what type of financing is made on the house. Some people still pay cash and you may not be able to fill this in exactly at the time. Some of the forms are a little simpler than this. If the price is $150,000; $10,000 is put down and the balance at close of escrow. That will do, too. This particular form is so designed to lock in the buyer, but you know that he must qualify first. And you want to be sure that he does not tie up your house for some period of time while he is applying for a loan that he may not get. So if you look at *paragraph four*, it states that he will need to "use his best efforts" to get a loan in the amount he needs. It also defines "best efforts." Any provisions that require somebody to get a loan, if it is going to be enforceable, and this is an important point to remember, has to specify certain basic things, such as *amount of the loan*, *term of the loan*, *interest rate*, and *points* he has to pay.

**Conditions.** Some deposit receipts are conditioned upon the buyer obtaining a loan. This is not sufficient from your standpoint. It gives the buyer a way out because he can say that he did not get a loan. If it says "conditioned upon buyer getting a loan in the amount of 80 percent of the purchase price" but it does not state the interest rate; he can tell you that he got a loan for 80 percent of the purchase price but the interest rate was higher than he wanted to pay. This cannot be enforced. If this contract said 80 percent of the purchase price, two-and-a-half points above prime, or calls for his interest to be whatever it is at time of close of escrow, that is specifying an interest rate.

There should be an objective means of establishing an interest rate. The prevailing rate at close of escrow is as good as saying two-and-a-half above prime or 15 percent or whatever it may be. Having it tied to something makes it a little more enforceable. You will have trouble if it is not specified and if there is no way for a third party (who does not know what the agreement was), to look at this agreement to determine the agreed upon interest rate.

The term of years must be specified. If the buyer can only get a 25-year loan but he wanted a 30-year loan, the contract cannot be enforced. Finally, if he does get the loan, but they want to charge him five points while he will not pay more than two, and you did not have points specified, you have given him a way out. Thus, if a condition of his performance is getting a particular loan, you must cover all of these items.

**Substitute of Materials.** *Paragraph nine* is a good provision to include—but it also requires care. You reserve the right to substitute materials of substantially equal quality as those specified in the plans and specifications. From your standpoint, it is advantageous to have that in there because you would like to have that freedom and flexibility, but there is a practical problem. If someone thought he was going to get a specific dishwasher and you put in another (of better quality) and he objects, then you can tell him to read the contract. Lawyers will advise their clients that it is a good provision and to include it for self-protection. But the builder is going to have to make a business decision as to whether he thinks he can accept the provision. One thing to remember here is that there is no form that cannot be changed at your discretion. You can negotiate with the buyer, and if a buyer is particularly difficult to deal with and does not want such a provision in there, you can cross it out, initial it, and change it for that buyer. There is a certain difficulty in doing that, because if you do it for one person and other people find out, they may ask for the same thing. It is still a good provision to have in your contract because it may be about 90 percent effective and it will do you a lot of good if you need it. It will alleviate the problem of having to install something that was in short supply, discontinued, or happened to cost more than you expected. If you have this provision, you can make a substitution.

**Liquidated Damages.** *Paragraph eleven* is in capital letters. For residential property, the code requires that the statement covering default be in capital letters and in ten-point type. The important thing is that *three percent* is the maximum amount that you can get if your buyer defaults and you want him to forfeit his deposit. The clause must be agreed upon and initialed by both parties. Some forms will state three percent of purchase price. Our form has a blank to be filled in. You just have to be certain that your salesmen know that the amount that goes in there is three percent of the purchase price of the house.

There is a lot of debate about liquidated damage clauses, which is what the three percent forfeit clause is called. The purpose of the clause, supposedly, is to avoid lawsuits. Both parties agree on a certain amount of money and, if there is a breach, that is it. There is some disagreement as to whether it is a good idea to have a liquidated damage clause in the agreement in view of the technical language and the code changes.

Some lawyers say they prefer not to have any clause at all in there—just leave the party to whatever he can prove. If he cannot prove that he was damaged at all, then he has to give the entire deposit back. If he can prove that he was damaged far in excess of three percent, then he can use that. However, some people feel the language of the code is so vague on this point that it leaves it open. Even if you comply with this provision, have a buyer who has defaulted, and there is a suit, the defendant (your buyer) could claim that there really was no damage; the builder resold the house for more money than the agreed price and that it was unconscionable for him to keep the three percent. And there is some indication that when such a case comes to court, under the proper facts, the buyer might win.

Most people are using the liquidated damage clause. Whether they will continue to do so will depend upon what happens in the next few years when some of these cases are tried and go up on appeal. There is a lag time of some three to five years, between the time that a new law such as this goes into effect and a suit is filed, tried, appealed, and decided before everyone understands that law. Often, when the legislature writes the code, it is not explicitly detailed.

**Extras.** Most forms used state that any extra items must be paid for in cash. This went to the builder. This is no longer allowed. Now when people start paying extra for upgrades—i.e., tennis courts, swimming pools, etc.—this money goes into escrow, not to you. Local Departments of Real Estate theory is that you cannot collect anything from a buyer until you have closed escrow, no matter what it is. You can get him to put it into escrow so he has the money, and if you run into problems and he defaults, the money is there. You can try to collect what is left, but you have to go to court. You cannot, however, take it out in advance.

**Color and Material Selections.** *Paragraph fourteen* deals with the selection of colors and materials. Sometimes you may have a buyer who is difficult to reach, and that will hold up proceedings. This provision gives you the right to make those choices; it gives you the legal right. However, you will have a practical problem with certain people if they do not like the tile that you have selected. But at least you have the choice; it is within your control to have this provision in there. If the provision is not in there, you must wait until you can reach them, and it will slow down your schedule.

**Assignment.** *Paragraph fifteen* concerns the assignment. The buyer cannot assign the agreement. This was put in the contract as a result of speculators buying houses and then cashing out on the close without putting up any money. You end up with an unknown third party in the house. This is designed to prevent that from happening, but all it really does, in a practical matter, is require your buyer to delay one day because you cannot stop him from reselling his house. You can stop your warranty from applying to the speculator. You can stop the speculator from the ordinary double escrow if he has no money in it and is relying on the third party to produce the loan and everything else to close the escrow.

You can force the buyer/speculator to acquire his own loan and his own cash in the escrow. Now, if he wants to open another escrow, you cannot stop him; but you can stop him from the one-step escrow, which will eliminate some of these speculators. We had problems with original buyers who would simply put an assignment in escrow. At closing, all the papers were from the new buyer—his loan papers, the deed drawn to him, his note, his deed of trust, etc. If you had this non-assignment clause, you could refuse to recognize your buyer's assignment to the third party because this is a violation of your contract. He would then have to close in his name, have his own instructions, and then get another escrow to close with the third party.

**Homeowners' Association.** *Paragraph sixteen*, of course, may or may not be applicable. This is a form for a PUD with a Homeowners' Association. If you have a standard single-family subdivision without an association, you would not need this provision.

## AGREEMENT FOR SALE OF REAL ESTATE

_____, California

Agreement Date: _____, 19__

RECEIVED by _____ (herein called "Seller") from _____

_____

(hereinafter called "Buyer"), the sum of _____ DOLLARS ($_____) as a deposit to be applied on the purchase price of the real property in the City of _____ described as Lot _____ as shown on the Subdivision Map of Tract No. _____ recorded in Book _____ of Maps at pages _____, official records of _____, California, together with the dwelling constructed or to be constructed thereon. (The lot and dwelling are hereinafter referred to as the "Property" and are part of the _____ Development (which is hereinafter called the "Development"). Seller agrees to sell and Buyer agrees to purchase the Property on the terms and conditions which follow.

### TERMS AND CONDITIONS

1. Seller has built or shall build upon the lot described above a Plan _____ Dwelling, substantially in conformity with the plans and specifications, and amendments thereto, on file with the City of _____, copies of which are located in Seller's office in _____, California; provided that in the event of a conflict between said plans and specifications and any model dwelling inspected by Buyer, said plans and specifications shall control. The dwelling, if not yet built, shall be completed no later than one (1) year from the date of this agreement but, if not so completed, Buyer may terminate this agreement by written notice, in which event all monies deposited by Buyer shall be returned and neither party shall have any further obligations hereunder.

2. This purchase and sale shall close through an escrow at a title insurance company authorized to transact business in the State of California upon ten (10) days notice to Buyer from Seller given after completion of the dwelling and the filing of a Notice of Completion with the County Recorder of _____ County; provided, however, the closing shall occur within one (1) year from and after the date of this agreement.

3. The purchase price for the Property is the sum of _____ _____ DOLLARS determined as follows:

BASE PRICE $ _____

OPTIONAL ITEMS

1. _____ $ _____

2. _____ $ _____

3. _____ $ _____

TOTAL PURCHASE PRICE $ _____

The purchase price shall be paid by Buyer to Seller at the closing of the sale and shall consist of:

(a) $ _____ cash deposit including any reservation fee.

(b) $ _____ remainder of purchase price to be paid by Buyer in cash (excluding closing costs).

(c) $ _____ cash proceeds of a loan made to Buyer pursuant to Paragraph 4 hereof.

_____

_____

_____

4. Immediately upon execution of this agreement, Buyer shall use his best efforts to obtain a loan in the loan amount designated in Paragraph 3 hereof from a lender designated to Buyer. Best efforts of Buyer shall include, but not be limited to, completing and submitting to the proposed lender a loan application and other written and oral information as may be required, disclosure of all facts which bear upon Buyer's ability or inability to obtain a loan, and compliance with and execution of such instruments as may be required by the lender to process and consummate the loan. If any lender to whom Buyer shall submit a loan application refuses to make a loan, Buyer shall likewise apply for a loan to such other lender or lenders who may evidence interest in making the loan. Buyer shall immediately furnish to Seller a copy of loan applications submitted and any loan acceptances received and, at Seller's request, true and correct copies of any other documents executed in connection therewith.

The loan to be made to Buyer shall bear interest at the lender's prevailing rate of interest at the time of closing for that classification of loan, shall be for a term which is customary for such loans and shall be subject to customary rules and regulations of the lender. All charges, costs and expenses payable in connection with the loan shall be paid by Buyer.

If Seller has failed to receive from Buyer or from a lender approved by Seller, written notice of approval of buyer's loan within thirty (30) days after the date of this agreement, Seller shall have the right to terminate this agreement by written notice to buyer in which case Buyer's deposit shall be refunded and neither party shall have any further obligations under this agreement, except Buyer shall pay for any charges incurred by Seller at the request of Buyer including, but not limited to, escrow or title charges and the cost of any optional items selected by Buyer.

5. At the closing of the sale of the Property, upon payment by Buyer in full of the purchase price and such other sums as may be required pursuant to the terms of this agreement, Seller shall convey to Buyer title to the Property by grant deed in condition to be insured by a standard form California Land Title Association policy of title insurance free and clear of all matters of record affecting title, except the lien of real property taxes not delinquent; all covenants, conditions and restrictions; all easements, rights or reservations of rights; and any liens or other matters imposed or suffered by Buyer at the closing of the sale. If seller is unable to convey title in the condition called for above, through no fault of Seller, then Seller shall not be liable to Buyer, but Buyer may terminate the agreement and the deposit of buyer shall be refunded and neither party shall have any further obligation hereunder. Buyer may designate the title insurance company from which he desires to purchase title insurance.

6. Seller shall pay for drawing the deed and the transfer tax on the conveyance. All other costs of the closing of the sale (title insurance, escrow fees, charges made by the lender, recording and notarization fees, etc.) shall be paid by Buyer. Taxes shall be prorated as of the date of delivery of the deed.

7. Seller's failure to have completed the paving and landscaping of the Development prior to the closing of the sale shall not excuse Buyer from taking title to the Property, although Seller's obligation to complete such work shall continue after the closing of the sale.

8. Buyer acknowledges and agrees that Seller is not acting as a contractor for Buyer in this transaction. Instead, Buyer is purchasing a dwelling and lot which are now, or shall be, completed by Seller substantially in accordance with the plans and specifications referred to hereinabove and available for Buyer's inspection.

9. Seller reserves the right to substitute materials, fixtures, equipment and appliances of substantially equal quality as those specified in the plans and specifications. Seller further reserves the right to make changes in construction as may be required from time to time by any lender making loans on the Property or the Development, by an entity or agency insuring, guaranteeing or purchasing loans or assisting in the financing of the Property or the Development, by an governmental law or regulation, by labor or material shortages or stoppages, or by emergencies involving the national defense. Seller may terminate this agreement and refund Buyer's deposit if Seller finds that commencement or continuation of construction of the Development has become impossible or impractical for reasons beyond Seller's control, including, but not limited to, labor or material shortages or stoppages, damage or destruction of the Property or of the Development, war, civil disorder or acts of God.

10. Any materials or equipment left by Seller on any part of the Property shall remain the property of Seller after the closing of the sale and Seller shall have the right to remove such materials and equipment.

11. BUYER AND SELLER, BY INITIALING BELOW, REPRESENT THAT BUYER AND SELLER (THROUGH SELLER'S AGENT) HAVE DISCUSSED THE IMPRACTICALITY AND EXTREME DIFFICULTY OF FIXING THE ACTUAL DAMAGES TO SELLER IN THE EVENT OF BUYER'S DEFAULT. AS A RESULT OF SAID DISCUSSION BUYER AND SELLER HAVE AGREED THAT THE AMOUNT OF $_____ IS A REASONABLE ESTIMATE OF THE ACTUAL DAMAGES WHICH SELLER WOULD INCUR IN THE CASE OF BUYER'S DEFAULT. THEREFORE, IN THE EVENT BUYER SHALL DEFAULT IN THE TIMELY PERFORMANCE OF HIS OBLIGATIONS UNDER THIS AGREEMENT, SELLER MAY TERMINATE THIS AGREEMENT BY WRITTEN NOTICE TO BUYER AND BE RELEASED FROM ITS OBLIGATION TO SELL THE PROPERTY TO BUYER AND MAY RETAIN THE SUM ABOVE DESIGNATED AS SELLER'S SOLE RIGHT TO DAMAGES.

BUYER INITIAL: _____    SELLER INITIAL: _____

12. Buyer realizes and acknowledges that ENTRY UPON THE DEVELOPMENT DURING CONSTRUCTION CAN BE DANGEROUS AND THAT HAZARDS MAY EXIST WHICH ARE NOT OBSERVABLE. BUYER'S ENTRY SHALL BE SOLELY AT HIS OWN RISK. Buyer does hereby waive any and all claims against Seller for any injury or loss to persons or property arising out of or in connection with such entry by Buyer or any other person accompanying him or entering at his direction, and Buyer shall defend and hold Seller harmless from and against any injury, loss, damage or expense to persons or property arising out of or in connection with any such entry.

13. At the closing Seller shall execute and deliver to Buyer the form of homeowner's warranty against defects in workmanship and materials which is attached hereto. BUYER AGREES TO ACCEPT SAID HOMEOWNER'S WARRANTY AT THE CLOSING IN LIEU OF ALL OTHER WARRANTIES WHATSOEVER, WHETHER EXPRESS OR IMPLIED BY LAW. The making of final payment by Buyer to Seller of the purchase price shall constitute a waiver and complete release of all claims by Buyer against Seller with respect to the Dwelling and this Agreement, except those as to which Seller is notified in writing and which are expressly covered by said homeowner's warranty. BUYER HEREBY ACKNOWLEDGES RECEIPT OF A SAMPLE COPY OF SELLER'S WARRANTY.

14. Buyer shall make selection of colors, materials and optional items (to the extent Seller permits such selection to be made) and pay any additional costs therefor, when requested to do so by Seller. If Buyer fails to make selections within ten (10) days after Seller's request, Seller may install colors and materials of Seller's choice.

15. Buyer cannot assign this agreement and any act in derogation hereof shall be null and void. Subject to this limitation this agreement shall inure to the benefit of, and be binding upon, the heirs, successors and assigns of the parties hereto.

16. Buyer understands that he is purchasing a dwelling in a planned development and that at the time he receives title to the Property he will automatically become a member of the _____ Association. Membership in the Association is mandatory for owners in the Development. The activities of the Association are fully described in the declaration of covenants, conditions and restrictions affecting the Development and the Bylaws of the Association, copies of which are available

from Seller. In general, the Association is responsible for the operation, maintenance and repair of the common areas, including landscaping and any recreational amenities. THE ASSOCIATION IS EMPOWERED TO LEVY ASSESSMENTS AGAINST ALL OWNERS FOR THE PURPOSE OF PERFORMING THESE AND OTHER DUTIES AND THESE ASSESSMENTS CONSTITUTE A LIEN ON THE PROPERTY.

  17. The provisions of this agreement shall continue beyond the closing of the sale and shall not merge in the deed delivered to Buyer. In this agreement, words used in the singular shall include the plural and words used in the masculine gender shall include the feminine and neuter. This agreement and the warranty described above constitute the entire agreement between the parties. NO REPRESENTATIONS, UNDERTAKINGS OR PROMISES, WHETHER ORAL, IMPLIED OR OTHERWISE, HAVE BEEN MADE BY SELLER TO BUYER UNLESS EXPRESSLY STATED HEREIN.

EXCEPTIONS: _____
    (Buyer to indicate; if none write "none" above.)

No amendments or modifications of this Agreement (including agreements for changes in construction or "Extras") shall be valid unless in writing and executed by both parties.

Buyer:            Seller:

_____

_____

Address _____  By _____
                (Its duly authorized agent)

Telephone _____

Salesman _____  Date _____

## COLOR SCHEDULES AND CHANGE ORDERS

Color schedules and change orders are forms used in the field, at the job site, that are generated and filled out by another department. Depending upon the project, they could be initiated by management or by the sales, architectural, or decorating department. In most cases, a buyer is involved and the cards are filled in with his/her requested colors and materials by the sales staff. This is the case in almost all subdivision and townhouse projects.

These forms are time-oriented. They must be in the field and out to the various subcontractors in time for ordering and scheduling, and they must be retained by the field superintendent for easy reference. He will need to check colors, materials, extras, and changes as the job progresses. This must be done in an orderly and efficient manner. The schedules, cards, and forms presented here are the time-proven method used by many major builders. They are easy to fill out and easy to read. They must be accurate and current and they must be dated and signed.

The forms must be completed and dated no later than the thirtieth (30) day of construction, which means the building will not yet be in the drywall stage. All free or uncompensated changes or alterations to the selections must be limited, if not entirely prohibited, beyond this point.

The subcontractors need this time to order and stock the ceramic tile, paint, carpet, linoleum, stucco color, masonry, and whatever other items are made available for customer selection. It is only fair that they be given as much time as possible to order these items without the possibility of changes.

The person making the decision on the color selection schedule must sign it. He is thereby attesting to the fact that these are his selections and that he agrees that there will be no changes.

The color selection and change order form package consists of the three forms that follow. The information from these forms must be sent to each subcontractor affected and a master sheet sent to the field.

### EXTERIOR COLOR SELECTIONS—FORM 660

If you are dealing with a PUD or townhouse project, you would not have exterior color selections as they would be part of your master planning and city/county approval. However, in single-family tracts, where you are offering up to three elevations per model and perhaps two or three color schemes per elevation, this becomes extremely important so that it may be coordinated in the field.

### INTERIOR COLOR SCHEDULE—FORM 670

This form is laid out for residential projects and, with some modification, it can be used for commercial and industrial jobs. The important points in any form of this type are that they are complete and correct. The job address, the tract, and lot number are just as important as the rest of the form. Above all, you should counsel and advise your client on *dye lot variations*. The color or sample on the board from which he is choosing, may, and usually does—especially in the case of some imported ceramic tile—vary from the material that he will receive.

## FIELD-COLOR SCHEDULE CARD—FORM 680

Form 680 is a 8½"-x-11" card which is sent to your superintendent or production man in the field and is his constant reminder of the parts that are necessary to make the house whole.

We have found that a three-ring binder or clipboard holding 50 of these cards is an invaluable asset in the field. As soon as the buyer has related his choice of colors, exteriors, extras, options, etc., management immediately sends the card to the field for inclusion in the aforementioned notebook. This affords the production man the opportunity of a fingertip review of any and all items that should be encompassed in a building during construction.

So many times the field is not made aware of the changes, extras, and colors; and a tremendous amount of money is spent redoing tile, carpets, and appliances, all because the office did not relay the message to the field. By using these forms, or similar ones, you will not encounter these costs.

# 660

## EXTERIOR COLOR SELECTIONS

| Tract Name | | | Tract No. | Lot No. | Plan No. | Elev. | 2-Car Garage ☐ |
|---|---|---|---|---|---|---|---|
| | | | | | | | 3-Car Garage ☐ |

| Ext. Color Scheme No. | Stucco No. | Fire-Place Style | Brick Type | | Yes No |
|---|---|---|---|---|---|
| | | | | Air Conditioning | ☐ ☐ |
| | | | | Wet Bar | ☐ ☐ |
| | | | | Mirrored Wardrobe Doors | ☐ ☐ |
| Paint Color No. | | | | No. of Bedrooms _____ | |
| Stain No. | | | | | |
| Base Siding No. | | | | | |

Approvals:

_____
Sales

_____
Date

_____
Buyer

_____
Date

| Date Received | Date Mailed |
|---|---|
| | |

## NOTES

**670**

## INTERIOR COLOR SCHEDULE

| Builder | | Tract Name | Tract No. |
|---|---|---|---|
| | Lot Number | Plan No. | Elev. | Date |
| Selected By: | | Garage | |

These color selections are final and no changes can be made after this date.

| Room | | Floor | |
|---|---|---|---|
| Living Room | | | |
| Halls | | | |
| Entry | | | |
| Dining Room | | | |
| Family Room | | | |
| Bed Rm. No. 1 | | | |
| Bed Rm. No. 2 | | | |
| Bed Rm. No. 3 | | | |
| Bed Rm. No. 4 | | | |
| Bed Rm. No. 5 | | | |

Your materials and color selections may vary in color, size and texture from samples utilized in your selection. In addition, there may be some inconsistencies in these same elements in your completed home.

Acknowledged By:

_____
Buyer

_____
Buyer

_____
Date

| | | | | Ceramic Tile | Hardware | Appliance |
|---|---|---|---|---|---|---|
| Den | | | | | | |
| Kitchen | | | | | | |
| Nook | | | | | | |
| Bath (Tub) | | | | | | |
| Bath (Shower) | | | | | | |
| Bath No. 3 | | | | | | |
| Laundry Room | | | | Distribution: | | |
| | | | Bar Top | | | |

# NOTES

## FIELD–COLOR SCHEDULE CARD

560/680

| Tract Name & Number | Lot No. | Plan No. | Elev. |
|---|---|---|---|
| | | | |

### INTERIOR COLOR SCHEDULE

| Room | Paint Walls | Paint Ceilg. | Paint Trim | Floors | Room | Paint Walls | Paint Ceilg. | Paint Trim | Floors |
|---|---|---|---|---|---|---|---|---|---|
| Living | | | | | Bdrm. 1 | | | | |
| Halls | | | | | Bdrm. 2 | | | | |
| Entry | | | | | Bdrm. 3 | | | | |
| Dining | | | | | Bdrm. 4 | | | | |
| Family | | | | | Bdrm. 5 | | | | |
| Den | | | | | Bath #1 | | | | |
| Kitchen | | | | | Bath #2 | | | | |
| Nook | | | | | Bath #3 | | | | |
| Garage | | | | | Laundry | | | | |

Doors: Int. _____ Front _____ Other Int. _____ Gar. _____ Ext. _____
Cabinets: Kit. _____ Bath _____ Bars _____ Other _____
Counter Tops: Kit. _____ Bath 1 _____ Bath 2 _____ Bath 3 _____ Other _____
Appliances: _____
Hardware: _____
Light Fixtures: _____

### EXTERIOR COLOR SCHEDULE

Exterior Color: Body _____ Trim _____ Gar Dr _____ Front Dr _____ Ext Dr _____
Stucco # _____ Masonry Veneer _____ Fireplace Style _____

### OPTIONAL ITEMS TO BE ADDED

| Extra | Yes | No | Extra | Yes | No |
|---|---|---|---|---|---|
| Air Conditioning | | | | | |
| Mirrored Ward. Doors | | | | | |
| Wet Bar | | | | | |

NOTES

# CHANGE ORDER—FORM 690

In subdivision tract homes and in townhouse projects there are usually very few, if any, changes allowed; especially buyer-instigated changes.

In custom contract, speculation building, commercial and, to a lesser degree, industrial construction, changes do occur and sometimes quite extensively.

In a seller's market there are few changes, because the seller needs to make no concessions to sell the product. In a buyer's market there can be many such changes and sometimes they are paid for by the seller.

If there are changes, corrections, additions, or deletions for any reason, there is a correct procedure to follow. The purpose of this process is:

1. To clarify the change and define the work in writing.
2. To provide a method of notifying all parties and documenting transmittal of the change order.
3. To agree to cost and/or terms.
4. To formalize the transaction by signatures and dates of agreement.

The whole thing is quite simple—so simple that it all too often does not get done. If you do not have good records, you may have trouble trying to substantiate a claim six months later. It will be difficult to defend your position that it was not part of the original agreement or that the cost is what you say it is.

It is best to have no changes at all. The next best thing would be to have changes paid for at the time they are ordered, with funds impounded in escrow.

The best routing procedure is to send written work orders (at the time the change order is signed, and acknowledged with a follow-up at the time the work is scheduled) to the field and to the subcontractor and/or material supplier involved.

The one major problem with extras or changes is that they are beyond the normal scheduled procedure and, because of this, they tend to be overlooked. Changes are a potential problem and the solution is coordination and communication.

# CHANGE ORDER

690

_____
CONTRACTOR

_____

_____
DATE

Job Location _____

Buyer's Name _____
_____

Subcontractor or supplier _____
_____

Work to be changed _____
_____
_____
_____
_____
_____
_____

Is plan change involved  ☐ yes   ☐ no   _____

**Charge or Reduction:**   ☐ add on   ☐ deduct   _____

$_____ Dollars   /100   ($        .      )

**Charge To:**

    Buyer - paid in full at time ordered, funds impounded in escrow _____
_____

    ☐ Builder   ☐ No charge   ☐ Other _____

Notification given to:

    ☐ Buyer   ☐ Sales   ☐ Field   ☐ Subcontractor   ☐ Lender

    ☐ Accounting Dept.   ☐ Other _____

This agreement executed on day and year first written above:

Buyer:                              Contractor:

_____            _____

_____            _____

# NOTES

# 7

# Warranty and Follow-Through

## WARRANTY

The warranty of the finished product is usually a personal thing with each builder. Most builders accept warranties as a necessary fact of life and they know they must honor it to the legal limits. Understandably, they are adverse to publicizing that the buyer can call any time for repairs due to defective workmanship and/or materials for one year, or the three years and longer now in effect in some states. They know that some buyers will and do take advantage of this privilege or obligation.

Most builders, especially the larger ones, are of the opinion that if the warranty is spelled out and agreed to at the time of purchase, much misunderstanding, ill feeling, time, and cost can possibly be avoided at a later date. They also know to limit complaints, except for emergencies, to written requests only. Emergencies can be reported by telephone during normal business hours.

A few words about warranty items:

1. They do not take care of themselves.
2. There is no substitute for doing it right the first time. If your repair people are quick, courteous, efficient, and on time, that service will go a long way towards maintaining your reputation and good customer relations.
3. Effective quality control during construction and a good cleanup before walk-through should cut warranty items to less than five.

258 / Warranty and Follow-Through

4. Prompt scheduling and communication is the fast way to get it done and off your books.

## WARRANTY CHECKLIST—FORM 700

Form 700 is a suggested checklist of items to include in a warranty form. There is a great deal of latitude in what can be included and the tolerances you are willing to concede. There are industry standards for wood products and manufactured items. The warranty must be credible. It is well to quote standards if you are going to work within their limits.

The warranty agreement does two things:

1. It tells your buyer what items you will repair and the standards you will follow.
2. It sets company policy and serves as a reference.

It is imperative that you have legal counsel on this extremely important part of the building process. It must be someone who is experienced in construction and, specifically, in contracts and warranties. The actual One-Year Warranty Form 705 that follows Form 700 was written by John Paul Hanna, who is one of the leading real estate attorneys in the state of California. He is the author of two books on real estate law and is an expert on warranty problems as they relate to the builder.

If there is any one chapter of this book on the building process that is more important than any other, this is it. Warranty work has discouraged more builders, given more ulcers, and sent more businessmen to other sectors of the profession—such as specializing in commercial or industrial—than all other problems combined. The warranty limits must be spelled out and the builder's exposure limited (the key word is *limit*) and that is the express purpose of the warranty form.

# WARRANTY CHECKLIST

CONTRACTOR _____

DATE _____

Address _____
Lot _____ Block _____ Tract _____ Job # _____
Buyer _____

I  **General Requirements**
Your Warranty Agreement could include, but not be limited to, the items in the following checklist. The final agreement should be provided or approved by your legal counsel.

    A. Warrantee period stated: number of years (one) (two) (three)
        Commencing when: close of escrow or occupancy, whichever is first.

    B. Method of repair - at builder's option: repair or replace.

    C. General exclusions: misuse  accident  normal wear/tear
        normal maintenance  casualties due to the elements

    D. Inspection by Buyer: walk-through inspection
        compliance inspection form

    E. Quality Standards

II  **Site Work**

    Yard accumulated water cannot drain toward and/or against foundation.

    Maximum settling of utility ditches 6 inches - repair to be made only once; builder not responsible for landscaping.

III  **Concrete**

    A. <u>Foundation</u>: nonstructural cracks less than 1/8 inch in width are considered normal. Cracks in excess of this to be repaired.

    B. <u>Slabs in habitable areas</u>: cracks 3/16 inch in width or less or 1/8 inch vertical displacement are considered normal. Cracks in excess of this to be repaired.

    C. <u>Slabs in nonhabitable areas</u>: (Garage, driveway, stoops, steps, walks, patios) - cracks 1/4 inch in width or less or 1/4 inch vertical displacement are considered normal. Cracks in excess of this to be repaired.

IV    **Masonry:** Nonstructural cracks less than 1/8 inch in width are considered normal. Cracks in excess of this are to be repaired.

V    **Conveyors and Equipment Elevators, Dumbwaiters:** covered by manufacturer's warranty or as each specific case requires.

VI    **Lumber and Millwork:**

    A.    Floors: warrantee covers
excessively squeaky floors that can be reasonably repaired.
by some codes floor slope cannot be more than 1/240 of room width or exceed 1/4 inch out of level in any 32 inch run.

    B.    Moldings, trim and millwork: cracks 1/8 inch or less will be considered normal shrinkage, cracks or openings greater than 1/8 inch will be repaired.

    C.    Exterior trim: cracks 1/4 inch or less not effecting weather control will be considered normal shrinkage. Cracks or openings greater than 1/4 inch will be repaired.

VII    **Thermal, Moisture Protection and Roof**

    A.    No water leak is acceptable if caused by work under the contractor's responsibility. This includes foundations, walls, roofs, windows, doors.

    B.    Air leaks are to be sealed off and minimized with caulking, flashing, weatherstripping.

    C.    Roof - roof and flashings leaks will be repaired.

VIII    **Doors and Windows**

    A.    interior wood doors warped more than 1/4 inch will be repaired or replaced.

    B.    Exterior wood doors warped more than 1/2 inch will be repaired or replaced - minor cracking will not be repaired.

    C.    Metal windows and doors should operate relatively easily without excessive air leakage.

IX    **Finishes**

    A.    Stucco: cracks greater than 1/16 inch are considered other than hairline cracks and will be repaired.

    B.    Drywall: nail pops and cracks due to normal shrinkage will be repaired one time. Defects caused by poor workmanship, blisters, excessive trowel marks, bad joints and corner beads will be repaired.

    C.    Ceramic Tile: grout problems caused by shrinkage and normal movement will be repaired one time during first year. Cracked or loose tile not caused by homeowner will be replaced with diligent effort but no guarantee of exact match.

D. Resilient Floor Covering: readily apparent ridges or depressions exceeding 1/16 inch - 3 inches on each side; bubbles, seams, width gaps greater than 1/16 inch, and scuffs, mars, stains, scratches noted before move-in shall be repaired or replaced with diligent efffort but no guarantee of exact match.

E. Painting: blistering, peeling, flaking, holidays or insufficient coverage, along with stains or soiling noted on inspection list will be repaired.

X  Specialties
Fireplace: must draw properly.

XI  Equipment

A. Kitchen Cabinets: doors and drawers to be adjusted properly, finish mars to be repaired.

B. Counter tops: delaminations, cracks, chips, mars noted on inspection list will be repaired.

XII, XIII, XIV  We are following the standard CSI format and these catagories do not apply.

XV  Mechanical

A. Plumbing: any leak in soil waste vent or waterpipe other than that caused by condensation will be repaired if reported within the warranty period. Faucet and valve leaks 30 days after inspection caused by worn or defective washers are not covered. Hot water heater is covered by the manufacturer's warrantee, and is not covered by this warrantee. Fixtures, appliances and fittings: mars, nicks or malfunctions noted on inspection to be repaired. Sewer: clogs and stoppages caused by the owner are not covered and will result in a charge back.

B. Heating and Air-conditioning
 1. Heating: the system must be capable of maintaining an inside temperature of $70°F$. measured at the center of each room 5 feet above the floor. As specified in ASHRAE handbook.
 2. Air-conditioning: the system must be capable of maintaining a temperature of $78°F$. measured at the center of each room 5 feet above the floor. As specified in ASHRAE handbook.
 3. Furnace and cooling system are covered by the manufacturer and not by this warrantee. It is the buyer's responsibility to clean filters and perform normal maintenance. In the event of a malfunction the service department of the heating and air-conditioning contractor should be notified.

XVI  Electrical: defective fixtures, outlets, switches and wiring will be repaired or replaced.

Acknowledged by:

_____    _____
Contractor        Date      Purchaser        Date

## WARRANTY AGREEMENT

There has been much debate over the years as to whether or not there should be a warranty agreement. Everyone knows there have been warranty agreements on automobiles and appliances for years and years. What people do not realize is that a lot of them are not worth the paper they are written on. The warranty form that General Motors used for years in California was effectively unenforceable. The General Motors form calls for twelve months or 12,000 miles. If you have a problem at fifteen months or 15,999 miles, you may still have a claim, as their warranty agreement does not comply with the law exactly.

Any warranty agreement that fails to meet the requirements of the law is only good as a psychological weapon. If you give someone something that appears to be the sum total of his legal rights, he will not bother you if the terms run out. There is some value to such a form. But, you do not want a form like that if you are going to have trouble using it. You want to have one that will be good if it comes to a legal battle.

## BUILDER'S LIABILITY EXTENDED

The courts have been extending the frontiers of builder's liability in many states on a regular basis. There is a statute of limitation, which is ten years, for latent defects. Latent defects refers to something that is not open and obvious, something hidden. For example, radiant heating pipes may burst beneath concrete slabs seven years after you sold the house. With the statute of limitations being ten years, you are liable. A myth surrounds a one-year warranty. It is the unwritten one-year warranty rule. Many people assume that there really is such a thing as a one-year warranty and that it is honored by contractors, subcontractors, developers, and buyers. It does not exist.

## TWO KINDS OF WARRRANTIES

There are two kinds of warranties: express warranties, which refers to those which are written and signed, such as the one that follows (Form 705); and implied warranties, which include those imposed legally. The statute states that there is a ten-year statute of limitations on major defects. This means there is an implied warranty that runs for at least ten years. It assures a buyer that the house you built is going to be good for the purpose of residence and that it was built to reasonable standards. If it is not, the buyer may make a claim.

An express warranty calls for, in effect, a definition of the areas of liability and the terms under which you are going to be liable. It is limited to that if it is agreed upon and signed. There are no other warranties outside of this document. You may have an inclination to make the terms as short as possible, make the warranty as brief as possible, and cover the minimum number of things that must be done. There is a danger here, because if you go too far and make this agreement too one-sided, the court may throw it out and say you took advantage of the buyer. The court may find your contract so tough that it is unconscionable and it may not allow you to enforce it against him. In the end, you will pay for the defect you excluded in your warranty. So, you must find the line, which will protect you as far as it can go, and try not to overstep those bounds. It is often difficult to find that "magic line," and even harder to put yourself on the "safe side." There are a great variety of warranty forms that are starting to surface now. These are relatively new instruments in the home-building industry.

## ONE-YEAR WARRANTY—FORM 705

The One-Year Warranty form is typical of many. It can be improved upon, as can any form. It goes into quite a bit of detail about various things which are covered and various things that are not covered. The first thing you want to do is make the basic decision. Do you want to have a warranty on your home at all—or just forget about it and leave it up to the courts? If you want to have a warranty, what terms do you want? This happens to be a one-year warranty form. Some people will advise going two or three years. Why? To make you seem more reasonable in court if a buyer or a group of homeowners sue you. You want to appear as reasonable as possible to that judge and jury, and if you have a very tough one-year warranty, you may be in trouble. If you have a reasonable two- or three-year warranty, you will look better but, of course, you have that additional exposure for two or three years. These are important things to consider when you are making your basic decisions.

The second thing you have to consider is how detailed do you want to be in your warranty form? How many things do you want to cover? Read Form 705 through and decide whether it contains more or less what you would like to have in your particular agreement.

The third thing you have to do is tailor this form to your project. There are some things in this form that would be applicable to some projects and other things you might want to include for another project. Over a period of time, people who stay in the building business will finally develop their own systems and their own forms. They will use them with confidence.

### PROVISIONS

You will notice that the form is for a one-year term. There is a notice provision, which is important and can be found in any warranty agreement. It states that you must be notified within a certain period of time of the nature of the defect. It is important that the form exclude anything that is not your fault, which, conversely, is the fault of someone else, including the buyer. It does not cover defects caused by misuse, accident, negligence, normal wear and tear, etc., or defects caused by manufacturer's, or other warranties (that is an important point, because you do not want double coverage).

**Buyer's Inspection.** The inspection is the key to your warranty (*see* first boldface paragraph, "Inspection by Purchaser"). You must have a walk-through, a checklist, and a detailed inspection. This is not something you want to rush through. You want to be sure that the buyer takes the proper amount of time and that you list everything, because that list is your protection and you want to be sure that it is right. You are not trying to get out of doing the pick-up work. You are trying to get out of having to do things which were caused by movers, children, dogs, etc. You want to be as sure as he is that you have listed every visible defect in that house.

There are provisions in the form for visible surface defects, such as foundations, concrete walks, floors, lumber, and mill work. These all have to do with shrinkage, cracking, movement, and all the normal things that crop up. You want to indicate to the buyer that you will take care of these things, within limits, but that he has to accept a certain amount of cracks, shrinkage, slight warping—that is normal. If you have that in the form and you tell him it is normal and he agrees to it, then you will save yourself a lot of problems later on. The buyer may genuinely want to have the house just perfect. We know a perfect house does not exist.

This form goes into detail on the various plumbing, electrical, and heating systems. You may want to tailor these sections to your particular development. If you have air conditioning, you may want to include that, too.

**Roof Warranty.** Some people claim that a one-year warranty on a roof really is not long enough. What if the roof leaks after two or three years, and it is a bad leak? If you exclude anything after the first year of the warranty, you might find yourself with a problem if there is a leak two years later. The buyer will take you to court and you may have to spend $5,000 to put on a new roof. This is one of the areas in which you have to waiver. Apply a one-year warranty to everything except the roof, and warranty that to three years. It makes you look a little better, and it is probably a little bit more realistic. But, you have to decide whether it is worth doing that from a business standpoint. You will have added exposure, but you have also made it a more saleable form to the judge or jury.

**Warranty After Sale.** The resale of the dwelling is a key point. Some people will say that the warranty is transferable on resales. This form does. Others will say it is only good for the first buyer. The people who say it is only good for the first buyer are doing it for obvious reasons. They want to cut off their liabilities as soon as possible. They know a certain number of homes are going to be sold within that year. But you are going to have the same problem. You may find that the buyer sold the house three weeks after he moved in because of hardship. He lived in it for three weeks, the roof leaks, and your nontransferable clause waives the warranty. The judge will say, "That's ridiculous. It leaks after six weeks? What's this roof for?" And you might say, "That's not in accordance with the contract." You will be faced with a long and expensive appeal and you will probably end up fixing the roof. So that is another thing you have to think about, whether you want to try to cut it off or make it transferable. Remember that it is only for the maximum of one year; it does not start a new one-year period. Between the two choices, we favor making the warranty transferable, whatever your period is.

**Nonwarrantive Conditions.** There is a list of nonwarrantive conditions in the final paragraph and there are 11 items listed. It could be 50 items or 100 items, but you should read that list and think about whether it is as long as you want it to be or whether it is too narrow and requires additions.

705

## ONE-YEAR WARRANTY

To: _____
                    Purchaser(s)
Community: _____
Lot/Unit Number: _____
Street Address: _____

The Building Company warrants the dwelling constructed at the above-described location against defects in the original material and workmanship for one (1) full year from the date of the closing of the purchase of the Dwelling or the date of occupancy by you, whichever occurs first (the "Warranty Period"), subject to the terms and provisions of this Warranty.

The Building Company will repair or replace, at its option, and at no charge, any component of the Dwelling which shall be found to be defective. All claims for correction of defects must be made within the Warranty Period by written notice addressed and mailed to the builder at the address set forth below, to the attention of the "Customer Service Department."

This Warranty does not cover (i) defects caused by misuse, accidents, negligent maintenance, normal wear and tear, casualties due to the elements, (ii) normal seasonal and other maintenance, and (iii) defects covered by manufacturers' or other warranties.

This Warranty is given and accepted in lieu of all other warranties or guaranties whatsoever, whether express or implied by law, or written or oral. This Warranty does not extend to incidental or consequential damages or injuries, including but not limited to, loss of usage, inconvenience or damage to persons or property.

**Inspection By Purchaser:** By your execution of this Warranty, you acknowledge that you have inspected the Dwelling and are thoroughly familiar with its condition. You further acknowledge that you have completed with a representative of the Building Company a list (the "Inspection List") of all visible surface defects which were present at the time of that inspection and such other defects as were apparent at inspection.

**Visible Surface Defects:** Visible surface defects are serious defects in finished surfaces, evident upon superficial examination. Examples are chipped, scratched, cracked or broken windows, mirrors or shower doors; chipped or scratched appliances, bathtubs or washbowls; scratched, gouged or scuffed flooring; stained or dirty carpeting; stained, scratched, gouged or dented walls, ceilings, doors or trim. Visible surface defects present upon inspection are covered by this Warranty <u>provided</u> they are noted on the Inspection List. <u>Visible surface defects not noted on the Inspection List are deemed to have occurred after transfer of title and are not covered by this Warranty.</u>

**Foundations:** Due to natural movement of soil and other conditions as well as to the natural shrinkage that takes place in concrete when it receives its final set, it is inevitable that minor cracks will appear in the foundation. The structural strength of the Dwelling is not adversely affected significantly by such minor cracks and it is unnecessary to repair them. The Builder does not warrant concrete foundations against such minor cracking. The Builder does warrant against leakage or seepage through walls, floors or cracks which may develop during the Warranty Period.

**Concrete Walks, Garage Floors, Driveways, Steps, Patios:** Concrete walks and garage floors, driveways, steps and patios are apt to settle and develop cracks. Minor cracking due to expansion and contraction is unavoidable and is not covered by this Warranty. However, if during the Warranty Period the concrete surface becomes unserviceable due to abnormal settling or cracking, the Builder will repair or replace said exterior concrete.

**Lumber and Millwork:** Some shrinkage of wood in the joists, studding, framing and rafters in your home is inevitable, and consequently some mouldings or trim may shift from their original position, joints in the woodwork may open, doors may warp, and cracks may appear in drywall. Wood is not affected by heat or cold, but it will shrink under extreme dryness as it loses moisture and swell under extreme humidity as it absorbs moisture. This characteristic of wood may cause joints in millwork to develop separations or gaps in the winter season. This minor shrinkage and expansion is to be expected and does not constitute any defect in material or workmanship.

**Interior Walls:** Minor cracks or nail pops may appear, due to normal shrinkage of lumber and/or normal settlement of the Dwelling. The Builder warrants the repair of these cracks or nail pops only. The Builder will, within the Warranty Period, return to your home one time and make these repairs.

**Interior Doors:** Interior doors which maintain more than one-quarter (1/4) inch of warp are considered defective and will be repaired or replaced.

**Exterior Doors:** Some warping of exterior doors is to be expected because of the differences between interior and exterior humidity. If an exterior door warps one-half (1/2) inch or more during the Warranty Period and does not straighten out to an acceptable tolerance during the summer, it will be repaired or replaced.

Normal shrinkage or warping may cause minor cracks to develop in wood door surfaces or panels. Such minor cracking or checking is not cause for replacement or repair. This Warranty, as it applies to exterior doors, is limited to those defects expressly described in this paragraph.

**Floors:** This Warranty covers extreme nail or seam popping, cracked or loose tile or linoleum, or imperfections in the subflooring. It further covers scratches, gouges, heel marks or other visible surface defects, provided they are noted in the Inspection List. Because shade, feel, and color will vary within each production run of a manufacturer's tile or linoleum, and may also vary as a result of use, cleaning and waxing, we cannot assure color match in case of repair or replacement.

**Plumbing:** The plumbing system and fixtures originally installed in your home are warranted as to proper function, with the following qualifications:

1. Thirty (30) days after inspection, leaking or dripping faucets are no longer the Builder's responsibility but are your responsibility and can easily be repaired by the installation of a new washer.

2. The hot water heater installed in the Dwelling is covered by a manufacturer's warranty, a copy of which has been supplied to you, and the hot water heater is accordingly not covered by this Warranty.

**Electrical System:** The electrical system and fixtures originally installed in your home are warranted as to proper function. Appliances and other electrical equipment connected to the system at outlets are not considered part of the electrical system and are covered elsewhere in this Warranty.

**Heating and Cooling Systems:** Heating and cooling systems, both central and individual room units, are warranted by the manufacturer and are consequently not covered by this Warranty. A copy of the manufacturer's warranty has been delivered to you. That warranty is contingent upon regular cleaning of filters, normal maintenance and periodic lubrication of motors in accordance with the instructions located near the furnace and cooling systems. In the event of any defects in the cooling or heating systems, the service department of the heating or cooling contractor should be notified.

**Countertops and Vanity Tops:** Serious scratches are covered by this Warranty provided they are noted on the Inspection List. Vanities and countertops are guaranteed against defects in workmanship and material during the Warranty Period. They are not guaranteed against burns or damage from frozen food.

**Roofs:** The roof, roof flashing, gutters and downspouts (if included) are guaranteed during the Warranty Period to be free from leaks or defects. They are not guaranteed against natural disasters or casualties beyond the control of the Builder. This warranty is void as to the items covered in this paragraph in the event the roof is used for any activity or if any structure or appurtenance is attached to the roof in such a way as to impair its structural or functional integrity.

**Appliances:** Appliances are guaranteed and/or warranted by the manufacturer and are not covered by this Warranty. All contact should be made with the service department of each manufacturer.

**Paint—Wood Siding:** The paint used inside and outside your home is of a type and quality appropriate to its use, and its application is warranted to be consistent with accepted standards of good workmanship. This Warranty covers blistering, peeling or flaking during the warranty period. It also covers serious smudges, stains or other soiling, <u>provided</u> they are noted on the Inspection List.

Paint will gradually change color with time, as no paint is completely color-stable when exposed to light, air and varying temperature and humidity. The Builder does not warrant against such color change. Wood siding is expected to change color with time.

**Expendable Items:** The Builder does not make any guarantee concerning expendable items which have been installed in the Dwelling, such as, but not limited to, light bulbs, fluorescent light, weatherstripping, or glass and glazing.

**Resale of Dwelling:** This Warranty is transferrable upon resale of the Dwelling, and will continue in effect for the balance of the Warranty period <u>provided</u> the original owners notify the Builder in writing that they have transferred their remaining rights and obligations under the Warranty to the new owners, not later than fourteen days after transfer of title.

**Non-Warrantable Conditions:**

1. The undersigned shall not be responsible or liable for any consequential or secondary damages and/or losses which may arise from or out of any and all defects including, but not limited to, personal injury or damage to personal property.

2. Prior to completion, any labor and/or material furnished by the lot/unit owner which is not included in the total contract price or which is part of any allowance and is paid for by the lot/unit owner, is excluded from this warranty.

3. Any addition, alteration, remodeling, and/or repair performed by or under the supervision of the lot/unit owner which has an adverse affect on any warrantable condition shall invalidate the warranty as to such warrantable condition.

4. Consumer Products: "Consumer Products" (as such term is used and defined by the Federal Trade Commission) including but not limited to any tangible personal property which is distributed in commerce and which is normally used for personal, family, or household purposes (including any such property intended to be installed in any real property without regard to whether it is so attached or installed) which are covered by the Magnuson-Moss Warranty act when sold as part of a home are EXCLUDED from this Limited Warranty.

5. Discoloration, non-uniformity of, or appearance of brick.

6. Marble: (man-made) variation in color or appearance of marble is a normal condition.

7. Broken glass.

8. Spots on carpeting not recognized on pre move-in inspection. Minor fading due to variety of exposure to light and slight dye lot variance.

9. Plumbing stoppage due to foreign material being deposited in line by occupants.

10. Service company meter problems, service lines installed by the undersigned, municipality or service company and earth, sand, rock, back filling or slump thereof.

11. Utility lines (water, sewer, gas and electric) installed by the undersigned after ninety (90) days.

Date: _____

By: _____
        President

_____

_____
        Address

_____
        Purchaser

**Acknowledgement of Receipt**

The undersigned on this _____ day of _____ 19__ acknowledge receipt of that certain ONE-YEAR WARRANTY given by _____ to the home at _____ and _____ understand and agree that the undertakings of _____, contained within this warranty constitute all of the undertakings of and obligations upon said company with respect to possible defects in the original material and workmanship in connection with its construction of the aforementioned home.

_____
        Purchaser

# COMPLIANCE INSPECTION REPORT—FORM 710

The Compliance Inspection Report is a very important form, if used properly, between the builder and the buyer. This is a very complex form which will be discussed in its entirety. The Compliance Inspection Report is filled out by the person who has been delegated the responsibility of making the walk-through with the client just prior to move-in.

## WALK-THROUGH

Too many builders give their buyer a key to their house and wish them "good luck." That is ridiculous. There is only one way to introduce a buyer to his new home and that is by a minute and detailed inspection of the home at the time of the presentation of the keys by a company representative or the builder and the buyer. This is the walk-through. The Compliance Inspection Report or Inspection List is the paper report of that walk-through.

The Compliance Inspection Report does many things. First, it notifies the builder that there are items that are not completed or correct and must be taken care of to the buyer's satisfaction. Second, it notifies the buyer that once they have signed for these items on the Compliance Inspection Report, no damage occurring from van-line movers, children, etc., are to be construed as builders' responsibility. This is extremely important. Far too many times, builders have gone back to houses and were told that when the people moved in, the tile on the counters were broken. The builder may know that this is not true, but he has the choice of a possible lawsuit, resulting in bad public relations, or to go ahead and do the repair. The Compliance Inspection Report is intended to forestall that eventuality.

## COMPLETING THE FORM

The boxes immediately to the right of *Item I*, 1 through 10, must be initialed at the time of the walk-through. It states that the client has found these items satisfactory and has so initialed. *Item II* states, "The following items have been fully explained to the buyer (buyer to initial each item)." Too many times, things such as grading swales, air filters, mechanical operations, grouting, and paint touch-up are not explained to the buyer and too many calls come in for warranty which are really home maintenance responsibility. *Swales*, for instance, are a case in point. The builder must put in the swale to either a city or county code or at least in conformance with good building techniques which is nominally a three percent grade away from the building and a one percent grade from backyard to front yard down the side yard swale. If the buyer interrupts this swale by planting rose bushes or other landscaping, the builder can no longer be held responsible for that action or the resulting ponding of water or misdirected water runoff. By having the buyer initial that part of the form, he has indicated his understanding, and this should alleviate any action on behalf of the buyer against the builder at some later date.

The other items are either in the same manner, or are just courtesy items such as location of gas shut-off and water.

*Item III*, which states "The following items are not in satisfactory condition," has space, *lines 1 through 18*, to record items such as nicks, cracks, missing items, defective doors, etc.

**Continuing Record.** In the right-hand column, we have set up boxes where you can indicate who will repair the items and when. This can also be a continuing record of all matters on this house.

Referring back to *Item III*, it states "Any number $x$ below is not warranted and will not be corrected, at this time." Once in a while, your walk-through specialist will find an item that he states is within normal construction standards and will tell the buyer it will not be corrected by the builder. In light of the fact that the buyer's bank or lender will be funding shortly, this box can be initialed by the buyer and then the items below can be x'd in the small box in the field in the left-hand side of the page. This is a very rare instance. Here is an example. If you are building a home with 6'-x-12' beams and some split longitudinally, this is acceptable from both a strength and engineering standpoint, but may be extremely alarming to the buyer. This item could be signed above and x'd out below. It might be necessary for a meeting with a higher echelon of management and, perhaps, an engineer, to soothe and allay any suspicions the buyer might have that he is buying a house that is structurally deficient.

In the paragraph "*We have inspected the home, etc.*", it further states that the buyer releases from responsibility for any damage which may occur, except as stated in their warranty. It states further that this is Page 1 of 2, or 3 of 4, etc. If you are receiving more than one page of items to be corrected, you should review your construction techniques, as there are major companies in the United States that average between five and eight items. That should be your goal.

**Permission to Enter.** The balance of the form has to do with move-in date and permission to enter. The permission to enter after move-in is very important. Do not let your warranty man enter a home without proper authorization. The suits on this are so numerous they cannot be added up. Everyone's 25¢ vase becomes a Ming Dynasty vase when it is missed right after your warranty man left.

# COMPLIANCE INSPECTION REPORT

**710**

I. Items excluded from warranty (buyer to initial each item as satisfactory, except as listed below in Section III).

| | Satisfactory | | Satisfactory |
|---|---|---|---|
| 1. Cabinetry (surface damage) | | 6. Windows (breakage) | |
| 2. Countertops (surface damage) | | 7. Shower doors (surface damage) | |
| 3. Plumbing Fix. (surface damage) | | 8. Mirrors (surface damage) | |
| 4. Lino. or Tile (surface damage) | | 9. Light Fixtures (breakage) | |
| 5. Hdwd. floors or carpeting | | 10. Concrete (cracks excessive) | |

II. The following items have been fully explained to the buyer (buyer to initial each item).

| | | | |
|---|---|---|---|
| 1. Grading swale (need) | | 4. Location of gas shutoff | |
| 2. Furnace Filters | | 5. Location of water shutoff | |
| 3. Ceramic Tile Grout | | 6. Location of elec. shutoff | |

III. The following items are not in satisfactory condition. Any number x below is <u>not</u> <u>warranted</u> and will not be corrected, at this time.

| | Not Warranted | Repaired By | Date Repaired |
|---|---|---|---|
| 1. | | | |
| 2. | | | |
| 3. | | | |
| 4. | | | |
| 5. | | | |
| 6. | | | |
| 7. | | | |
| 8. | | | |
| 9. | | | |
| 10. | | | |
| 11. | | | |
| 12. | | | |

|  | Not Warranted | Repaired By | Date Repaired |
|---|---|---|---|
| 13. |  |  |  |
| 14. |  |  |  |
| 15. |  |  |  |
| 16. |  |  |  |
| 17. |  |  |  |
| 18. |  |  |  |

We have inspected the home and items above, and have found them in good condition except as noted. We therefore release the seller and builder from responsibility for any damage which may occur except as stated in their Warranty. We realize that cracks in concrete, masonry, stucco and interior walls and ceilings may develop from natural causes beyond the control of the seller or builder, who, under such circumstances, are not liable for these cracks. We have received one copy of "Your New Home, Its Care and Safety." We further understand that we must obtain the permission of the sales office prior to storing personal property in and/or occupying this home.

Builder's Representative _____ Purchaser _____

Job No. _____ Plan No. _____ Address _____

Insp. Date _____ Anticipated Move-In Date _____ Permission to enter after move-in ☐ Yes ☐ No

**Warranty Office - Job File** The above items have been repaired to my satisfaction except as noted in Sec. III. above.

Date _____, 19__ Purchaser _____
Signature

## ONE-MONTH INSPECTION—FORM 720

A builder does not want to have a buyer calling him on a daily basis. He is not trying to become friends. He is building a commodity properly and in a timely manner. At the time of the walk-through, the buyers are notified that complaints or corrections will only be received by mail and that only items that are emergencies will be accepted by telephone. An emergency is not an oven that is not working. An emergency can only be of an electrical or plumbing nature. Of course, this would be at your discretion. The One-Month Inspection Form insures that you receive notification of those minor items that need correction at one time. This cuts down on your management time and also helps your subcontractors. It keeps your lines of communication clear.

# 720

## ONE-MONTH INSPECTION FORM

Buyer _____  Date _____

Address _____  Phone _____

_____  Job # _____

In the event no one is at home, permission to enter is granted: ☐ Yes ☐ No _____

If permission to enter is not given, at what times are you generally at home, or how can an appointment be arranged?

_____

_____

_____

Complaint including Location, Size, Color, Dimension, as required:

_____

## NOTES

# Epilogue

## A FEW FINAL WORDS

The people or companies who make the big profits are the ones who prepare themselves to do so. They set high standards, value their time and product at a maximum, and systematically set out to achieve their goals.

They take no marginal jobs and operate at sufficient volume to achieve the greatest buying power. They select their subcontractors and associates with care, not always taking the low bid, but rather contracting with the people who can consistently be relied upon to do good work and to do it on schedule.

They build no "monuments" to their ego or to anyone else's ego unless they are paid for it. They operate within the limits of marketability and make their decisions very carefully.

They are paid for everything they do. They use work orders, change orders, contract checklists, and all the other forms—checklists and controls—that have been introduced or reintroduced to you in this book. Their secret is organization and their method is good business management.

They know that construction depends upon systematic and efficient management methods. They know that they must work with others to accomplish all of the many details involved, and that success depends upon the quality of their personnel management. Common sense must be applied along with forward thinking and conscientious effort. And they:

1. Plan carefully *what is to be done.*
2. Prepare and execute realistic schedules for *when it is to be done.*
3. Effectively supervise *how it is done.*
4. Regularly review performance and cost data to determine *how well it was done.*

# Index

AAA, *see* American Arbitration Association
Absorption: Market Study of a Specific Site (Form 240), 38-39, 41, 45
Accounting, 104-113
    choosing an accountant, 104-106
    systems of, 109-110
Administrative expenses: Cost and Profit Analysis (Form 400), 122-123, 127
Advertising, 214-216
    Alamo Bridge project, 220-221
    Cost and Profit Analysis (Form 400), 122 127
    Sales and Marketing Planning Checklist (Form 600), 225-226, 228-230, 232
Advertising agencies, 214
Aesthetics: Preliminary Site Study (Form 100), 12
Agreement for Sale of Real Estate (Form 650), 234-243
Agreements and contracts, *see* Contracts and agreements
AIA, *see* American Institute of Architecture
Air-conditioning, 84-85
    Warranty Checklist (Form 700), 261
Alamo Bridge project, California, 218-223
"Already sold," as marketing element, 213
Alter ego doctrine, of corporations, 64
Amenities, 77-78
    Building Design (Form 306), 81
    Cost and Profit Study of Tentative Program (Form 110), 15
    Market Study Conclusions (Form 250), 51
    Market Study of a Specific Site (Form 240), 41
American Arbitration Association, 144
American Institute of Architecture, 142-144
Annexation requirements: Preliminary Site Study (Form 100), 11
Anticipated land use: Preliminary Site Study (Form 100), 11
Apartment site: location criteria, 9
Arbitration, 144
Architect, 75
    DRE processing, 70-71

Architectural controls, from local ordinances: Site Feasibility Study (Form 200), 23
Architectural operation: Forward Planning Schedule (Form 300), 59
Architectural style: Market Study of a Specific Site (Form 240), 42
Assembly Bill 884, California, 70
Assignment of agreement: Agreement for Sale of Real Estate (Form 650), 237-238, 242
Attorneys, *see* Legal counsel
Audited financial statement, 106
Avco case, California, 68

Bankruptcy rate, in building industry, 2
Banks and bankers, 106-107, 110-111
Bidding, 89
    Bid Proposal-Subcontractors (Form 320), 93-96
    Bid Proposal-Suppliers (Form 325), 93, 97-98
    Bid Summary Sheet (Form 330), 99-102
    Invitation to Bid (Form 310), 90-92
    letting the bid, 103-104
    preparation for, 84-88
    shortcuts, 88-89
    starting time, 75-76
Bid file, 85-86
Bid list, 89-90
    subcontractors phone bid list, 87-88
Bid Proposal-Subcontractor (Form 320), 93-96
Bid Proposal-Suppliers (Form 325), 93, 97-98
Bid request form, *see* Invitation to Bid (Form 310)
Bid Summary Sheet (Form 330), 99-102
Billing:
    Bid Proposal-Subcontractor (Form 320), 96
    Bid Proposal-Suppliers (Form 325), 98
    cutoff date, 118
Bond notices, 145

## 282 / Index

Bookkeeping, *see* Accounting
Borrowing, *see* Loans
Broker: sales forms, 234
Budget, 109
Builder/developer: bidding, 104
Building codes: Site Feasibility Study (Form 200), 23
Building department requirements: Site Feasibility Study (Form 200), 23
Building Design (Form 306), 78, 81-82
Building development cost budget, 88
Building industry, *see* Construction industry
Building permits, 67, 141
    Preliminary Site Study (Form 100), 11
    Site Feasibility Study (Form 200), 23
Business, forms of, 62-64
Business failures, in construction industry, 2
Business management:
    contractors, 2
    front office managerial functions, 53-54
    records as a tool of, 108-109
Buyer, consideration of, in marketing, 202
Buyer's inspection: One-Year Warranty (Form 705), 264, 267

Capital, in incorporating, 63
Carpentry: Quality Control-Itemized Form (Form 550), 180
Cash flow cycle, 118-119
Cash management, 112
Ceramic tile:
    dye lot variations, 245
    Warranty Checklist (Form 700), 260
Change Order (Form 690), 253-256
Checks, joint, 146
Children, influence of, on housing, 203-204
City agencies: Site Feasibility Study (Form 200), 22-25
Clean-up:
    for marketing, 217
    Quality Control-Itemized Form (Form 550), 178, 182, 185
    Subcontract Agreement (Form 510), 154
    by subcontractor, 87
Color selection and schedules:
    Agreement for Sale of Real Estate (Form 650), 237, 242
    Exterior Color Selections (Form 660), 244, 247-248
    Field-Color Schedule Card (Form 560/680), 190-192, 245, 251-252
    Interior Color Schedule (Form 670), 244-245, 249-250

Commercial site:
    location criteria, 9
    Preliminary Site Study (Form 100), 12
    tentative study of site potential, 13
Commissions on sales: Cost and Profit Analysis (Form 400), 122, 127
Competition:
    Market Study Conclusions (Form 250), 52
    Market Study of a Specific Site (Form 240), 40-45
Compliance Inspection Report (Form 710), 271-274
Concrete work:
    One-Year Warranty (Form 705), 268
    Quality Control-Itemized Form (Form 550), 171-172, 181-182
    Warranty Checklist (Form 700), 259
Conflict of interest, of insurance companies, 66
Constitutional guarantees of property rights, 69
Construction, 141-199
    Construction Contract Checklist (Form 500), 146-148
    contracts, 142-146
    Cost and Profit Analysis (Form 400), 122, 127
    Cost and Profit Study of Tentative Program (Form 110), 15
    Employee Record Card (Form 570), 193-195
    Field-Color Schedule Card (Form 560/680), 190-192
    Forward Planning Schedule (Form 300), 60-61
    Job Summary (Form 590), 193, 199
    lien problems, 144-146
    mobilization, 141-142
    Quality Control-Itemized Form (Form 550), 163-164, 169-189
    Quality Control-Outline Form (Form 540), 163-168
    Subcontract Agreement (Form 510), 149-154
    Subdivision Schedule (Form 520), 156-158
    tentative program, cost of, 13-16
    Timecard (Form 580), 193, 197
    Weekly Construction Schedule (Form 530), 159-162
    Work in Process Budget-Indirect (Form 410), 124, 129-130
Construction Contract Checklist (Form 500), 146-148

Construction industry, 1-3
    control systems network, 2-3
    failure rate, 2
    forms of business, 62-64
    legal organization of company, 62-74
    opportunities in, 2
Consumer preference: Market Study of a Specific Site (Form 240), 50
Contingency, 13
    Cost and Profit Study of Tentative Program (Form 110), 15
Contracting:
    bidding, preparation for, 84-88
    early involvement, 83-84
Contract payment schedule, 88
Contracts and agreements, 17, 142-146
    Agreement for Sale of Real Estate (Form 650), 234-243
    Bid Proposal-Subcontractor (Form 320), 96
    Bid Proposal-Suppliers (Form 325), 98
    Construction Contract Checklist (Form 500), 146-148
    remedies, 143-144
    Subcontract Agreement (Form 510), 149-154
Control systems network, 2-3
Cooling system:
    One-Year Warranty (Form 705), 269
    *see also* Air-conditioning
Corporate expense: Cost and Profit Analysis (Form 400), 123, 127
Corporation, 63-64
Cost:
    analysis, 121-140
    attorney's fees, 65-66
    budget for building development, 88
    budget for land development, 88
    Cost and Profit Analysis (Form 400), 122-123, 127
    Cost and Profit Study of the Tentative Program (Form 110), 15-16
    and design, 75, 83-84
    Financing Tax Budget (Form 440), 124-125, 137-138
    Forward Planning Schedule (Form 300), 57, 59-60
    of high quality work, 163-164
    history of, for cost evaluation, 107
    Model Excess Budget (Form 450), 125, 139-140
    in preliminary site study, 5-6
    Product Line Detail Support work sheet (Form 430), 124, 135-136
    of tentative program, 13-16

    Work in Process Budget-Direct (Form 420), 123-124, 131-134
    Work in Process Budget-Indirect (Form 410), 123, 129-130
County agencies: Site Feasibility Study (Form 200), 22-25
County clerk, filing of negative EIR with, 69-70
Credit, in two-income families, 203
Creditor action against corporate stockholder (piercing the corporate veil), 63
Credit rating, 118
Curb appeal, of home, 77

Damages:
    contractor and subcontractor: Subcontract Agreement (Form 510), 153
    liquidated: Agreement for Sale of Real Estate (Form 650), 236-237, 242
Data catalogue: Market Study of a Specific Site (Form 240), 43-44, 49
Data processing, 110
DBA, defined, 62
Debris removal, *see* Clean-up
Default by home buyer: Agreement for Sale of Real Estate (Form 650), 236-237, 242
Demand, 202-203
    Market Study of a Specific Site (Form 240), 38-39
Demand pocket, 207
Density of housing, 205
Department of real estate: processing of documents, 70-71
Deposits, 17
    conditioned receipts: Agreement for Sale of Real Estate (Form 650), 235, 241
    forfeiting of: Agreement for Sale of Real Estate (Form 650), 236-237, 242
Design, 75-82
    alternatives and costs, 83-84
    Building Design (Form 306), 78, 81-82
    effect of inflation on, 206
    and selling dissatisfaction, 206-207
    Site Design (Form 305), 78-80
Developed land cost, 14
Developed lot cost, 13
    Cost and Profit Analysis (Form 400), 122, 127
    Cost and Profit Study of Tentative Program (Form 110), 15
Development, ease of, 9
    Preliminary Site Study (Form 100), 11-12

Development, legal problems in, 67–68
Direct costs:
    Cost and Profit Analysis (Form 400), 122, 127
    Work in Process Budget-Direct (Form 420), 123–124, 131–134
Distribution of units: Market Study of a Specific Site (Form 240), 45
Documents:
    for construction mobilization, 141–142
    processing with government agencies, 67–74
Doors:
    One-Year Warranty (Form 705), 268
    Quality Control-Itemized Form (Form 550), 175
    Warranty Checklist (Form 700), 260
Drainage:
    Preliminary Site Study (Form 100), 11
    Site Feasibility Study (Form 200), 21
DRE, *see* Department of real estate
Drywall:
    payment schedule, 88
    Warranty Checklist (Form 700), 260
Dye lot variations, 245

Ecological requirements: Preliminary Site Study (Form 100), 11
Economic base of town or city, 202–203
Ego state of purchaser, 211
EIR, *see* Environmental impact report
Electrical system:
    One-Year Warranty (Form 705), 269
    Quality Control-Itemized Form (Form 550), 173, 177–178, 185
    Site Feasibility Study (Form 200), 24
    Warranty Checklist (Form 700), 261
Elevations:
    Building Design (Form 306), 81
Employee Record Card (Form 570), 193, 195
Employee taxes, 112
Employment:
    Market Study of a Regional Area (Form 220), 31
    Market Study of a Specific Site (Form 240), 39, 42
Encroachment permits, 141
Energy conservation, value of, 210–211
Engineer: DRE processing, 70–71
Engineering agency of county or city: Site Feasibility Study (Form 200), 22
Entrance to site: Sales and Marketing Planning Checklist (Form 600), 226

Environmental impact report, 69–70
    Forward Planning Schedule (Form 300), 59
Environmental-law specialist, 65
Environmental quality of area: Market Study of a Specific Site (Form 240), 36
Equal Credit Act, 203
Equipment: Warranty Checklist (Form 700), 261
Escrow: money paid by buyer for extras, 237
Escrow fees: Cost and Profit Analysis (Form 400), 122, 127
Estimated cost of tentative program, 13
Exclusivity, as motivating factor in purchase, 212
Express warranty, 262
    One-Year Warranty (Form 705), 263–270
Exterior Color Selections (Form 660), 244, 247–248


Failure rate, in building industry, 2
Families, types of, 203–204
Feasible cost, 13–14
Feasibility study, 19–52
    for financing, 114–117
    Forward Planning Schedule (Form 300), 57
    information gathering, 19–20, 28
    Market Study Conclusions (Form 250), 51–52
    Market Study of a Regional Area (Form 220), 28–32
    Market Study of a Specific Site (Form 240), 33–50
    Preliminary Site Study (Form 100), 12
    Site Feasibility Study (Form 200), 20–26
Field cards:
    Employee Record Card (Form 570), 193, 195
    Field-Color Schedule Card (Form 560/680), 190–192, 245, 251–252
    Job Summary (Form 590), 193, 199
    Timecard (Form 580), 193, 197
Field-Color Schedule Card (Form 560/680), 190–192, 245, 251–252
Field investigation: Site Feasibility Study (Form 200), 21
Field superintendent, 142
Filing, 87
Final map, 68
Finance charge, 14
    Cost and Profit Study of Tentative Program (Form 110), 15

# Index / 285

Finance Feasibility Study (Form 360), 114-116
Finance Package Checklist (Form 370), 114, 117
Financial statements, 106-108, 110-111
Financing:
    for home buyers, 217-218
    of limited partnership, 63
    *see also* Loans
Financing Tax Budget (Form 440), 124-125, 137-138
Finishes: Warranty Checklist (Form 700), 260
Fireplace:
    Quality Control-Itemized Form (Form 550), 176-177
    Warranty Checklist (Form 700), 261
Flat, 205
Flood Control: Site Feasibility Study (Form 200), 24-25
Floor covering: Quality Control-Itemized Form (Form 550), 183, 186
Floors:
    One-Year Warranty (Form 705), 268
    Warranty Checklist (Form 700), 261
Forms:
    Agreement for Sale of Real Estate (Form 650) 234-243
    Bid Proposal-Subcontractors (Form 320), 93-96
    Bid Proposal-Suppliers (Form 325), 93, 97-98
    Bid Summary Sheet (Form 330), 99-102
    Building Design (Form 306), 78, 81-82
    Change Order (Form 690), 253-256
    Compliance Inspection Report (Form 710), 271-274
    Construction Contract Checklist (Form 500), 146-148
    contract forms of AIA, 142-144
    Cost and Profit Analysis (Form 400), 122-123, 127
    Cost and Profit Study of the Tentative Program (Form 110), 13-16
    Employee Record Card (Form 570), 193, 195
    Exterior Color Selection (Form 660), 244, 247-248
    Field-Color Schedule Card (Form 560/680), 190-192, 245, 251-252
    Finance Feasibility Study (Form 360), 114-116
    Finance Package Checklist (Form 370), 114, 117
    Financing Tax Budget (Form 440), 124-125, 137-138
    Forward Planning Schedule (Form 300), 54-61
    Interior Color Schedule (Form 670), 244-245, 249-250
    Invitation to Bid (Form 310), 90-92
    Job Summary (Form 590), 193, 199
    Market Study Conclusions (Form 250), 51-52
    Market Study of a Regional Area (Form 220), 28-32
    Market Study of a Specific Site (Form 240), 33-50
    Model Excess Budget (Form 450), 125, 139-140
    One-Month Inspection (Form 720), 275-278
    One-Year Warranty (Form 705), 263-270
    Preliminary Site Study (Form 100), 10-12
    Product Line Detail Support work sheet (Form 430), 124, 135-136
    Quality Control-Itemized Form (Form 550), 163-164, 169-189
    Quality Control-Outline Form (Form 540), 163-168
    Sales and Marketing Planning Checklist (Form 600), 223-233
    Site Design (Form 305), 78-80
    Site Feasibility Study (Form 200), 20-26
    Subcontract Agreement (Form 510), 149-154
    Subdivision Schedule (Form 520), 156-158
    Timecard (Form 580), 193, 197
    Warranty Checklist (Form 700), 258-261
    Weekly Construction Schedule (Form 530), 159-162
    Work in Process Budget-Direct (Form 420), 123-124, 131-134
    Work in Process Budget-Indirect (Form 410), 123, 129-130
Forward Planning Schedule (Form 300), 54-61
Forward planning stage, 53-119
    accounting, 104-113
    contracts and purchasing, 83-102
    Forward Planning Schedule (Form 300), 54-61
    government approval, 71-74
    legal organization of company, 62-74
    letting the bid, 103-104
    money management, 118-119
    project design implementation, 75-82
Foundations:
    One-Year Warranty (Form 705), 267

Quality Control-Itemized Form (Form 550), 170-171
Framing, 87
    Quality Control-Itemized Form (Form 550), 171, 174-175, 178
Front office managerial functions, 53-54
Full disclosure, in sales operation, 218
Funding: Forward Planning Schedule (Form 300), 57

Gas for utilities: Site Feasibility Study (Form 200), 23
General/administrative expense: Cost and Profit Analysis (Form 400), 122-123, 127
General contractor, 103, 142
General partner, 62-63
Geological studies: Site Feasibility Study (Form 200), 22
Geologist, 75
Government agencies, regulations and requirements:
    document processing, 67-74
    permits, 141-142
    Preliminary Site Study (Form 100), 11
    record-keeping for, 107-108
    Site Feasibility Study (Form 200), 22-25
    and site selection, 9
Grading:
    Quality Control-Itemized Form (Form 550), 169, 181, 184
    Site Feasibility Study (Form 200), 22
Gross margin: Cost and Profit Analysis (Form 400), 122, 127

Hardware: Quality Control-Itemized Form (Form 550), 183
Heating system:
    One-Year Warranty (Form 705), 269
    Quality Control-Itemized Form (Form 550), 173, 177, 184
    Warranty Checklist (Form 700), 261
High-density housing, 205
Homeowners' associations, 216
    Agreement for Sale of Real Estate (Form 650), 238, 242-243
Housing:
    design criteria, 77-78
    and family size, 203-204
    single-family detached house, 203
    types of, 204-208
Housing market studies:
    Market Study of a Regional Area (Form 220), 31
    Market Study of a Specific Site (Form 240), 37
    and preliminary site study, 6

Implied warranty, 262
Improvements:
    Cost and Profit Analysis (Form 400), 122, 127
    Cost and Profit Study of Tentative Program (Form 110), 15
    Forward Planning Schedule (Form 300), 60
Incorporation process, 63
Indirect costs:
    Cost and Profit Analysis (Form 400), 122, 127
    Work in Process-Indirect (Form 410), 123, 129-130
Industrial site:
    location criteria, 9
    Preliminary Site Study (Form 100), 12
    tentative study of site potential, 13
Inflation, effect of, on housing design, 206
Information-gathering process, for feasibility study, 19-20, 28
Inspection:
    Compliance Inspection Report (Form 710), 271-274
    One-Month Inspection (Form 720), 275-278
    One-Year Warranty (Form 705), 264, 267
Insulation:
    perceived value, 210
    Quality Control-Itemized Form (Form 550), 178
Insurance:
    Cost and Profit Analysis (Form 400), 122, 127
    lawsuits, 66
    Model Excess Budget (Form 450), 125, 139
    Subcontract Agreement (Form 510), 152-153
    subcontractors' liability, 106
    subcontractors' release, 113
Integrated plans, 75-76
Interest rates:
    Agreement for Sale of Real Estate (Form 650), 235, 240
    for bank loans, 111
    Cost and Profit Analysis (Form 400), 122, 127
Interior Color Schedule (Form 670), 244-245, 249-250

Interior decoration: Sales and Marketing Planning Checklist (Form 600), 226, 228, 231
Inventory management, 217
    Alamo Bridge project, 221-222
    *see also* Land inventory, 208
Invitation to Bid (Form 310), 90-92
Invoice file, 87

Joint checks, 146
Joint venture, 62
Job Summary (Form 590), 193, 199

Land:
    Cost and Profit Analysis (Form 400), 122, 127
    Cost and Profit Study of Tentative Program (Form 110), 15
    development cost, 13, 88
    documents, in acquisition, 141-142
    value, changes in, 202
Land inventory, 208
Land planner: Forward Planning Schedule (Form 300), 58
Land planning units: Forward Planning Schedule (Form 300), 58
Land purchase agreement forms, 17
Landscape designer, 75
Landscaping:
    Forward Planning Schedule (Form 300), 59
    Sales and Marketing Planning Checklist (Form 600), 226, 229-230
Large-volume builder, 8, 27
Latent defects, 262
Lawsuits, 66, 144
Legal counsel, 64-66
    DRE processing, 70-71
    in property acquisition, 17
    for warranty forms, 258
Legal organization of company, 62-74
Legal problems in building and development, 66-68
Legal requirements, *see* Government agencies, regulations and requirements
Letter of intent, 17
Letting the bid, 103-104
Liability, 63, 262
    insurance coverage, 66
Licenses, 64
Lien problems, 144-145

Lien releases, 145-146
    Bid Proposal-Subcontractor (Form 320), 96
    Bid Proposal-Suppliers (Form 325), 98
    Subcontract Agreement (Form 510), 152
Life-style, of target group, 205
Lighting, 217
    Sales and Marketing Planning Checklist (Form 600), 229
Limited partnership, 62-63
Liquidated damages: Agreement for Sale of Real Estate (Form 650), 236-237, 242
Liquidity, and governmental approval of project, 72
Loan points/fees: Cost and Profit Analysis (Form 400), 122, 127
Loans, 106-107, 110, 112-114, 119, 141-142
    Agreement for Sale of Real Estate (Form 650), 235-236, 240-241
    borrowing against real estate, 209
    Finance Package Checklist (Form 370), 114, 117
    Financial Feasibility Study (Form 360), 114-116
    Financing Tax Budget (Form 440), 124-125, 137-138
    home purchases, 217-218
Location, 9, 76, 202
    Cost and Profit Study of the Tentative Program (Form 110), 15
    Market Study Conclusions (Form 250), 52
    Market Study of a Regional Area (Form 220), 31
    Market Study of a Specific Site (Form 240), 35, 42, 44
    Preliminary Site Study (Form 100), 11-12
Lot coverage rules, 77
Lot layout: Quality Control-Itemized Form (Form 550), 169
Lot size, 76-77
Lot yield, 77
Low-density housing, 205
Lumber:
    One-Year Warranty (Form 705), 268
    Quality Control-Itemized Form (Form 550), 171
    Warranty Checklist (Form 700), 260

Management, *see* Business management
Maps, 67-68

## 288 / Index

Market feasibility study, 6, 9, 27–52
   Market Study Conclusions (Form 250), 51–52
   Market Study of a Regional Area (Form 220), 28–32
   Market Study of a Specific Site (Form 240), 33–50
   Preliminary Site Study Form (Form 100), 12
Marketing, 201–256
   advertising, 214–216
   buyer, 202
   Change Order (Form 690), 253–256
   Cost and Profit Analysis (Form 400), 122, 127
   Cost and Profit Study of Tentative Program (Form 110), 15
   demand, 202–203
   energy conservation features, 210–211
   evaluation of project, 218–223
   Exterior Color Selections (Form 660), 244, 247–248
   Field-Color Schedule Card (Form 560/680), 190–192, 245, 251–252
   financing home purchases, 217–218
   Interior Color Schedule (Form 670), 244–245, 249–250
   inventorying land, 208
   inventory strategy, 217
   location, 202
   market motivators, 76
   Market Study of a Specific Site (Form 240), 41–45
   market survey, 209–210
   odds of success, 213
   pricing and profit, 213–214
   Sales and Marketing Planning Checklist (Form 600), 223–233
   strategy, 211–213
   target groups, 203–204
   types of housing, 204–208
   *see also* Sales
Marketing agent and consultant, 215, 224
Market standards: Market Study of a Specific Site (Form 240), 43
Market Study Conclusions (Form 250), 51–52
Market Study of a Regional Area (Form 220), 28–32
Market Study of a Specific Site (Form 240), 33–50
Masonry: Warranty Checklist (Form 700), 260
Masonry veneer: Quality Control-Itemized Form (Form 550), 181
Material Selections: Agreement for Sale of Real Estate (Form 650), 237, 242

Mechanic's lien, 144–145
Medium-volume builder, 7, 27
Millwork:
   One-Year Warranty (Form 705), 268
   Warranty Checklist (Form 700), 260
Model:
   clean-up, 217
   Cost and Profit Analysis (Form 400), 122, 127
   description: Agreement for Sale of Real Estate (Form 650), 234, 239
   entrance, 213, 223
   flow, in showing to buyers, 217
   maintenance: Model Excess Budget (Form 450), 125, 139
   site, changes in, 222
Model Excess Budget (Form 450), 125, 139–140
Moisture protection: Warranty Checklist (Form 700), 260
Money management, 118–119
Money market, 114
Motivation, in real estate purchase, 212

Negative declaration, on environmental impact report, 69–70
Neighborhood, 76
   Market Study of a Specific Site (Form 240), 42
Neighborhood preference: Market Study of a Specific Site (Form 240), 50
Neighborhood profile: Market Survey of a Specific Site (Form 240), 47–49
Non-warrantable conditions: One-Year Warranty (Form 705), 265, 270
Notice provision, of warranty agreement, 263

Off-site field investigation: Site Feasibility Study (Form 200), 21
One-man corporation, 64
One-Month Inspection (Form 720), 275–278
One-Year Warranty (Form 705), 263–270
One-year warranty, unwritten, 262
On-site field investigation: Site Feasibility Study (Form 200), 21
Option to purchase, 17
   Preliminary Site Study (Form 100), 12
Overhead:
   Cost and Profit Analysis (Form 400), 122–123, 127
   Cost and Profit Study of Tentative Program (Form 110), 15

Paint:
- Exterior Color Selections (Form 660), 247
- Field-Color Schedule Card (Form 560/680), 191, 251-252
- One-Year Warranty (Form 705), 269
- Quality Control-Itemized Form (Form 550), 180-182, 186
- Warranty Checklist (Form 700), 261

Palo Alto, California: property restriction case, 69
Parking, 205
Parks: Site Feasibility Study (Form 200), 25
Partnership, 62
Payments:
- Bid Proposal-Subcontractors (Form 320), 96
- Bid Proposal-Suppliers (Form 325), 98
- contract payment schedule, 88
- delayed, 118
- Subcontract Agreement (Form 510), 153
- timing, 118

Perceived value, 210
- Alamo Bridge project, 219-220

Permission to enter after move-in: Compliance Inspection Report (Form 710), 272, 274
Permits, 141-142
  see also Building permits; Use permits
Per unit fixed column: Cost and Profit Analysis (Form 400), 123, 127
Phone bid list, 87
Piercing the corporate veil, 63-64
Planning agencies and commissions:
- Site Feasibility Study (Form 200), 22
- subdivision map, consideration of, 67

Plans, 84-86
Plumbing:
- One-Year Warranty (Form 705), 268
- Quality Control-Itemized Form (Form 550), 172, 176, 184-185
- Warranty Checklist (Form 700), 261

Population growth:
- Market Study of a Regional Area (Form 220), 31
- Market Study of a Specific Site (Form 240), 38

Preliminary site study, 5-12
- Preliminary Site Study (Form 100), 10-12

Pre-opening of new homes: Sales and Marketing Planning Checklist (Form 600), 225-233
Pre-opening party: Sales and Marketing Planning Checklist (Form 600), 230, 232

Prestige items, 78
Price:
- Agreement for Sale of Real Estate (Form 650), 235, 240
- based on worth, 212
- Bid Proposal-Subcontractors (Form 320), 95
- Bid Proposal-Suppliers (Form 325), 97
- as home design criterion, 78
- Market Study Conclusions (Form 250), 51-52
- Preliminary Site Study (Form 100), 12
- and profit, 213-214

Prime interest rate, 111
Privacy, as motivating factor in purchase, 212
Production costs: Forward Planning Schedule (Form 300), 59-60
Product Line Detail Support work sheet (Form 430), 124, 135-136
*Professional Builder* market survey, 210
Profit, 121, 140
- Cost and Profit Analysis (Form 400), 122-123, 127
- Cost and Profit Study of Tentative Program (Form 110), 15-16
- Forward Planning Schedule (Form 300), 57-58
- preliminary site study, 5-6
- pricing and, 213-214

Project design implementation, 75-82
- Building Design (Form 306), 81-82
- Site Design (Form 305), 79-80

Project selection, 5-8
Property acquisition, 17
Proposition 13, 205
Proprietorship, 62
Public attitude: Market Survey of a Specific Site (Form 240), 46-50
Public health: Site Feasibility Study (Form 200), 24
Public transportation: Market Study of a Specific Site (Form 240), 35
Public utilities, see Utilities
Public works agencies: Site Feasibility Study (Form 200), 22
Purchasing:
- bidding, preparation for, 84-88
- early involvement, 83-84
- property, 17
- terms of purchase and site selection, 9

Quality Control-Itemized Form (Form 550), 163-164, 169-189

290 / Index

Quality Control-Outline Form (Form 540), 163–168
Quality inspector, 164

Real estate, department of, see Department of real estate
Record-keeping, 106–109
Recreation: Cost and Profit Analysis (Form 400), 122, 127
Regional Area, Market Study of a (Form 220), 28–32
Reputation, importance of, 78
Resale and warranty transfer: One-Year Warranty (Form 705), 264–265, 269
Residential site, 9, 13
    Preliminary Site Study Form (Form 100), 11
Responsibility in sales and marketing, 224
    Sales and Marketing Planning Checklist (Form 600), 225–233
Retentions, 89, 146
    Bid Proposal-Subcontractors (Form 320), 96
    Bid Proposal-Suppliers (Form 325), 98
Rezoning, 67–68
    Preliminary Site Study Form (Form 100), 11
Roads and streets:
    Market Study of a Regional Area (Form 220), 31
    Market Study of a Specific Site (Form 240), 35
    Preliminary Site Study (Form 100), 11
    Site Feasibility Study (Form 200), 21, 22
Roof:
    One-Year Warranty (Form 705), 264, 269
    Quality Control-Itemized Form (Form 550), 175, 177
    Warranty Checklist (Form 700), 260

Safeguard accounting system, 110
Safety, personal:
    Market Study of a Specific Site (Form 240), 37
Sales:
    Agreement for Sale of Real Estate (Form 650), 234–243
    budget, 14
    Cost and Profit Study of Tentative Program (Form 110), 15
    and ego state of buyer, 211
    Market Study of a Specific Site (Form 240), 41–45

    operation, 218
    Preliminary Site Study (Form 100), 12
    price, 6
    Sales and Marketing Planning Checklist (Form 600), 223–233
    see also Marketing; Target sales price
Sales area:
    Model Excess Budget (Form 450), 125, 139
Sales office and staff, 218, 220
    Sales and Marketing Planning Checklist (Form 600), 226, 229–230
Schools:
    Market Study of a Specific Site (Form 240), 37, 42
    Site Feasibility Study (Form 200), 25
Selling dissatisfaction, 206–207
Sewers:
    Preliminary Site Study (Form 100), 11
    Quality Control-Itemized Form (Form 550), 172
    Site Feasibility Study (Form 200), 22–23
Shortages, 202
Single-family detached house, 203
Site engineer, 75
Site engineering:
    Site Design (Form 305), 79
Site Feasibility Study (Form 200), 20–26
Site selection and design, 5–13, 76–80
    Market Study Conclusions (Form 250), 52
    Market Study of a Specific Site (Form 240), 35–50
    Site Design (Form 305), 78–80
Site work: Warranty Checklist (Form 700), 259
Small-volume builder, 7, 27, 33, 53
Soils engineer: Forward Planning Schedule (Form 300), 59
Sole proprietorship, 62
Speculators, control of, 237–238
Statute of limitations, for latent defects, 262
Stock notices, 145
Structural engineer, 75
Stucco:
    Quality Control-Itemized Form (Form 550), 179–180
    Warranty Checklist (Form 700), 260
Subcontract Agreement (Form 510), 149–154
Subcontractors:
    agreements, 142; Subcontract Agreement (Form 510), 149–154
    bidding, 84–90, 103; Bid Proposal (Form 320), 93–96; Invitation to Bid (Form 310), 90–92

billing cutoff date, 118
checklist, 87; Construction Contract Checklist (Form 500), 146-148
contract payment schedule, 88
insurance liability, 106
relationships with, 84, 88-89
taxes, 112
Subdivision processing, 67-68
Subdivision Schedule (Form 520), 156-158
Substitution of materials: Agreement for Sale of Real Estate (Form 650), 236, 241
Success atmosphere, creation of, 212
Suppliers:
  agreements, 142
  bidding, 89-90, 103; Bid Proposal (Form 325), 93, 97-98; Invitation to Bid (Form 310), 90-92
  billing cutoff date, 118
  Construction Contract Checklist (Form 500), 146-148
Supply: Market Study of a Specific Site (Form 240), 39
Swales: Compliance Inspection Report (Form 710), 271-273
Sweep-up, *see* Clean-up

Takeout and loan points/fees: Cost and Profit Analysis (Form 400), 122, 127
Target dates:
  Building Design (Form 306), 81
  Site Design (Form 305), 79
Target groups, in marketing, 203-206
Target sales price, 14
  Cost and Profit Study of Tentative Program (Form 110), 15
Taxes:
  Cost and Profit Analysis (Form 400), 122, 127
  effect on housing market, 209
  Financing Tax Budget (Form 440), 124-125, 137-138
  subcontractor/employee, 112
Tax-law specialist, 65
Tax shelter, 63
Team selling, 224
Telephone bid, 87-88, 99
Tentative map, 67-68
Tentative program, 13-14
  Cost and Profit Study (Form 110), 15-16
Terrain: Preliminary Site Study (Form 100), 11
Theft costs: Model Excess Budget (Form 450), 125, 139

Thermal protection: Warranty Checklist (Form 700), 260
Thirty-day invoices, 118
Timecard (Form 580), 193, 197
Time documentation: Forward Planning Schedule (Form 300), 54-61
Time limits:
  Agreement for Sale of Real Estate (Form 650), 234-235, 239
  negative EIR, 69-70
  subdivision Map Act, 67
Title:
  Cost and Profit Analysis (Form 400), 122, 127
  joint venture, 62
  Site Feasibility Study (Form 200), 21
  transfer, 141-142
Title company, 70-71, 141
Total cost of sales: Cost and Profit Analysis (Form 400), 122, 127
Total dollars column: Cost and Profit Analysis (Form 400), 123, 127
Townhouse, 9, 13, 205
Transactional analysis, 211-212
Transferable warranty: One-Year Warranty (Form 705), 264-265, 269
Transportation:
  Market Study of a Regional Area (Form 220), 31
  Market Study of a Specific Site (Form 240), 35-36, 42
  *see also* Roads and streets
Treasury bills, 112
Trenching: Quality Control-Itemized Form (Form 550), 170
Trial lawyer, 65
Two-income families, 203

Unwritten warranty, 262
Use permits, 74
Utilities:
  cost of, and buying decision, 210-211
  Preliminary Site Study (Form 100), 11
  Quality Control-Itemized Form (Form 550), 170, 172-173, 179
  Site Feasibility Study (Form 200), 23-24

Value engineered, 76
Vandalism costs: Model Excess Budget (Form 450), 125, 139
Vested rights document, 67-68
View: Preliminary Site Study (Form 100), 12

Visible surface defects: One-Year Warranty (Form 705), 264, 267

Walk-through, 271
Walls and wall covers:
    One-Year Warranty (Form 705), 268
    Quality Control-Itemized Form (Form 550), 176, 178
Warranty, 257-270
    Bid Proposal-Subcontractors (Form 320), 96
    Bid Proposal-Suppliers (Form 325), 98
    One-Year Warranty (Form 705), 263-270
    Warranty Checklist (Form 700), 258-261
Water:
    Quality Control-Itemized Form (Form 550), 173
    Site Feasibility Study (Form 200), 24
Weekly Construction Schedule (Form 530), 159-162
Windows:
    Quality Control-Itemized Form (Form 550), 175
    Warranty Checklist (Form 700), 260

Women's income, and family credit, 203
Work in Process Budget-Direct (Form 420), 123-124, 131-134
Work in Process Budget-Indirect (Form 410), 123, 129-130
Work schedules:
    Subdivision Schedule (Form 520), 156-158
    Weekly Construction Schedule (Form 530), 159-162

Youngblood case, California, 68

Zoning, 74, 205
    Preliminary Site Study (Form 100), 11
    rezoning, 67-68
    Site Feasibility Study (Form 200), 22